T5-BAR-547

PONTIAC

Since 1945

Also by the author

BMW: Since 1945
Jaguar: Since 1945

W·W·NORTON & COMPANY·New York·London

PONTIAC

Since 1945

RICHARD L. BUSENKELL

Published simultaneously in Canada by Penguin Books Canada Ltd.,
2801 John Street, Markham, Ontario L3R1B4.

Printed in the United States of America.

The text of this book is composed in Times Roman
with display type set in Helvetica Bold Condensed.
Composition by PennSet, Inc.
Manufacturing by The Murray Printing Company.
Book design by Jacques Chazaud.

First Edition

Library of Congress Cataloging-in-Publication Data

Busenkell, Richard L.
Pontiac since 1945.

1. Pontiac automobile—History. I. Title.
TL215.P68B87 1989 629.2′222 88–25368

ISBN 0-393-02589-6

W. W. Norton & Company, Inc. 500 Fifth Avenue, New York, N.Y. 10110
W. W. Norton & Company Ltd., 37 Great Russell Street, London WC1B 3NU

1 2 3 4 5 6 7 8 9 0

To all the people at Pontiac Motor Division of General Motors for their efforts to produce the most interesting cars in America; and to my wife, Deborah Lynn Busenkell.

Contents

Acknowledgments

The author would like to thank William J. O'Neill, Pontiac's director of public relations, and the following people in Pontiac's public relations department: Chuck Licari, Elizabeth Robertson, Richard Thompson, and Jill Witzenburg. They were tolerant of my lengthy investigation of Pontiac's historical files and unfailingly polite whenever my questions interrupted their current work.

Thanks also to Carl Sheffer, formerly with Pontiac public relations and now in GM's west coast office in Los Angeles, for his support and interest in this project.

No one could write a book about an automobile company without repeated examination of the cars themselves at the retail level. The sales and service staffs at Hyman Brothers Pontiac in Richmond, Virginia, and Bob Hix Pontiac in Costa Mesa, California, were enthusiastic and helpful in providing information about technical specifications and sales policies of late-model Pontiacs.

A special thanks is due to Robert C. Stempel, who was Pontiac's general manager at the time of my factory research. Despite his busy schedule he always greeted me by name, and was more enthusiastic and inquisitive about this book than anyone else at Pontiac. The inside word among the Pontiac staff at the time was that the dynamic Bob Stempel was unquestionably going to become the president of General Motors. Today that is indeed his title, and he has thus reaped the rich reward that should come to all those who encourage historians.

The most special thanks of all goes to my former wife, Dr. Margaret Ellen Mayo, who was supportive far and above the mere requirements of marital duty, during a difficult time in our lives. Thank you very much, Maggie.

Richard L. Busenkell
Costa Mesa, California
March, 1988

PONTIAC

Since 1945

The Early Years
1926–1939

The Pontiac automobile is named for the city in which it is built: Pontiac, Michigan. Located some 25 miles northwest of Detroit, Pontiac is the seat of Oakland County. The city is named after the great Ottawa Indian of the eighteenth century, who became chief of the combined Ottawa, Chippewa, and Potawatomie peoples. Opposing the Treaty of Paris in 1763 because it seized Indian lands, Pontiac won a number of victories over British forces, including the capture of eight forts. After besieging Detroit for six months, he concluded a peace treaty in 1765. Pontiac is remembered for his military and diplomatic skills, but even more for his eloquent articulation of Indian rights. The Pontiac automobile adopted an Indian head as its symbol in tribute to this great native American.

The Pontiac originated in 1926 as a "companion" marque to the Oakland, an upper-middle-class GM car in existence since 1907, also manufactured in the city of Pontiac. The onset of the Great Depression killed the Oakland in 1931. Pontiac eventually became the only "companion" car to become a permanent part of GM's marketing array.

Introduced in 1926 as a lower-priced companion car to Oakland, Pontiac quickly established a reputation for durability and value. Dignified yet handsome bodies like this 2-door sedan, finished in Du Pont's new "Duco" lacquer, proved so popular that within a few years GM discontinued Oakland.

PONTIAC SINCE 1945

Sober yet sporty, this 1926 coupe exhibits excellent proportions and period stylishness. Extolling its 6-cylinder engine with slogans like "Chief of the Sixes," Pontiac attracted buyers who wanted more performance than 4-cylinder Fords and Chevrolets, but at a comparable price.

The early Pontiac was esteemed for its 6-cylinder engine, an advantage over the 4-cylinder Chevrolet. Even after 1929, when Chevrolet introduced its overhead-valve six, Pontiacs continued to sell well due to snappy styling, reliability, and low cost.

In 1933 Pontiac blossomed by dropping its 6-cylinder engine and introducing a powerful new straight eight. With this engine and rakish new styling, Pontiac's sales doubled. In 1934 the division received GM's new independent front suspension, and in 1935 it introduced a redesigned six to supplement the eight.

Pontiac sold a record 236,189 cars in the recovery year of 1937. By the end of its first decade, the division had comfortably weathered the storms of the Depression and established its own distinctive identity.

Introduced in the depths of the Depression, the 1933 Pontiac combined a new straight-8 engine with smashing new styling to create one of the most rakishly handsome cars of its time. With low-priced models as pretty as this roadster, the "tin Indian" flourished when many other marques were failing.

Prewar Conservatism
1940–1942

The 1940 DeLuxe touring sedan was a handsome six-window car with Buick-type styling and crisp window detailing. Available with a six or an eight, it was the first Pontiac with faired-in headlights. Running boards were optional.

The headlights of all Pontiacs for 1940 were faired into the front fenders, a new styling treatment. The bodies were wider and rectangular in shape, whereas the grille and frontal aspect were almost identical to the Buick.

At the bottom of the 1940 Pontiac array was the Special Six with a 117-inch wheelbase. The Deluxe series had a 120-inch wheelbase and offered a choice of a 6-cylinder or 8-cylinder engine.

Adding excitement was the completely new "torpedo" body. Compared to the standard body, the torpedo was lower, wider, had blind rear quarters, no running boards, more steeply raked glass areas, and a fully integrated trunk. Pontiac's Torpedo Eight was available only as a 4-door sedan or 2-door sport coupe on a 122-inch wheelbase, powered by a 103-hp version of the eight. The sedan was 7¾ inches longer, 3 inches wider, and 1⅜ inches lower than a Deluxe Eight sedan.

New for 1940, the Torpedo Eight was Pontiac's luxury model. Longer, lower, and wider than the DeLuxe body, the torpedo became Pontiac's standard body the following year.

The 1940 engines were old friends to Pontiac customers. The straight eight displaced 248.9 cubic inches and developed 100 hp; a special version for the Torpedo Eight had a dual-throat carburetor and three more horsepower. The six had a displacement of 222.7 cubic inches and 87 hp. Both designs were flatheads with a single downdraft carburetor and long strokes. Head, block, and pistons were cast iron. The forged steel connecting rods were drilled for pressure lubrication of the wrist pins, and both engines had a compression ratio of 6.5:1.

The X-braced channel-section Pontiac chassis frame was robust and orthodox. The three-speed manual transmission had synchromesh on the second and third gears, and Pontiac had used a crankshaft harmonic balancer and hypoid rear axle gears for years. Since 1937 the independent front suspension had been a simple A-arm arrangement with coil springs, superseding the Dubonnet system introduced in 1934; Pontiac, however, still used the original "Knee Action" term to describe it. The rear suspension had the traditional solid rear axle and semi-elliptic "Duflex" leaf springs.

The bright face of the '41 Pontiac was emphasized by fender creases and a crisp grille with fine detailing.

1941

All Pontiacs this year had torpedo bodies. Either engine was available in any model, the eight costing only $25 extra.

The Deluxe Torpedo was the bottom range, with a new 119-inch wheelbase. The medium range was a new fastback body style, the Streamliner Torpedo, on a 122-inch wheelbase. Optional was a "Super-Streamliner" trim package with finer upholstery, thicker carpeting, sponge rubber seat cushions, electric clock, folding rear armrest, and spring-spoked steering wheel.

At the top of the '41 line was the Custom Torpedo, and joining the sedan and sedan coupe in this range was a surprise: the station wagon. In a major upgrading the wagon now had a 122-inch wheelbase, carried Pontiac's best trim, and was available with an eight. There was even a luxury trim option called the Special Station Wagon, which had leather seats and full carpeting.

All three of Pontiac's basic bodies for 1941 were shared with other GM divisions. The Deluxe was the "A" body, shared with Chevrolet and the smaller Olds and Buick models; the Streamliner was the "B" body, shared with Olds, Buick, and the new Cadillac Series 61; the Custom was the "C" body, shared with the bigger Olds and Buick models and the Cadillac Series 62.

All 8-cylinder engines for 1941 were the 103-hp version with its dual-throat carb. The six received a bore increase of ⅛-inch to 3 9/16 inches, which raised its displacement to 239.2 cubic inches and its power to 90 hp.

The most expensive Pontiac in 1941 was the wagon at $1,133 for the 8-cylinder version. Its beautiful timber body was available with two seats or three.

One of the options offered in 1941 was a heater-defroster underdash unit called "Weather Chief," the first piece of Pontiac hardware with the name "chief." Previous usage had been confined to advertising, such as the description of early Pontiacs as "Chief of the Sixes."

So successful was the torpedo body throughout the GM range in its original C-body form that an A-body version was introduced in mid-year. This new model was called the Metropolitan at Pontiac, and fitted into the Deluxe line. Available only as a 4-door sedan, the Metropolitan shared the Deluxe 119-inch wheelbase and appointments, yet it resembled the top-line Custom Torpedo sedan.

A new record of 330,061 Pontiac cars were produced during the model year, an astonishing 40 percent more than the previous best year of 1937.

Introduced in mid-year, the 1941 Metropolitan was an A-body copy of the C-body Custom Torpedo touring sedan. Priced at $921 with a six and $946 with an eight, it was $131 cheaper than its lookalike bigger brother.

Revised styling for 1942 made the Torpedo body seem longer and lower by extending the front fender back into the front door and emphasizing the triple "speed lines."

1942

By the time the 1942 models were introduced, Pontiac had been building 20mm Oerlikon anti-aircraft guns for the Navy for six months. Due to this military work, the entire C-body Custom Torpedo line was dropped. "Torpedo" became the name of Pontiac's lowest-priced line. Streamliners equipped with the luxury trim option were then called "Streamliner-Chieftains," the first appearance of the name that Pontiac would use extensively in the future.

Mechanical changes in 1942 were few. The convertible coupe now had wind-up rear quarter windows and a top operated by two electric motors rather than engine vacuum.

Like all auto manufacturers, Pontiac was restricted in its use of chromium plating after January 1, 1942; chromium was an alloying element in stainless steel which was used by the military. When production was stopped on February 10 by government order, Pontiac had already produced 83,555 1942-model cars.

For the next 3½ years Pontiac produced only war materiel. Its contracts included the Swiss-designed Oerlikon 20mm gun for the Navy, the Swedish-designed 40mm Bofors gun for the Army, aircraft-launched torpedoes for the Navy, the front axle for the Army's M5 medium tank, castings for truck engines, and various parts for 2-stroke diesel engines made by GM's Detroit Diesel division.

Army officers and Pontiac officials inspect a twin 40mm Bofors gun on an improvised mount. Pontiac built great quantities of the Bofors during WWII. Other wartime Pontiac work included the 20mm Oerlikon gun and air-launched torpedoes for the Navy, tank axles for the Army, and parts for diesel engines and trucks.

Postwar Placidity
1946–1948

During the years 1945–47, GM spent the gigantic sum of $588 million to modernize and expand its manufacturing capacity. Pontiac's share was $30 million to enlarge the assembly areas and the foundry.

For Pontiac the years 1946–48 can be summed up simply: more of 1942. Only two lines were offered: the A-body Torpedo with 119-inch wheelbase and the B-body Streamliner with 122-inch wheelbase. The only major innovation was the introduction of Hydra-Matic as an option in 1948. Yet sales boomed. Despite strikes and material shortages, in 1947 and 1948 Pontiac enjoyed sales almost equal to its second-best year of 1937.

Pontiac's auto production resumed on September 12, 1945, with the Streamliner sedan coupe, followed by the station wagon. The A-body Torpedo line did not re-enter production until June 10, 1946. Left unresumed were the Metropolitan and the upmarket Chieftain trim option for the Streamliner.

The Streamliner Eight outsold the Streamliner Six, continuing a growing preference for the 8-cylinder engine first noticed in the 1942 Streamliner and 1941 Custom.

Except for slightly changed grillework, 1946 Pontiacs were almost indistinguishable from 1942 models. This timber-bodied station wagon remained Pontiac's most expensive model.

1947

Changes in 1947 were few and minor. New spark plugs had longer insulators made of aluminum oxide instead of aluminum silicate. The 6-cylinder engine now used the same ignition coil as the eight, providing 15 percent greater output voltage. Both engines had vacuum-metering carburetors and improved head gaskets.

The convertible's top mechanism now used a single electric motor to drive a hydraulic pump.

The Streamliner sedan coupe, here in 1947 form, was Pontiac's most popular body style in the early postwar years.

1948

Chief engineer Benjamin H. Anibal retired in 1947, having held that post since Pontiac's origin in 1926. He was succeeded by George Delaney. Due to the conservatism of Anibal and general manager Harry Klingler, Pontiac did not offer Hydra-Matic earlier. Developed by GM Research and first introduced by Oldsmobile in 1939, Hydra-Matic was instantly popular and was offered by Cadillac for 1941. In the postwar period Buick and Chevrolet developed their own automatics, Dynaflow and Powerglide. Pontiac finally offered Hydra-Matic as a $185 option in 1948, and it was an immediate hit, ordered on no less than 73 percent of all 1948 Pontiacs.

The luxury trim package, last offered in 1942, returned in 1948 as the Deluxe option, and was offered on every model except the Torpedo 2-door sedan and business coupe. Pontiac considered this Deluxe package the same as an additional model, and rather cheekily advertised that it offered the greatly expanded range of 15 models for '48 compared to only nine in '47.

The convertible's instrument panel was now painted body color rather than the "quarter sawed mahogany" imitation wood finish of the closed cars.

The customer preference for the 8-cylinder engine was turning into a stampede; fully 67 percent now chose the larger engine.

Hydra-Matic became a best-selling option in 1948, the last year for the prewar body design. Styling clue for '48: the speed lines were replaced by a single trim spear and a rear fender gravel guard.

The Old Order Changeth
1949–1954

The old body with its separate fenders and towering grille was swept away by GM's 1949 styling revolution. The new Fisher A-body, shared with Chevrolet and Oldsmobile, was a clean and masterful design with a high straight-through fenderline, low hood, and strong horizontal grille.

Pontiac offered ten variations of it in two series. The Streamliner series was a fastback, and included a 4-door sedan and sedan coupe. The new Chieftain series, replacing the Torpedo, was a notchback; it had a 4-door sedan, 2-door sedan, sedan coupe, business coupe, and convertible coupe. In a separate group were two 4-door wagons: the Station Wagon, which had an all-steel structure with genuine wood applied as exterior decoration, and the All-Steel Station Wagon, identical except for exterior metal panels painted to resemble wood. A new model was the 2-door sedan delivery. Of these ten models, seven were available with a choice of standard or Deluxe

An all-new Chieftain delights two ladies in 1949. Lighter and smaller than the previous Torpedo, the Chieftain had more interior room and more glass area.

trim, so Pontiac claimed a total of 17 models. Both series had a wheelbase of 120 inches and an overall length of 202½ inches. The new body was one inch narrower, two inches lower, and two inches shorter than a '48 Torpedo, and weighed 150 pounds less.

Even more significant was the increase in interior room. The engine and seats were moved farther forward, which brought the rear seat out from between the wheel arches and allowed an astonishing 9½-inch increase in rear seat width.

Major chassis improvements included 15- x 5.5-inch wheels, low-pressure 7.10-15 tires, tubular shock absorbers, a redesigned "Gentleflex" front suspension, and a stiffer frame. In addition the doors were much larger, and so was the trunk, with a wider and counterbalanced lid. The rear window was eight inches wider and three inches taller, while the new "Wide-Horizon" windshield—still in two pieces—curved impressively.

The car that almost was: a 1949 Catalina. Pontiac's handsome hardtop did not actually debut until the following year. This fully finished car was displayed at a number of early GM shows touting the entire corporate line, but was then withdrawn.

The 1949 Fisher A-body was a milestone design. Lower, shorter, and narrower than its predecessor, it nevertheless had more interior room, larger openings, better visibility and less weight, yet was no more expensive to manufacture. It was also much handsomer.

Inside the new Pontiac, the instrument panel was finished in two-tone gray. The "Dial-Cluster" arrangement grouped four minor gauges around the speedometer, which had a clever molded-in magnifying lens. A starter button replaced the previous foot starter, and a "Nite-Lite" illuminated the ignition switch.

Ignition timing marks were moved from the flywheel to the harmonic balancer on both engines. One horsepower was gained by the eight by an increase in carburetor venturi size from 1¼ to $1\frac{5}{16}$ inches.

To compensate for the smaller 15-inch wheels, which might have caused brake overheating, the front brake shoes were widened by ¼-inch, which increased the total lining area from 159 to 171 square inches.

The best new option was the completely redesigned "Venti-Heat" system, which cost $68.25 and was located under the front seat. The small underdash Weather Chief unit was discontinued.

Another popular option was the illuminated hood ornament—Chief Pontiac's face of amber plastic was lit up by a small bulb at night. Still fondly recalled today, this accessory would last until the V-8 era.

Sales for 1949 were 304,819, second only to 1941. Hydra-Matic (67 percent) and the 8-cylinder engine (77 percent) remained overwhelming preferences.

Another view of the '49 Catalina shows its graceful shape and large 3-piece backlight. The production version of 1950 was identical to this car except for model year identification. Harley Earl's "hardtop convertible," introduced into all five GM divisions in 1949–50, would soon sweep the industry.

1950

A name that would last for 30 years made its debut this year: the Catalina. This was Pontiac's version of GM styling head Harley Earl's spectacular 2-door hardtop, introduced in 1949 as the Cadillac Coupe de Ville, Buick Riviera, and Oldsmobile Holiday. The Catalina and Chevrolet's version, the Bel Air, did not appear until 1950.

Where did the Catalina get its name? Airplane lovers might recall the graceful Navy twin-engine patrol bomber of World War II, the Consolidated PBY Catalina. However, the new hardtop was named for the island of Santa Catalina, some 30 miles off the coast of

Pontiac's big news for 1950 was the Catalina hardtop. This is the Super Deluxe version, with its standard 8-cylinder engine, leather interior, and exclusive exterior colors of San Pedro Ivory and Sierra Rust.

Southern California, and simply called "Catalina" by Californians. Discovered in 1542 and named for the fourth-century martyr St. Catherine of Alexandria, it has been owned since 1919 by the Chicago-based Wrigley family of chewing gum fame. The island's only settlement is the harbor town of Avalon, famed for its unusually clear waters. Though Pontiac's 1950 Catalina brochure never mentioned the island directly, it was full of lush resort scenes. And on its cover was the giveaway to anyone familiar with the island: a yacht harbor nestled next to a large circular white-pillared building which could only have been the Casino, Avalon's most famous and prominent structure.

With its wide-sweeping 3-piece rear window and lack of center posts, Pontiac's Catalina had the open airy feeling of a convertible. This convertible impression inside a Catalina was heightened by several clever touches. A molding running around the roof edge above the glass areas resembled the reinforced edge of a convertible top. A small rectangular corner light was placed in this molding on each side of the car just above the rear seat, while transverse chrome trim strips across the headliner mimicked a convertible's crossbows.

Two Catalina trim levels were offered: the Deluxe, finished like a Deluxe sedan and costing $2,069; and the Super Deluxe, which cost $2,127.

Only two exterior colors were available for the Super Deluxe Catalina, both indicative of the California influence: Sierra Rust and San Pedro Ivory. The Sierra Nevada range is the mountainous backbone of the state, and San Pedro is the port city for Los Angeles; the Catalina steamship made its round trip between Avalon and San Pedro.

The Super Deluxe Catalina was the most luxurious car in America for its price. Top-grain genuine leather covered the seats, with cushions in rust and the bolsters in ivory. The rust/ivory motif was carried out on the door panels, instrument panel, and even the steering wheel. The driver had a choice of ordering either engine or transmission.

The year brought many major changes. The wood-trimmed station wagon was discontinued. The bore of the 8-cylinder engine was enlarged to 3⅜ inches, increasing the displacement to 268.2 cubic inches. With standard 6.5:1 compression ratio it was now rated at 108 hp; the optional 7.5:1 ratio raised this to 113 hp.

The auto industry had a boom year, and Pontiac set a soaring new sales record of 446,429 cars. However, the Korean War started on June 25, and would eventually cause material shortages.

The Catalina's distinctive interior was strongly evocative of a convertible. It had a ribbed and pleated headliner, stainless steel trim, heavy molding above the windows, rear quarter lamps, and leather upholstery matched to the body exterior colors.

1951

Both engines were uprated for Pontiac's silver anniversary. With standard 6.5:1 compression ratio the eight had 116 hp, the six 96 hp; the optional 7.5:1 ratio raised these outputs to 120 and 100 hp.

Pontiac's flagship, the Super Deluxe Catalina, was again offered in two exclusive colors with a color-keyed interior, Sapphire Blue and Malibu Ivory. The Streamliner, however, was dying. The sedan was dropped, leaving only the sedan coupe in the series which was once the height of fashion.

The Korean War took its toll as certain critical materials were rationed, and production fell to 370,159. Eight-cylinder preference rose again to 85 percent, and 80 percent of the eights had Hydra-Matic.

"The Pontiac Motor Trial this month is one of the most thorough inquisitions ever performed in a road test conducted by any publication," according to *Motor Trend* who subjected a 1951 Chieftain Eight Deluxe 4-door sedan to a sound thrashing. This 3500-mile "motor trial" was the longest in *Motor Trend*'s young history, and the first road test of a Pontiac by any motoring magazine. *MT* liked the overall fuel economy of 17.49 miles per gallon, the brakes, the cooling system, and the rock-solid reliability. The ride was "as reasonable a compromise as the steering" and the acceleration "about average." The top speed was 87.7 mph. The Hydra-Matic, however, exhibited a major flaw: "Going downgrade through the mountains, and particularly when following a stream of traffic . . . I had to constantly apply the brakes . . . a downshift to the Low range is impractical since it is too low a gear." Unknown to *Motor Trend*, Pontiac was about to remedy that Hydra-Matic deficiency.

The Silver Anniversary models for 1951 had only minor trim changes from 1950, as shown by this Chieftain Deluxe Eight.

Harry J. Klingler, who retired in 1951, had been Pontiac's general manager since 1933. His 18-year span as Pontiac's boss would remain unrivaled in divisional history.

1952

The improved Dual-Range Hydra-Matic appeared this year on Pontiacs, as well as Cadillacs and Oldsmobiles. Hydra-Matic consisted of a fluid coupling and three planetary gearsets, which provided four forward speeds and reverse. Prior to 1952, there were only four positions in the H-M shift quadrant: N, DR, LO, R. In LO, the transmission would start in first gear, shift up to second, then stay there; in DR, it would start in first gear and shift up through the

All Pontiac convertibles had an attractive line and a fully disappearing top, as this '52 version demonstrates. The new Dual-Range Hydra-Matic greatly improved the '52's driving characteristics.

other three gears in sequence. As *Motor Trend* pointed out, there was a problem with this arrangement which became glaringly evident in mountain driving: you could not downshift above 40 mph, the maximum speed for LO range (second gear).

In the new Dual-Range Hydra-Matic, DR was actually two positions, indicated by little triangles on either side of the "DR" letters. In the △ DR position the automatic behaved in its usual manner, shifting up 1-2-3-4 sequentially. In DR △ it shifted 1-2-3 and then stopped. This was the "traffic" or "mountain" range, in which third gear became top gear. Shifting between the two DR positions could be done at any speed, though the transmission would not actually downshift to third gear at speeds much greater than 60 mph.

In either DR range the traditional H-M feature of downshifting by flooring the throttle was retained.

The dual DR range was not the only H-M improvement. In LO range it now started out in second gear; first gear was engaged only if the driver floored the throttle, and then only if car speed was less than 10 mph. This new arrangement made the car smoother, more economical, and easier to control at low speeds under slippery conditions.

For $150, the D-R H-M was an immense improvement. Only two criticisms could really be leveled at it. One was that there was no "Park" position; the driver had to select R with the ignition off to engage the parking pawl. The other was that N (neutral) should logically have been placed between forward and reverse positions.

Offered only with D-R H-M was a new 3.08 axle ratio, the highest ratio yet offered in Pontiac's history.

All engines had higher compression ratios. The standard 6.8:1 resulted in 118 hp for the eight and 100 hp for the six; the optional 7.7:1 ratio raised these to 122 and 102 hp.

A '52 Pontiac is barely distinguishable from a '51, as the whole auto industry kept changes to a minimum to avoid problems with tooling suppliers, who were busy with military contracts. The model lineup was simplified. Gone was the last of the Streamliners, the sedan coupe, as well as the Chieftain sedan coupe and business coupe.

By contrast, the Catalina was becoming a runaway success. In the Super Deluxe version, the special colors offered for 1952 were pale Seamist Green and dark Belfast Green.

A Catalina exclusive was the new "flipper" door seal. A metal spring-loaded flap, mounted in the roof over each door, flipped down over the window glass and provided a positive weather seal.

Motor Trend's 1952 Chieftain Deluxe Eight accelerated through a quarter-mile a half-second quicker than the '51 test Pontiac, had a top speed five mph greater, and obtained notably better fuel economy.

Production dropped to 271,373 for the model year, reflecting the slowdown in the whole auto industry. Eight-cylinder preference now reached a whopping 92.7 percent, and 87 percent of the eights had Hydra-Matic.

A new design for the 1949 models, Pontiac's simple and sturdy chassis received only minor modifications for the next five years; this is the 1953 version.

1953

A bigger body was the big news in 1953. At 122 inches, the wheelbase was longer by two inches, the additional floor length being used in the rear passenger area. The overall length increased by just 0.2 inches, however, due to a redesign of the trunk and rear bumper. Visibility was improved by the new one-piece windshield and wraparound rear window.

All Pontiacs were now Chieftains, either Special or Deluxe. Included in the Deluxe series was the Custom Catalina, the new name

Introduced in 1953, "Curve Control" (right) was a modification of the front suspension arms which reduced wheel camber change during cornering.

In 1953 the Pontiac body received the first sheet metal changes since 1949. The new one-piece windshield and larger wraparound backlight improved visibility, while the bulges and flares on the fenders gave the illusion of a heavier car.

for the former Super Deluxe Catalina. It still retained its pair of exclusive colors; this year they were Laurel Green and Milano Ivory.

Entrance and exit from any 2-door model was aided by new front seats which tilted inward as they were folded forward.

The 6-cylinder engine now had a dual-throat carburetor, 7:1 compression ratio, a hotter cam, and 115 hp, or 118 hp with an optional 7.7:1 compression ratio. The eight received a larger oil pump. Optional power steering was available for the first time, costing $177.40.

The front suspension was revised to reduce camber change and brake dive. Combined with longer coil springs, stronger A-arm supports, and revised shock absorber valving, this improved suspension was dubbed "Curve Control."

For $53.65, the wondrous "Autronic Eye" automatically dimmed the headlights.

Sales recovered nicely to 418,619 cars, the second-highest in history. A setback, however, was the disastrous fire at GM's Hydra-Matic plant in Livonia, Michigan, in August. Chevy's Powerglide was temporarily substituted in Pontiacs, 17,797 of which were built.

The most famous Pontiac accessory of all was the illuminated face of Chief Pontiac, available from 1949 to 1954. The Chief's vertical headdress and the twin silver streaks mark this as a '53 version.

1954

Introduced this year was a whole new upmarket series, the Star Chief, which was bigger, pricier, and more luxurious than any previous Pontiac.

The Star Chief's wheelbase was two inches longer than that of a Chieftain and its overall length was an immense eleven inches greater, most of which went into the cavernous trunk. As its sales brochure shamelessly noted, the Star Chief had the "unmistakable stamp of a highway aristocrat" with "dramatically long lines—barely short of eighteen feet overall!"

There were two Star Chief lines, Deluxe and Custom. The top Custom models, a 4-door sedan and a Catalina, were offered in special colors—Coral Red, Maize Yellow, Biloxi Beige—with color-matched leather-and-nylon interiors. As Pontiac's lushest 4-door, the Star Chief Custom sedan was the production version of its 1953 show car, the Avalon. Too bad it didn't carry that lovely name. All Star Chiefs had the 8-cylinder engine as standard equipment.

The Chieftain series had its usual two lines, Special and Deluxe, and also a third new line, the Chieftain Custom. This contained only one model, a Catalina, which was a shorter version of the Star Chief Custom Catalina, but with a choice of either engine.

For the Star Chief Deluxe convertible appeared a new upholstery material: Morrokide. Described as "an extra-durable and extra-weatherproof coated fabric," Morrokide was what we today call vinyl—a polyvinyl plastic coating on a stretchable backing of knitted nylon. In a few short years Morrokide would supplant all other fabrics to become Pontiac's dominant upholstery material.

One of two spectacular show cars unveiled by Pontiac at the 1954 GM Motorama was the Bonneville Special, a fiberglass-bodied 2-seat sports coupe. This car had a 100-inch wheelbase, 4-carburetor straight-8 engine, Hydra-Matic transmission, and a plexiglass canopy with flip-up panels. Pontiac general manager Bob Critchfield (right) poses with GM president Harlow Curtice. Behind the wheel is Betty Skelton, a record-setting driver who competed frequently at Bonneville and Daytona speed events.

The other 1954 Pontiac show car was the Strato Streak II, a futuristic 4-door hardtop. Made of fiberglass, it had the same 124-inch wheelbase as a production Star Chief. Four bucket seats were fitted; the front two could swivel up to 90 degrees for easy entrance and exit.

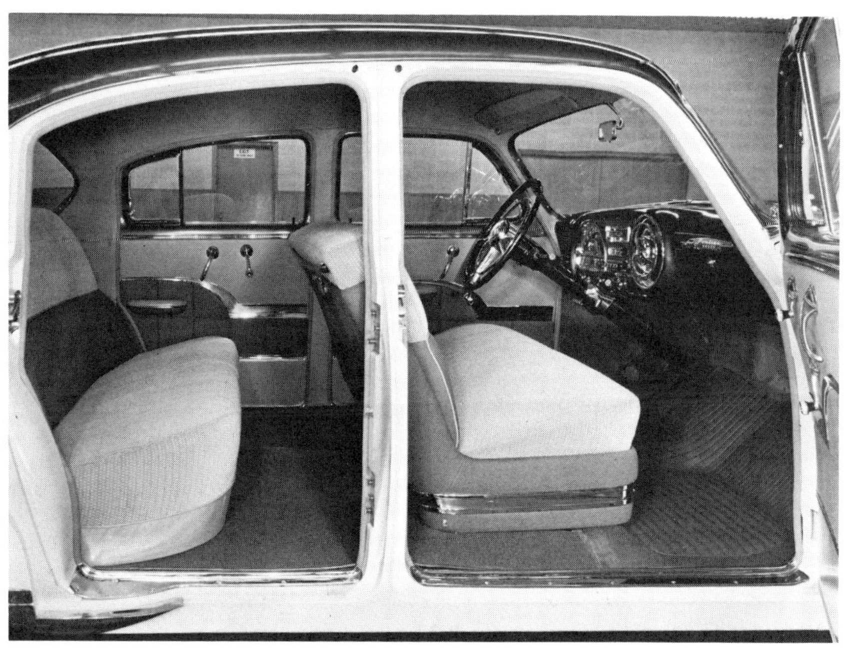

A typical Pontiac sedan of the early '50s was upholstered in nylon and broadcloth. Pontiac's vinyl upholstery material, "Morrokide," first appeared in several 1954 models.

The optional "Comfort-Control" seat, introduced in 1954, was Pontiac's ingenious answer to the "power seats" of rivals. Though it contained no electric motors, this seat could be adjusted to 360 positions.

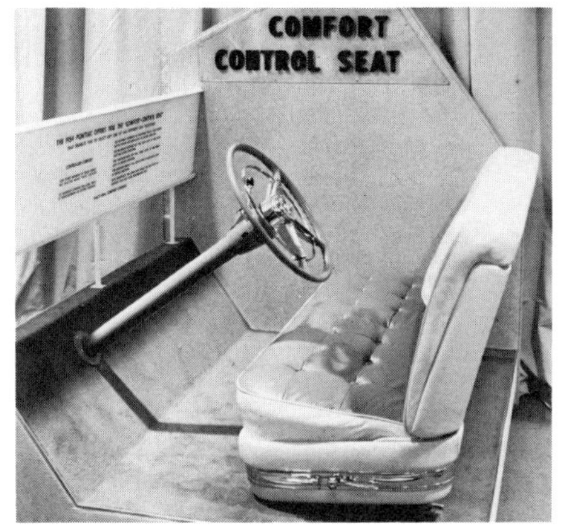

The new air conditioning system was a breakthrough. For the first time an automotive air refrigeration system had all of its components under the hood, an arrangement made possible by a compact evaporator. The A/C system weighed 110 pounds, and was available only with the 8-cylinder engine. Pontiac made a number of modifications to A/C-equipped cars, including a 6-bladed fan, heavy-duty fuel-vacuum pump, larger battery, 50-amp generator, 13-psi radiator cap, stiffer front springs, 7.60 x 15 tires, and a lower axle ratio.

Air conditioning was a marvelous option, but it cost the earth: $594, or about one-quarter the cost of an entire car!

Other new options were a vacuum-boosted power brake system for $35, and electric front window lifts for $49.

The "Comfort-Control" front bench seat was an ingenious oddity that used no electric motors. Its motions came from cleverly arranged ratchets, controlled by one button and two levers on the driver's side. Pontiac claimed that this seat could be adjusted to 360 different positions.

The *Motor Trend* summation of the 1954 Star Chief Deluxe sedan could be the perfect definition of all that the division had been trying to do since 1926: "It is not a car with lightning acceleration, it doesn't ride like an easy chair with sponge rubber wheels, and it won't corner like a Ferrari. But people don't buy Pontiacs

The Parisienne was a show car for the 1953 GM Motorama. Based on a standard '53 chassis, it was an updated interpretation of a classic-era town car.

The Star Chief was a completely new line for 1954. This is a Star Chief Custom Sedan, which had richer interiors than the Star Chief Deluxe. All Star Chiefs had 8-cylinder engines.

for . . . those reasons. The '54 Pontiac simply continues its old, admirable role as a top family car at a down-to-earth price."

Motor Trend meant to be kind, but it made a Pontiac sound like the next best thing to a sleeping pill. For the same price as a Star Chief Custom sedan a buyer could have the 185-hp Oldsmobile Super 88 or Buick's blazing new 200-hp Century, exciting and handsome cars which could effortlessly blow the doors off any Pontiac. In an automotive age that was becoming hooked on horsepower, Pontiac's unspectacular virtues were often interpreted as uncaring obsolescence.

The division's sales for 1954 nosedived to only 69 percent of its '53 sales. Worse, it dropped from its traditional fifth place in the industry (behind the "low-priced three" and Buick, which had outsold Pontiac since 1938) to sixth, passed by the Rocket-powered Oldsmobile fleet. Though next lowest in price to Chevrolet, Pontiac was in the embarrassing position of being outsold by every other GM division except Cadillac.

One lesson was now crystal-clear: power sold, and more power sold more. Pontiac desperately needed an injection of raw muscle. Just in time, it arrived.

New Engine, New Image, New Boss 1955–1956

Nineteen fifty-five was one of the most significant years in the history of the American auto industry, as fresh new designs powered by brilliant new engines appeared everywhere. Pontiac's own turnaround was equally dramatic, highlighted by a new V-8 engine.

Experimental work on V-8 engines had been going on at Pontiac since 1945. The first design was a flathead V-8 displacing 269 cubic inches, similar in concept to the then-current Cadillac 346 V-8. Between 1946 and 1949, eight examples were built.

The flathead investigations were abandoned when revolutionary new overhead-valve V-8s appeared in the 1949 Cadillac and Oldsmobile. Using the Olds block, Pontiac built seven examples of a 272 V-8 which were used to test various combustion chamber designs and overhead valve mechanisms.

By 1950, work was started in earnest on a third design intended to be the production version, an overhead-valve design displacing 268 cubic inches. It had a number of outstanding features—notably its revolutionary stamped stud-mounted rocker arms—and shared a common bore diameter and interchangeable pistons with an overhead-valve six, then also under development. Eleven examples were built. Influenced by information leaking out about Chevrolet's planned 265 V-8, in 1951 this engine was enlarged to 287 cubic inches. By the end of 1952, 42 examples of this "V-287" engine had been built and exhaustively tested.

Pontiac engineers were aiming at two targets: they wanted a better engine than their own straight eight, and a cheaper engine than the Oldsmobile Rocket 303 V-8.

Success was achieved on all points. The V-8's dry weight was 630.3 pounds, 43 pounds less than the 673-pound straight eight. Its overall length was 29 inches, a whopping 10.6 inches shorter than the straight eight. It could be manufactured for $208.75, compared to $190.60 for the straight eight and $228.51 for the Olds V-8.

Dubbed the "Strato-Streak V-8," it had a bore and stroke of 3.75 by 3.25 inches, and was Pontiac's first engine with overhead valve gear and oversquare cylinder dimensions. (It was not, however, the first Pontiac V-8; in 1932 the division had offered a leftover 1931 Oakland flathead V-8.)

With 8:1 compression ratio and 2-bbl. carburetor, the Strato-Streak V-8 was rated at 180 hp, and was standard on all models. Optional only with manual transmission was an economy version with 7.4:1 compression ratio and 173 hp. At the last minute came a $35 option: a 200-hp version with a 4-bbl. carburetor.

The V-8 had an advanced lubrication system with four oil galleries—one on each side of the block and one in each cylinder head—which delivered oil under pressure to the valve train as well as the usual crankshaft and camshaft bearings.

The new 287 "Strato-Streak" V-8 powered all 1955 Pontiacs. This marvelous engine would soon push Pontiac to the forefront of the performance field, and successive modifications would keep it competitive for nearly a quarter-century.

An all-new body appeared in 1955; this 2-door wagon was one of four models in the low-priced Chieftain 860 line.

The engine's most unusual feature was its rocker arm arrangement. Instead of the traditional forged arms mounted on a shaft, the new V-8 used stamped rocker arms which pivoted about hemispherical "ball" retainers. Each retainer was secured by a lock nut onto a stud. The holes into which the studs were pressed terminated in the cylinder head's oil gallery, and each stud was drilled lengthwise. In operation, oil from the gallery came up through the stud and out another hole near the ball-pivot, thus lubricating the rocker arm where it pivoted on the ball. Additional lubrication was provided by oil which was forced up through the hollow pushrods.

The chief advantage of the ball-pivot rocker arms was that they automatically aligned themselves squarely on the pushrods. They were also cheaper, lighter, and stronger than forged rocker arms, reduced valve train inertia, and eliminated the rocker shafts.

During development of its own V-8, Chevrolet learned of Pontiac's experimental ball-pivot rocker arms and requested information. Pontiac assented, and this feature then appeared on Chevy's own 265 V-8 in 1955. The notion persists even today that Chevrolet was the originator of this ingenious design, even though the engineering team responsible for the new Chevy engine—Harry Barr, Ed Kelley, and Chevrolet chief engineer Ed Cole—repeatedly gave credit to Pontiac.

The 1955 Star Chief was quickly identified by three stars ahead of the side trim strip.

Top of the line for 1955 was the Star Chief Custom series, a sedan and this Catalina. Star Chief Customs had a bright trim strip above the side windows and a large stainless steel molding on the lower rear fender.

Firing the V-8 was Pontiac's first 12-volt electrical system, which gave a hotter spark, faster cranking speed, and greater capacity for auxiliaries.

Such was the Pontiac V-8, a classic engine design. In the years to follow it would grow rapidly in size and power and fame, establishing Pontiac's performance image and eventually propelling the division into third place in U.S. auto sales.

No 6-cylinder engine was offered in 1955, though Pontiac did preliminary investigation on a modern overhead-valve design. Its developments was halted in 1951, as it became clear that a detuned version of the V-8 would be far more satisfactory as an economy engine. What finally emerged in 1955 was the low-compression 173-hp version of the V-8.

Numerous refinements improved the ride and handling. The all-new body was 2.7 inches lower and 1.2 inches narrower than the 1949–54 body, yet hip room was 2 inches wider in front and 2.4 inches wider in the rear. This was GM's B body, shared with Olds and smaller Buicks. Its most obvious change was the wraparound panoramic windshield.

The front brake drums were increased one inch in diameter to 12 inches, and the total lining area grew from 171 to 178 square inches. In the chassis the frame was revised for greater rigidity and a lower floor. The front suspension now had vertical king pins—formerly inclined inwards by five degrees—and shorter upper control arms. A recirculating-ball steering gearbox replaced the previous worm-and-roller type, while the forward perches of the rear leaf springs were moved to the outside of the frame rails. All models now had tubeless tires as standard equipment.

Introduced in mid-1955, the Safari was a special luxury station wagon. The roof structure, glass areas, and rear fenders were quite different from standard Chieftain wagons. Fitted with Star Chief Custom interior and exterior trim and packing a 200-hp engine as standard equipment, the Safari was Pontiac's most expensive 1955 model.

The air conditioning system was revised to mate with the new cowl ventilation system, offering a choice of fresh or recirculated air, and electric window lifts now operated on all four windows.

In January 1955, at the Motorama Show in the Waldorf-Astoria Hotel in New York City, GM displayed a pair of sporty 2-door station wagons. The Pontiac Safari had a 122-inch wheelbase while the Chevrolet Nomad had a 115-inch wheelbase, but they shared a common roof, windows, doors, tailgates, and inner fender panels. Both were announced as production models in February.

Since Pontiac already had three wagons in its two Chieftain lines, the Safari was marketed as a Star Chief. It carried the exterior trim of the Star Chief Custom line, offered a choice of Morrokide or leather upholstery, and had the 200-hp engine as standard equipment. Its base price was $2,962, making the Safari the most expensive model yet in Pontiac's history.

Motor Trend tested three '55 Pontiacs: a Star Chief sedan with the standard 180-hp engine, a Star Chief Custom Catalina with the optional 200-hp engine, and a Safari.

Loaded with automatic transmission, power steering, and power brakes, the 4,060-pound Star Chief sedan scooted to 60 mph in 13.8 seconds, a full 3.6 seconds quicker than *MT*'s 1954 Star Chief. It topped out at 100.3 mph, the first Pontiac *MT* had ever been able to coax past 100 mph.

Two features which *MT* praised were its roadability and brakes. "We place it among the top handling cars of '55," the magazine stated. "After numerous acceleration runs and hard, fast stops, there is absolutely no indication of brake fade."

MT found that in the other Pontiacs the 200-hp Custom Catalina was notably quicker than the sedan. It jumped out to 60 mph in 1.1 seconds less time, and knocked 2.1 seconds off the 50–80 mph time.

The Safari was wrung out on a week-long 2,600-mile tour of the American southwest. *MT* liked the visibility—"like sitting in a Vista-Dome Greyhound or train"—its convenience, and "better-than-average roadability," and the average fuel economy of 16.6 miles per gallon.

In just one year Pontiac had made great strides, but so had everyone else. As *Motor Trend* put it, the '55 Pontiac "will appeal to the same crowd that used to like it, plus a number of new friends." The old family-car image was still there. Enough of the same crowd and new friends responded to set a new sales record of 554,000 cars.

On September 18, GM president Harlow H. "Red" Curtice addressed a meeting of Pontiac sales personnel in Detroit. "Your penetration of the market represents a 93 percent increase over your 1954 model year—an outstanding accomplishment." He predicted more of the same. "I think this high level of activity will continue for 1956. We have more people working today for high wages, taking home more money, than ever before in the history of this great country. I can see no reason why that full employment should not continue." Curtice, soon to be chosen *Time* magazine's "Man of the Year" for 1955, had cause for ebullience. The auto industry had its best-ever year, selling 7.2 million cars, and every one of GM's divisions had set new sales records. Pontiac was now fully recovered, nipping at Oldsmobile's heels for fifth sales spot. Yet Curtice's prediction would prove to be wrong.

Pontiac's 1955 show car was the Strato Star. The 2-door 6-passenger coupe was finished in metallic silver, with vermilion red for the interior and wheel wells. Only 53 inches high, it featured hinged roof panels which automatically raised when the doors were opened.

The only new body style for 1956 was the 4-door Catalina; this is the Star Chief version. Both 2-door and 4-door Catalinas were offered in every Pontiac line for '56.

1956

After the great splurge of changes in 1955 came the refinements of 1956: a new body style, larger engine, improved Hydra-Matic, and line re-evaluations. The new body was a 4-door hardtop. Like the 2-door version, this was an idea conceived by Harley Earl and brought to production throughout GM. Pontiac's version was unimaginatively named "4-door Catalina." It is unfortunate that another name like "Avalon" was not used, preserving the hard-won prestige of the Catalina name for the 2-door hardtop.

The Star Chief Custom series was dropped. Instead, all Star Chiefs except the sedan were finished, as was the previous Star Chief Custom line, with lush leather-trimmed interiors harmonizing with exclusive exterior colors.

The two Chieftain lines were no longer called Chieftains, but 860 and 870. Catalinas were added to both lines, so Pontiac could advertise that both Catalina variants were available in all three of its lines.

All '56 models were 2.4 inches longer, due entirely to the more massive front bumper. At $3,124, the Safari was again the most expensive model.

Pontiac wasted little time enlarging its V-8. The bore was increased 3⁄16-inch to 3.94 inches, raising the displacement to 316.6 cubic inches. An economy version had 7.9:1 compression ratio, 2-bbl. carburetor, and an unspecified power output. Standard on 860 and 870 with Hydra-Matic was a compression ratio of 8.9:1, a hotter cam, and 205 hp. Standard on Star Chief was 4-bbl. carburetion and 227 hp. Dual exhaust was a separate option on either of the high-compression versions, raising their outputs to 215 hp for the 2-bbl. and 240 hp for the 4-bbl.

In January Pontiac announced a special engine for stock-car racing. For the astonishingly low price of $31, this "Extra Horsepower" option had 10:1 compression ratio, two 4-bbl. carbs, dual exhaust, a hot camshaft with 71° of valve overlap instead of the standard 58°, stiffer valve springs, and a special racing distributor. Rated at 285 hp, it was the first Pontiac engine aimed at the high-performance market. Although it started late in the horsepower race, Pontiac was catching up fast.

The Dual-Range Hydra-Matic was modified so extensively that it had a new name: Strato-Flight Hydra-Matic. The principal change was the substitution of a small hydraulic coupling and a sprag clutch in place of the previous band and multiplate clutch in the front unit, which resulted in a much smoother shifting action. Other improvements were a larger capacity front oil pump, a transmission cooler, and—at last—a "Park" position on the shift quadrant.

Motor Trend's first test Pontiac this year was a Star Chief 4-door Catalina loaded with everything except air conditioning. It accelerated to 60 mph in 11.1 seconds, from 50-80 mph in 13.7 seconds, and had a top speed of 106.2 mph.

A few months later the magazine got its eager hands on a 285-hp 860 with automatic transmission. Unfortunately, this car had only 66 miles on the odometer, and *MT* apologized for its poor performance with such a tight engine. Nevertheless, it turned in a 50-80 run which took only 12.1 seconds. Properly broken in, this model should have been capable of 115 mph and a 0-60 time of 10 seconds.

The Club de Mer is carried away in a Motorama van—with Chevrolet's name! This view emphasizes the small size of the roadster, and shows the engine air outlets incorporated into the doors.

More auto show hoopla as Pontiac's Club de Mer roadster is surrounded at the 1956 Motorama. Only 38 inches high, the body was aluminum alloy anodized in cerulean blue—the leather interior was vermilion red. A rear-mounted manual transmission allowed room in the snug cockpit, and a 4-carb 300-hp V-8 provided plenty of motive power.

Changes also occurred in the administration at Pontiac. On July 1 Semon E. Knudsen became Pontiac's general manager, bringing a famous name to the division. His father was William S. "Big Bill" Knudsen, a Danish-born engineer with a talent that matched his 6-foot 3-inch 235-pound size. For ten years Bill Knudsen was Henry Ford's production ramrod, pushing the massive assembly lines in Highland Park that made the Model T Ford the wonder of the industrial age. Eventually he had a falling out with Ford, and joined Chevrolet in 1922. In 1932–33 he was Pontiac's general manager, and eventually GM president 1937–40. His son, Semon, nicknamed "Bunkie" from boyhood camping trips, was the first and only son to follow his father as general manager of a GM division.

Opportunities to make major personnel changes soon came Knudsen's way. In September George Delaney retired, and to replace him as chief engineer Knudsen tapped Elliot M. "Pete" Estes. A graduate of the General Motors Institute and University of Cincinnati, Estes had worked at the GM Research Laboratories under the legendary Charles F. "Boss Ket" Kettering. Joining Oldsmobile, he participated in the design of its epochal 1949 V-8 engine and became its assistant chief engineer in 1954. Knudsen appointed John Zachary DeLorean as director of advanced engineering under Estes only a few months later.

Semon E. "Bunkie" Knudsen became Pontiac's general manager on July 1, 1956. Son of former GM president William Knudsen, Semon is given credit for transforming Pontiac into a maker—in his words—of a "young man's car."

In Estes and DeLorean, Knudsen chose well indeed. Both would succeed him as Pontiac's general manager, both would follow him as general manager of Chevrolet, and Estes became president of General Motors. Taken together, the Knudsen-Estes-DeLorean years of 1956–69 would be Pontiac's years of glory.

Pontiac sales fell to just over 400,000; the 1955 boom did not continue despite Curtice's best hopes. Most notable about the sales figures was the astonishing rise in popularity of the hardtops. In 1950, the first year of the Catalina, it accounted for 8.06 percent of Pontiac production. By 1956, with 2-door and 4-door Catalinas in every line, they amounted to *60.04 percent* of all Pontiacs produced.

Pontiac's burgeoning performance image was given a huge boost just before Knudsen took office. In June, perennial Bonneville contender Ab Jenkins drove a 285-hp 860 2-door sedan to a new NASCAR 24-hour distance record. Using a huge circle ten miles in circumference on the Utah salt flats, Jenkins covered 2,841 miles at an average speed of 118.375 mph; he broke the previous record by 219 miles.

The six millionth Pontiac, a Star Chief 2-door Catalina, rolled off the assembly lines on August 17 making it a real red-letter day.

"Pontiac" Means "Performance" 1957–1958

Knudsen quickly used his position to put his stamp on Pontiac design. Viewing the prototypes for the upcoming '57 models shortly after he took office, he took an immediate dislike to one minor but hallmark feature: the time-honored silver streak, a traditional Pontiac styling feature which dated back to 1935. On the new cars this was scheduled to be a pair of trim strips near the outside edges of the hood. Knudsen ordered them removed, causing a panic among the production engineers since only a few weeks remained for new tooling to be installed for the annual model change. This action carried great psychological weight, for it showed everyone that the new general manager was determined to forge a new image.

The Strato-Streak V-8 was enlarged again to 347 cubic inches by lengthening the stroke from 3¼ to 3⁹⁄₁₆ inches. There were four power ratings, ranging from a 227-hp economy version to 270 hp. All main bearings were enlarged by ⅛ inch to 2.62 inches. The block casting was stronger, the bearing caps heavier, oil rings improved, and the valve guides vented.

Originally, a special high-performance engine using two 4-bbl. carbs, similar to the 1956 285-hp engine, was planned. However, it

Though chrome-laden, 1957 Pontiacs had graceful proportions, shown well by this Star Chief Custom Catalina Sedan.

was shelved in favor of a pair of triple 2-bbl. engines which were announced in December 1956 under the general name "Tri-Power." The "Triple Carburetor" engine had 290 hp and was available only with Hydra-Matic; it was the standard 10:1 high-compression engine fitted with three Rochester 2-bbl. carbs. The "Extra Horsepower" engine was considerably modified for sustained high output and available only with manual transmission.

There were two versions of the Extra Horsepower engine. One had a hydraulic-lifter cam, the other had mechanical tappets and a camshaft with higher lift but less radical timing. This latter version was a factory-approved installation of an Iskenderian aftermarket cam kit. Pontiac rated both versions at 317 hp @ 5200 rpm.

As a graphic example of the rapid change of Pontiac's image, the *least* powerful engine in 1957 had exactly one hundred *more* horsepower than its *most* powerful engine just three years before!

Again there were body refinements. The hood was 1.6 inches lower, overall height was ½ inch lower due to the switch to 14-inch wheels, and bigger bumpers increased the overall length by 1.2 inches.

Making a return from 1955 was the Star Chief Custom line with its leather interiors; it included 2-door and 4-door Catalinas and a sedan. The Star Chief line had another sedan and a convertible. "Super Chief" was the new name for the 870 line, while the familiar "Chieftain" name returned for the 860 series.

All station wagons for 1957 were called Safaris. The top model was the 2-door Star Chief Custom Safari, which retained the distinctive roof shape and leather interior. There was a 4-door, 2-seat

This late styling prototype of the '57 Pontiac shows the twin silver streaks intended for production. Knudsen removed them at the last minute.

Safari in the Super Chief line, while the Chieftain line had its usual 2-door, 2-seat and 4-door, 3-seat wagons.

Pontiac displayed three cars at the National Automobile Show in New York in January, two of which became production models. "La Parisienne," however, a Star Chief Custom sedan finished in Coral Mist and White Pearl with an asymmetric-pattern interior, did not see production. One of the three cars displayed was a 4-door luxury wagon, officially called the "Star Chief Custom Four-Door Safari." Pontiac tried to get around that awkward name by also calling it the "Transcontinental," but the name didn't stick. Transcontinental was an upmarket version of the Super Chief and Chieftain wagons; it did not have the distinctive roof shape and glass areas of the 2-door Star Chief Custom Safari.

The third of the New York Show trio carried a name destined for immortality: Bonneville. It was a Star Chief convertible with magic words on the front fenders and trunk lid: "fuel injection."

The Rochester injection system on the Bonneville was the same as that available as an option on '57 Chevrolets and Corvettes. With it, Chevrolet claimed to be the first U.S. manufacturer to achieve one horsepower per cubic inch of displacement from a production engine. (The 1956 Chrysler 300B with its optional high-compression engine was actually the first.) Pontiac, however, was unexpectedly

Rarest of 1957 Pontiacs was the Bonneville, introduced in mid-year. All '57 Bonnevilles were fuel-injected convertibles.

reticent about the Bonneville engine, stating only that it had "in excess of 300 horsepower." This discretion was caused by the fact that the injected engine produced 310 hp; this was not only less than one hp per cubic inch, it was even less than Pontiac's own carbureted Extra Horsepower engine. The injected engine did, however, idle more smoothly and obtain better fuel economy than any Tri-Power version.

In February the Bonneville was placed in limited production. Included in its list price of $5,782 was virtually every accessory Pontiac manufactured. The only options offered were air conditioning and an externally mounted spare tire. Only 630 Bonnevilles were made during the model year, making a '57 Bonnie one of the most sought-after collectible Pontiacs today.

Motor Trend tested two Super Chief Catalina coupes with the 270-hp engine and Hydra-Matic and found blistering performances: 0 to 60 in 8.7 seconds, 50 to 80 in 8.3 seconds, and the quarter-mile in 16.6 seconds. "Acceleration is simply fantastic in any speed range," the tests reported glowingly. "The Pontiac is the fastest-accelerating Detroit family car that *Motor Trend* has tested yet this year, which surprised us."

Also sampled were two Tri-Power Pontiacs and an experimental injected Star Chief. The two Tri-Powered cars were both sedans on the short 122-inch wheelbase; one had 290 hp, the other the hydraulic-tappet 317-hp engine, and both had Hydra-Matic. The 317-hp version did 0–60 mph in 8.4 seconds and 50–80 in 8.0 seconds, while the injected car did 0–60 in 8.1 seconds and 50–80 in 8.8 seconds.

The brakes drew pointed criticism from *Motor Trend*; they were unchanged from the previous year. The new 14-inch wheels tightly shrouded the brake drums, allowing in very little cooling air. The unfortunate result was that heavy usage caused rapid overheating and fading.

The triple-carburetor "Tri-Power" engine first appeared in December 1956, and became the division's most famous performance option.

Nineteen fifty-seven can be pinpointed as the year in which Pontiac's image truly did change. After two years of dramatic improvement, the firebreathing '57 models, aided by the glamorous Bonneville, succeeded in transforming the public's perception of Pontiac. No longer would auto magazines and car buffs overlook Pontiac when discussing Detroit's hottest cars. Never again would anyone be surprised when a Pontiac turned in a sizzling performance. Pontiac was well on its way to becoming something unthinkable a few short years before: the yardstick by which the performance of every other American sedan was measured.

1958

Major chassis changes, a bigger engine, and a new Bonneville series marked 1958. In the seven models of the Chieftain line was a surprise: the convertible, previously available only as a Star Chief. Both wagons were now 4-door models.

The Super Chief received an upgrading by sharing the Star Chief's 124-inch wheelbase and 215.5-inch overall length. The Star Chief array was reduced by the elimination of the convertible and 2-door Safari.

The new Bonneville series had two models, a Sport Coupe and a convertible; both had the short 122-inch wheelbase of the Chieftain. The Sport Coupe was a new body style, shared with Chevrolet where it was known as the Impala Sport Coupe.

All engines now had a displacement of 370 cubic inches, obtained by increasing the bore ⅛-inch to 4.06 inches. The general name "Tempest" was applied to all engines, replacing the Strato-Streak name used since 1955. There were four standard versions, from 240 to 285 hp.

Optional on any model were five high-performance engines. The Special Equipment engine had the same 285-hp rating as the Star Chief/Bonneville engine, but substituted stiffer valve springs for sustained high-rpm use. The Triple Carburetor engine added a higher 10.5:1 compression ratio and different valves for 300 hp, the Fuel Injection engine had 310 hp, and in December 1957 came two powerhouses with long-duration camshafts and low-restriction exhaust systems: the Super Tempest 395-A engines, the "395" designating their torque output in foot-pounds. The 395-A-PK version had a 4-bbl. carburetor and 315 hp; the 395-A-PM was a Tri-Power with 330 hp.

Four headlamps, a wide mesh grille, and protruding parking lamps identified the 1958 Pontiacs with their all-new bodies and chassis. This Chieftain Catalina Sedan shows the hubcaps and three fender stars marking the low-priced line.

Available as a separate option with the Super Tempest engines was a Borg-Warner heavy-duty gearbox with wide-ratio gears. A new frame, combined with a 2-piece driveshaft and step-down floor design, was responsible for the dramatic 3.1-inch reduction in body height. The front suspension was a new design with ball joints in upper and lower control arms, greater suspension travel, and larger-diameter coil springs.

Coil springs were used in the rear suspension for the first time in the division's history. Three trailing links located the axle; two long links which ran underneath the axle and supported the coil springs, and a large stamped A-arm which was attached to the top of the differential housing. The sales department coined the term "Quadra-Poise" to describe the new all-coil suspension system. An option that aided in maintaining traction under slippery or high-power conditions was a new limited-slip differential named "Safe-T-Track."

Quite unexpected was the air suspension option. This revolutionary system was developed by Cadillac as an adaptation of that used on GM buses. It first appeared on the exclusive 1957 Cadillac Eldorado Brougham, and in a corporate decision which was certainly premature, was rushed into volume production and made available for every division for 1958.

Each GM division had its own pet name for this system. Oldsmobile's was the cleverest—"New-Matic"—while Pontiac called it "Ever-Level Air Ride." At $188, it replaced the steel springs with four air springs which were supplied with air at a pressure of 140 psi from an engine-driven compressor and a storage tank. Three leveling valves sensed vehicle position and routed air to maintain a standard vehicle height; a delay switch prevented the system from

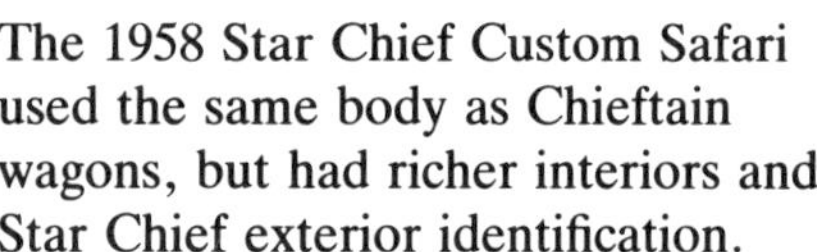
The 1958 Star Chief Custom Safari used the same body as Chieftain wagons, but had richer interiors and Star Chief exterior identification.

attempting to compensate to momentary road disturbances. Pontiac added an anti-roll bar to the rear suspension of all air-suspended cars.

In theory, the air suspension had the advantages of a softer ride and automatic height adjustment. In practice, it was a disaster. In a comparison test of two '58 Buicks, *Motor Trend* found that the air-suspended car raised its nose on acceleration and dropped it on deceleration, bottomed out on sharp dips, rolled badly on corners, and on rough roads had wheel patter so violent "the hood and front fender assembly of the car would clatter like a tin barrel half full of tin cans rolling down a hill." Additionally, there was no detectable improvement in the ride. And if all this were not bad enough, the air suspension also required much greater maintenance. Along with every other division except Cadillac, Pontiac dropped this troublesome system after only one year.

Motor Trend's test Pontiac this year, a Star Chief Catalina coupe with a 300-hp Tri-Power engine and Hydra-Matic, was quicker and more economical than the sensational '57. *MT* also sampled the hottest '58 version: racer Vicki Wood's Chieftain 2-door sedan with a Tri-Power Super Tempest engine and manual transmission. This powerful car stormed to 60 mph in 7.2 seconds and had a top speed greater than 130 mph.

Despite all the horsepower, Pontiac's sales dropped sharply in this recession year to 217,000 cars. Something besides more power was needed. Pontiac was ready.

Split Nose, Wide-Track, and the 389 1959–1960

In this watershed year there were three developments that had a major influence upon Pontiac's destiny: Wide-Track, the split-nose styling, and the immortal 389 engine.

The all-new body was daringly different, exceptionally wide at 80.7 inches, up 3.3 inches over the '58. Its length varied from 213.7 inches for the new low-priced Catalina line to 220.7 inches for the Bonneville. The Sports Coupe and convertible were only 54 inches high, making the '59 editions the longest, lowest, and widest Pontiac family yet.

Matching the wide new body was a substantial increase in track: from 58.7 to 63.7 inches at the front, and from 59.4 to 64 inches at the rear. This was the widest track in the U.S. auto industry; Pontiac called it "Wide-Track." The new styling accentuated the width. The twin-grille design was not only new for Pontiac, but broke new ground for American styling. The glass area was increased enormously. The new "Vista-Panoramic" windshield alone was no less than 50 percent larger than the previous windshield.

Welcome attention was paid to the brakes; the total lining area was increased to 191 square inches by widening the shoes and drums. Heat dissipation ability was improved by reducing front drum diameter from 12 to 11 inches, adding a cooling flange, and moving the rear brakes inboard by one inch.

The displacement of the new 389 engine was obtained by lengthening the stroke ⅛ inch to 3.75 inches. This was the fourth straight year for a size increase for the V-8, now more than 100 cubic inches larger than its 1955 introductory displacement. The really significant change, however, was the great increase in size of the main bearings from 2⅝ to 3 inches, which allowed a much stiffer crankshaft.

All 1959 engines carried a "Tempest 420" name. They ranged from a 420E economy version with 215 hp to the 420A high-performance engine, which had 330 hp with 4-bbl. carburetor and 345 hp with Tri-Power.

The time-honored "Chieftain" series name was replaced by "Catalina." In nine years the Catalina name had been gradually stripped of its exclusivity; now it was simply a general name for the lowest-priced line.

A split nose and gigantic windshield marked the 1959 models, the third year in a row for all-new bodies. "Catalina" was now the name of Pontiac's lowest-priced line, and "Vista" denoted a 4-door hardtop with a distinctive wraparound backlight and overhanging roof; this is a Catalina Vista.

The Super Chief was dead after only two years. Its sales were disappointing, and it now clashed with the Star Chief in the middle range. The top Bonneville line was expanded to four models: convertible, Sports Coupe, Vista 4-door hardtop, and Custom Safari.

All Pontiacs were painted with a new GM-developed acrylic lacquer, which Pontiac called "Magic-Mirror Finish," and all received a foot-operated parking brake.

Among the minor improvements were a new electric windshield wiper system—single-speed for Catalinas, 2-speed for Star Chiefs and Bonnevilles—and an optional electric windshield washer system.

In a head-to-head test, *Motor Trend* found that a 300-hp Catalina Vista was unexpectedly slower than a Dodge Custom Royal sedan and a Mercury Montclair hardtop, but had the best handling and ride.

Nevertheless, in a major publicity accolade, *Motor Trend* selected Pontiac as "Car of the Year."

In citing its reasons, *MT* singled out Wide-Track. "The stability of the 1959 Pontiac is . . . the outstanding automotive advance of the year." The greater roll stability of a wider tread allowed a lower suspension rate, thus giving a softer ride, without reducing handling. In '59 Pontiacs the rear spring rate was reduced 9 percent from '58, yet roll stiffness was 14 percent greater. In *MT*'s words, this was "a significant step toward resolving the compromise between ride and handling."

The magazine also applauded Pontiac's development of the 420E economy engine as well as the 420A performance versions. Even in

A cutaway Star Chief Vista shows the full coil suspension, low seating position, massive glass area, and enormous trunk space of the 1959 Pontiacs.

its first year, the 389 V-8 was recognized as an outstanding powerplant with a brilliant future.

The division's sales happily recovered strongly to 383,320 cars. Rather unexpectedly, this surge carried Pontiac past divisional rivals Buick and Oldsmobile as well as hot-selling Rambler. Excluding imports, Pontiac's share of the market rose to 6.9 percent, and it found itself in the unfamiliar but welcome position of fourth place in sales, nipping at Plymouth's heels! Could anything be more wonderful? It could. And in a few years, it was.

1960

Nineteen sixty saw the inception of a whole new series, namely, the Ventura. Wedged in between the Catalina and Star Chief lines, the Ventura offered only Sports Coupe and Vista hardtops. These were mechanically identical to their Catalina counterparts, differing only in trim.

The Ventura was another example of name-snitching from Southern California. Ventura is the county between Los Angeles and Santa Barbara counties, and also the city which is the county seat. Both derive their name from Mission San Buenaventura, one of the California missions established in the eighteenth century.

There were no major changes to the 389 engine, but several new variants appeared. Standard with manual transmission in the Bonneville was a 235-hp version, while a 281-hp version was available only with heavy-duty manual transmission. The rest of the 1960 engines had three more horsepower than their 1959 counterparts, due to a small increase in compression ratio.

Motor Trend tried two 1960 Pontiacs with the top-line 348-hp Tri-Power engine. A hefty 4800-pound Bonneville Safari with Hydra-Matic was sluggish, achieving 0 to 60 in 11.5 seconds and the quarter-mile in 18.6 seconds at 76 mph. A Ventura Sport Coupe with 3.42 axle ratio, however, limited-slip differential, and a heavy-duty manual transmission ripped off 0 to 60 mph in 7.9 seconds, 50 to 80 mph in 6 seconds flat, and the quarter-mile in 14.8 seconds at 89 mph. Top speed was estimated at 138 mph if the car were fitted with the optional 2.69 axle ratio.

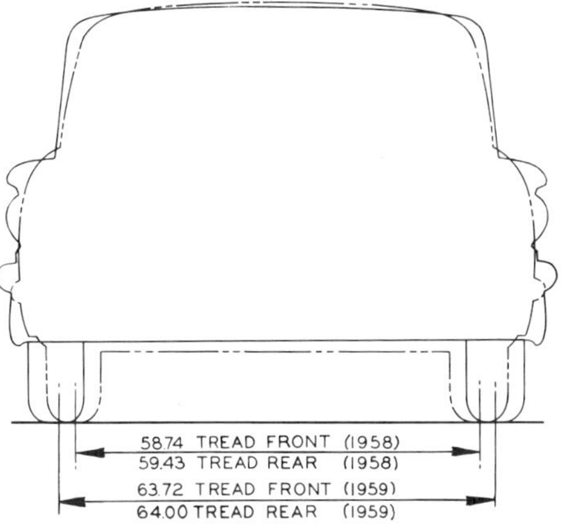

Pontiac's famous "Wide-Track" appeared in 1959; this sketch shows the substantial difference in tread between the 1958 and 1959 models.

The 1960 face-lift temporarily removed the split-nose grille, which would return the following year. Besides the Catalina shown here, the Vista 4-door hardtop was available in the Bonneville, Star Chief, and new Ventura series.

Though 1960 was only a "face-lift" year at Pontiac, it was able to comfortably extend its sales lead over Olds and Buick. However, it was pushed down to fifth place overall by the fast-rising Rambler, which soared past Pontiac and even Plymouth to take over third place. To counter Rambler, VW, and the new compact cars from the "Big Three," Pontiac needed its own compact. In 1961 it got one, and it proved to be a blockbuster.

A Tempest Rises
1961

Following the lead of Chevrolet's revolutionary Corvair, all the other GM divisions except Cadillac issued their own compact model for 1961. Buick's was named the Special, Oldsmobile's the F-85; Pontiac called its version the Tempest.

These models all shared a Fisher unibody structure with a wheelbase of 112 inches. There were only two body styles, a 4-door sedan and a 4-door, 2-seat station wagon. To give the Tempest a Pontiac identity, divisional stylists returned to the successful 1959 split-grille theme. For power, the Tempest had two new engines: an inline four developed by Pontiac, and an aluminum V-8 borrowed from Buick.

The inline four was derived from the right-hand cylinder bank of the 389 V-8. It had the same bore and stroke, so its displacement was half the V-8's at 194.5 cubic inches. Parts interchangeability with the V-8 was quite extensive, which saved immense sums in tooling costs. Of 44 major parts or assemblies, no fewer than 28 were completely interchangeable, and a further five required only minor modification.

Big news for 1961 was the Tempest, Pontiac's first compact. Loaded with revolutionary features, the Tempest was easily the most unusual American car of its time.

The new engine had the same five husky 3-inch main bearings as the V-8, resulting in one of the stiffest crankshafts in the world. Excluding the flywheel, the new engine weighed 479 pounds; by comparison, the 389 V-8 was 654 pounds. When installed in the car, this engine was tilted over on its right side at a 45° angle, just as if it were still part of a V-8. For this reason, Pontiac literature referred to this engine—named the "Trophy 4"—as a "slant 4" or "inclined 4." To offset this tilt, the crankshaft centerline was placed 1.4 inches to the left of the car's centerline, resulting in an equal left/right weight distribution.

This engine had a major problem, and the design engineers, J. P. Charles and M. R. "Mac" McKellar, did not shy away from admitting it. With its large displacement, it was especially subject to that old 4-cylinder hobgoblin, unbalanced secondary forces. "In a 4-cylinder engine of 195 cubic inch displacement," Charles and McKellar stated in a technical paper, "such forces are more than considerable; they are colossal. At 4,000 rpm, for example, a force of 2,588 pounds changes direction by 180° twice each revolution of the engine." To deal with this vibration all the engine-mounted accessories received special strengthening.

Pontiac offered five versions of the Trophy 4, from 110 to 155 hp.

Great things were expected from the optional aluminum V-8. *Sports Car Illustrated* bubbled with praise: "We'll wager the most widely copied engine in the next ten years will be the superb new aluminum V-8 by Buick." Unfortunately, the magazine would have lost that bet.

The little V-8 had oversquare cylinder dimensions of 3.50 x 2.80 inches for a displacement of 215 cubic inches. Aluminum was everywhere; the only major parts of iron were the exhaust manifolds, cylinder liners, crankshaft, camshaft, and rocker shafts. Even the rocker arms and supports for the rocker shafts were made of diecast aluminum.

From a manufacturing standpoint, the V-8's most unusual feature was its iron liners; they were not pressed into the block in European fashion, but were held in position during the foundry process while the molten aluminum was cast around them.

With fan, water pump, and generator, this remarkable engine weighed only 318 pounds, or 161 pounds *less* than the smaller Trophy 4. Pontiac's version had only one power rating: 155 hp @ 4600 rpm.

The Tempest's "compression strut" front suspension resembled a conventional arrangement, except that the lower control arm was attached to the subframe at only one point. Fore-and-aft rigidity for this control arm was provided by the strut. The inboard end of this strut was threaded, allowing adjustment of the caster angle. The suspension was mounted on a subframe, which was then attached to the car's unibody structure with six bolts.

The Tempest's rear suspension, with a transaxle and swing arms, was derived from the Corvair.

Both manual and automatic transmissions were offered. The manual was a floor-shifted 3-speed in unit with the differential, with which it shared a common lubricant. The optional "TempesTorque" 2-speed automatic consisted of three major components arranged in a startling manner: a differential/final drive housing in the center, with a planetary gearbox mounted ahead and a torque converter mounted behind. The bulky torque converter was not mounted in its normal position in front of the gearbox, as this would have encroached upon rear-seat passenger room. To connect the converter with the gearbox therefore required three hollow concentric shafts running through the differential housing. Since the characteristics of automatic transmission fluid and final-drive lubricant were so different, a common lubricant could not be used as it was with the manual transmission. Therefore, more hollow shafting was needed to transfer hydraulic fluid back and forth from converter to gearbox through the differential housing.

Pontiac claimed a first for the way the automatic's high-gear

The all-welded unibody of the Tempest was derived from the Chevrolet Corvair, with a wheelbase 4 inches longer at 112 inches.

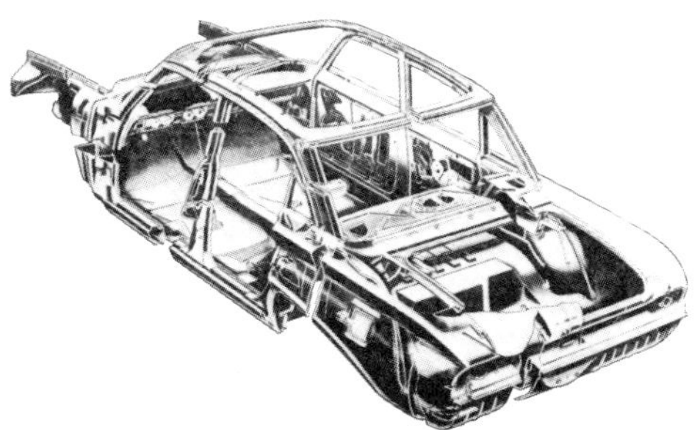

Independent rear suspension, torque tube enclosing the curved driveshaft, and rear transaxle of the 1961 Tempest are evident here. This is the automatic version, with the torque converter mounted at the rear of the transaxle.

Standard engine for the 1961 Tempest was the "Trophy 4," essentially the right-hand bank of the 389 V-8. It was economical to produce since it shared so many parts and common tooling with the V-8, but was plagued with vibration.

clutch worked. It fed 40 percent of engine torque straight through the gearbox and 60 percent through the torque converter. In Pontiac's words, "this split-torque principle results in a solid drive feel and minimum slip or efficiency loss."

Final drive ratio for both sedan and wagon was 3.55, regardless of engine or transmission choice.

The swing axles of the independent rear suspension were located by semi-trailing arms which also supported the coil springs and shock absorbers. In typical swing-axle fashion the wheels underwent a large change in camber as they moved up and down, the effect of which was pronounced since the Tempest used large 15-inch wheels. This rear suspension and the transaxle were mounted on a subframe, which was attached to the unibody with four bolts.

The attachment of engine to transmission was the most arresting feature of the Tempest's design: its curved one-piece driveshaft. It had no universal joints since engine and transmission were mounted rigidly to the unibody structure, and thus did not move relative to each other. The shaft came in two diameters and lengths: .75 x 81.94 inches for the manual transmission, and .65 x 87.24 inches for the automatic. This shaft was not inexpensive. Made of heat-treated triple-alloy steel, it was finish-ground over its entire length to assure absolute circularity and concentricity, and then shot-peened to relieve surface stresses and improve fatigue life.

The Tempest's unique driveshaft could be so slim for two reasons: it transmitted only unmultiplied engine torque, and it was freed from critical vibrations since it was bent into a curve. The flexibility of this driveshaft gave rise to its famous nickname: the "rope-shaft drive."

Knowing that public skepticism would focus on this flimsy-looking shaft, Pontiac development engineers tried hard to break it during 2,600,000 test miles. Not a single shaft broke.

The driveshaft was enclosed in a torque tube, which served several functions. It bolted rigidly to the engine's bell housing and the transaxle, thus precisely connecting the two together and eliminating misalignment; it provided a mounting for the two steady bearings for the shaft; and it greatly helped absorb those huge torque reactions of the slant-4 engine.

The braking system employed 9-inch drums with 108.9 square inches of effective lining area; power assist was not offered.

The 1961 Tempest was easily the most radical car in Pontiac's history. The list of "firsts" claimed for it was a lengthy one:

World's first automobile with a front-mounted engine and rear-mounted automatic transaxle.
World's first automobile with a curved one-piece driveshaft.
First American car with front engine, rear transmission, and 4-wheel independent suspension.
World's largest 4-cylinder automobile engine in production.
First Pontiac with 4-wheel independent suspension.
First Pontiac with a transaxle.
First Pontiac with a 4-cylinder engine.

Both *Road & Track* and *Sports Cars Illustrated*, which had previously ignored Pontiacs, featured lengthy articles about the Tempest. *SCI* called it the "terrific Tempest" and "Detroit's most modern car." *R&T* observed, "Pontiac's Tempest deserves high praise. The approach is unique, the thinking behind it is sound. . . . In short, the Tempest is exactly the kind of car we have been asking and hoping for."

In actual road tests, however, the press reactions were mixed.

R&T was enthusiastic about its test model, which was a sedan with stick shift and the 110-hp, 4-cylinder engine. It praised the quick throttle response, instant availability of torque, the position of the shift lever, the outward visibility, comfortable ride, easy accessibility of underhood components, and the low-maintenance design. Criticism was directed at certain aspects of the drivetrain. "By deliberately adopting 'little-old-lady-from-Pasadena' habits we provoked a really remarkable display of throbbing and snatching from the car. For that reason, we really do think Mr. Average Driver will be much happier with the automatic transmission version."

A much more advanced engine for the 1961 Tempest was its optional V-8, built by Buick. This lightweight 215 V-8 was conventional in design but radical in its extensive use of aluminum. It developed as much power as the Trophy 4 but was much smoother and weighed 160 pounds less.

R&T was surprised that the independent rear suspension did not improve the handling. "The all-independent suspension appears to be valuable only from the standpoint of comfort—the car's road-holding isn't any better than others of similar size and type that feature the old standby live axle." And: "When the car is cranked into a corner with any real vigor it exhibits a substantial oversteer."

SCI also felt that the automatic transmission was "far and away the preferred box for the Tempest. It is quieter at all times . . . any oscillations in the drive shaft are completely hidden, and it felt better in hard cornering." The magazine found that the Tempest's suspension not only had strange behavior when pressed hard, but was also sharply sensitive to tire pressures.

The Tempest coupe was introduced in May 1961. This is a special show version, named "Le Mans," which appeared at the 1961 New York Auto Show. The production use of the Le Mans name occurred the following year.

Motor Trend awarded its "Car of the Year" prize to Pontiac for the Tempest. "In a year of outstanding cars, it is clear that the Tempest is the car most outstanding for progress in design." This was the second time in three years that Pontiac had won this prestigious award.

In May 1961 came a 2-door version of the GM compact body shared by Buick, Olds, and Pontiac. All three GM divisions brought out special versions of this coupe with a plush interior and front bucket seats. Buick and Olds turned these coupes into new models with new names—Olds F-85 Cutlass Sports Coupe and Buick Skylark—and powered them with a hot new 185-hp version of the aluminum V-8. Pontiac temporarily ignored its sister divisions and offered no new engines for its version, which it simply called the Tempest Coupe.

The most surprising change to the big Pontiacs was that they became smaller. The wheelbase of the Catalina and Ventura was reduced 3 inches to 119 inches, while that of the Star Chief and Bonneville dropped one inch to 123 inches. The '61 Pontiacs were also about 200 pounds lighter than their '60 counterparts. The principal reason for this reduction was a new perimeter frame, which even allowed room for a single-piece driveshaft to replace the previous 2-piece affair.

The front suspension had stronger lower control arms, while the coil-spring rear suspension now employed four trailing links; the large trailing A-arm was deleted.

Wide-Track was reduced from 64 to 62.5 inches; however, since this reduction was less than the 2.5-inch reduction in overall car width, Wide-Track was now proportionately even wider.

The engine lineup was the most comprehensive in Pontiac history; ten variations of the 389 V-8 were offered.

Two new transmissions appeared for the big Pontiacs. A new automatic had three forward speeds and a torque converter. It was lighter than the 4-speed Hydra-Matic, employing a one-piece flywheel housing, a simpler valve body, an aluminum case, and a lubricant capacity of 12 pints instead of 18. This new automatic was used only in the Catalina and Ventura series, with the older H-M reserved for the Star Chief and Bonneville.

Since Pontiac used both automatics, its advertising tended to downplay the significance of this new development. The new automatic was not given a totally new name and was initially described only as a "lighter, compact, and simplified three-speed Hydra-Matic transmission." Only later was it given its curious name: Roto Hydra-Matic.

The other new transmission was an enthusiast's dream: a Warner all-synchromesh 4-speed manual gearbox with a floor-mounted shift lever. It was available in any model, but only teamed with either of the two high-performance engines (333 and 348 hp) or the 318-hp Tri-Power.

Motor Trend tested 12 medium-priced 1961 cars head-to-head; a Bonneville Vista was the fastest-accelerating car of the group. Sizzling performances like this gave rise to a notion that became widespread: Pontiac's horsepower ratings were deliberately conservative. This opinion was not hurt by racetrack comparison, as Pontiac was dominating NASCAR stock car racing.

Detroit's hottest car of 1961 was conceded to be a Pontiac Catalina Sport Coupe with a 4-speed floor shift and 348-hp Tri-Power

Introduced in 1961, the optional 4-speed all-synchromesh manual transmission was capable of taking the power and torque of the 389 V-8.

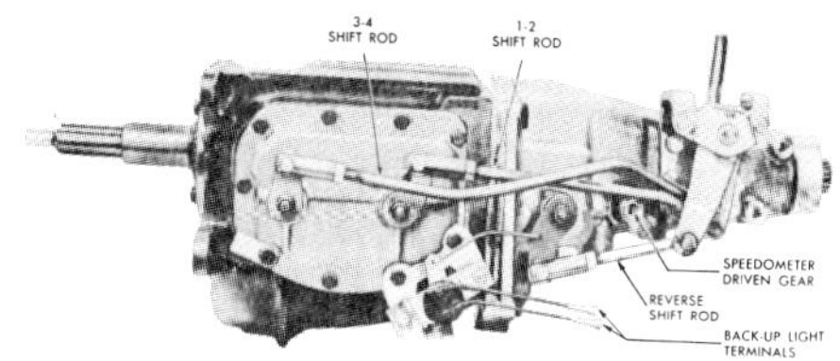

The 1961 full-size Pontiacs were slightly smaller and lighter, with a new body, all-new perimeter frame, and shorter wheelbases; this is a Ventura Vista.

engine. In mid-year, however, Chevrolet fielded a mighty challenger, the Impala Super Sport with a new 360-hp 409 engine. This landmark car would provoke immediate countermeasures from other manufacturers, forcing Pontiac to defend its position with a significant new engine in 1962.

In 1961 a minor slump hit the U.S. auto industry. Pontiac sales declined to 340,635 from 396,716 and its market share dropped from 6.6 percent to 6.3 percent. However, this was enough to edge out Plymouth, and Pontiac moved up a notch to fourth place behind Chevy, Ford, and Rambler. Just over 100,000 of Pontiac's sales were Tempests, a remarkable introduction for the new compact.

In the fall of 1961 Bunkie Knudsen was promoted to general manager of Chevrolet. Pete Estes moved up to succeed him as Pontiac's general manager, and John DeLorean became Pontiac's chief engineer.

The Power of Success 1962–1963

For 1962 Pontiac's program was a refinement of the Tempest, a deeper involvement in racing, the dropping of a whole series, and the introduction of a new model destined to become an industry style leader.

The big Tempest changes were the appearance of a convertible and the Le Mans trim option. Offered only on the sports coupe and the convertible, the Le Mans option was a trim package consisting of Morrokide upholstery, individual front seats, full carpeting, a revised instrument panel, special wheel covers, and power operation of the convertible's top.

Five versions of the Trophy 4 engine were offered. The 4-bbl. high-performance version now had 166 hp due to a new intake manifold. The only aluminum V-8 offered was the hot 185-hp version used by the Olds Cutlass and Buick Skylark. In mid-1962, Pontiac upped the power a bit to 190 hp by boosting the compression ratio to 11:1.

A new Tempest transmission was available: a 4-speed all-synchromesh manual, the same as that introduced on the Corvair

Biggest changes for Tempest in 1962 were the addition of the upmarket Le Mans option and a new convertible body style, sold only in Le Mans trim.

the previous year. The rear suspension was improved by tilting the pivot axis of the lower control arms by three degrees.

Motor Trend tested a Le Mans coupe with the 166-hp Trophy 4 engine, 4-speed stick shift, and 3.73 axle ratio. It scooted to 60 mph in 10.5 seconds and covered the quarter-mile in 18.2 seconds at 80 mph. *MT* criticized the inadequate fade resistance of the brakes and didn't like the handling. "In tight corners . . . you can scare yourself real easy. The rear end breaks loose with very little warning."

Among the big Pontiacs, the Catalina's wheelbase grew by one inch. The three Safaris, however—two Catalinas and a Bonneville—retained their 1961 wheelbase length of 119 inches.

Like the Super Chief, the Ventura did not sell well enough, and was dropped. The name, however, would soon be reincarnated.

Pontiac's entry in the "personal luxury" market was the brand new Grand Prix. This was essentially a Catalina sports coupe, fitted with a plush interior and a more powerful engine. Standard equipment included individual front seats, a console which contained a tachometer and floor-mounted shift lever, and the 303-hp engine. Optional were the 230-hp economy engine and all of the high-performance engines.

Motor Trend tested a Grand Prix with the standard engine, automatic transmission, power steering, and power brakes. It went 0 to 60 mph in 8.0 seconds and the quarter-mile in 17.2 seconds at 85 mph.

The car tested was fitted with a truly significant option rarely seen today and all but forgotten: the combination aluminum brake drum and wheel hub.

Introduced in 1960, the unique aluminum drum/hub was Pontiac's answer to the growing problem of brake fade. It employed a hefty 11-inch cast aluminum brake drum with deep fins. Because aluminum is incompatible with brake lining, Pontiac followed the usual aluminum-brake practice of bonding an iron liner to the inside of the drum.

When such drums were installed in place of ordinary cast iron drums, the improvement was enormous. However, there still remained the problem of the wheel itself, which acted as a barrier between the drum and cooling air. To solve this problem, Pontiac designed wheels that had no center section; the brake drum itself was the wheel center. The wheel mounted on eight studs on the periphery of the drum. The advantage of this arrangement was that the drum surface was now exposed directly to the air.

Motor Trend was lavish in its praise of these brakes. "They did an excellent job of dissipating any heat buildup that occurred during our braking tests, and on our last run we experienced the same quick, no-swerve stop that we did on the first. There was absolutely no fade, pedal harshness, or tendency to lock the wheels." *MT* was surprised that these potent brakes, a $122 option, required only "feather-light" pressure.

For several years Pontiac had built its reputation as the hottest name in NASCAR and drag racing by developing the "over-the-counter" performance parts business to a fine art. Though the 348-hp Tri-Power was officially the most powerful engine, everybody knew that Pontiac dealers had a long list of high-performance parts that would turn the 389 into a genuine competition engine.

Destined for a great future, the first Grand Prix appeared in 1962. Essentially a Catalina Sports Coupe loaded with options, the Grand Prix had a different grille and tail lamps from other 1962 Pontiacs, and boasted a standard 303-hp engine, bucket seats, console, and floor shift. This particular car is fitted with the optional hub/drum aluminum wheels, as handsome as they were efficient.

This careful attitude of speaking softly but carrying a big racing stick was copied by other manufacturers. Chevrolet had a 360-hp 409, Dodge a 340-hp 383; in 1961 Ford announced a special dealer-assembled version of its 390 engine with three 2-bbl. carbs and 401 hp.

Then the National Hot Rod Association, the sanctioning body for American drag racing, forced this issue of covert racing engines out into the open. For the 1962 season it decreed that only complete engines available *from the manufacturer*— not from dealers or speed shops—would be eligible to compete in its Super Stock division, the extremely popular class for the hottest street cars. This rule forced all the manufacturers to publicly designate competition engines. Ford responded by enlarging their triple-carb 390 to 406 cubic inches and claimed 405 hp. Chevrolet added a second 4-bbl. carb, bigger valves, and high compression to its 409 and came up with 409 hp. Chrysler announced 380-hp and 405-hp versions of its husky 413 engine. Dodge raided Chrysler's parts bin and fielded its own versions of the 413, a 375-hp street version and an awesome 410-hp "Ramcharger" option.

Elliott M. "Pete" Estes was Pontiac's general manager from 1961 to 1965, succeeding Semon Knudsen. He later became general manager of Chevrolet and president of General Motors.

Pontiac's response was two "Super Duty" competition engines, the first of which was a 389 rated at 385 hp. It had a single 4-bbl. with large venturis, a special aluminum intake manifold, large valves, forged aluminum pistons, a forged and heat-treated crankshaft, heat-treated connecting rods, a 6-quart oil pan, high-pressure fuel and oil pumps, special light flywheel, heavy-duty clutch, a dual-breaker distributor with no vacuum advance, and a large-diameter dual exhaust system.

The SD 389's solid-lifter camshaft had 308° of duration on the intake valves and 320° on the exhaust valves. It operated through high-ratio rocker arms and stiff valve springs. In fact, the valve springs installed at the factory were recommended for break-in and nonracing use, while the *really* stiff valve springs intended for use *only* on the racetrack were supplied in a separate package.

As if all this were not enough, Pontiac still supplied special dealer-installed options for use where the rules permitted. These included a 9-quart oil pan, other camshafts, other cylinder heads with even larger ports and valves, and three other carburetion systems: a single 4-bbl. with larger primaries, a triple 2-bbl., and a dual 4-bbl.

The second Super Duty powerplant was even more potent. The displacement was enlarged to 421 cubic inches by increasing the bore 1/32 inch and the stroke by 1/4 inch. The main bearings were

3.25 inches in diameter instead of the 389's 3-inch mains, and dual 4-bbl. carburetion was standard. Pontiac claimed 405 hp at 5600 rpm for the SD 421.

The two Super Duty engines were available only in the Catalina Sport Coupe and 2-door sedan, the lightest full-size Pontiac bodies. The price of the SD 389 option was $1,090; the SD 421 was $1,240.

Why two SD engines? The new 421 was aimed at drag racing, where displacement and torque meant everything. Despite its big main bearings, the durability of this new long-stroke version at sustained high speeds was unknown, so the proven 389 remained available for oval track racing.

Pontiac emphasized that these SD engines were meant for competition use only, and could not be ordered with such fripperies as automatic transmission or air conditioning. They were not included in any sales brochures. They were not considered standard production engines, and therefore are not listed in Appendix II of this book.

At Detroit Dragway *Motor Trend* tested one of the first SD 421-powered Catalina coupes, fitted with 4-speed transmission, Hurst shifter, and 4.30 axle ratio. "And BOOM. . . . Low gear was a rubber-burning fishtail, with the indifferent traction available. A snap shift to second at 5500 rpm, and 60 mph came up in a bit over five seconds. The bellowing open exhaust rattled the whole countryside. Second and 3rd gears almost tore my head off. Then across the finish line at 5300—stopping the watch at 13.9 seconds and 107 mph!"

In 1962 the U.S. auto industry came roaring back from the mini-recession, increasing its production by 1.3 million units to 6.7 million cars. Almost all of this increase was due to GM cars. Pontiac's production increased 53.1 percent to 521,933, the largest percentage increase of any GM division and the second-best year in the division's history. This stellar performance put Pontiac solidly in third place in the industry, the first time the division had ever occupied this lofty position.

1963

Flushed with sales success, Pontiac charged into 1963 with dramatic new styling and several hot new engines.

Handsomely restyled for 1963, the Tempest's overall length increased by five inches. The Trophy 4 remained the standard engine, but the optional aluminum 215 V-8 was replaced by an iron 326 V-8. This is a Le Mans, a separate series for 1963.

The Tempest's Trophy 4 engine was slightly lighter, and continued with the same power ratings as in 1962 except for the deletion of the base 110-hp version.

Replacing the aluminum V-8 as a Tempest option was a new cast-iron 326 V-8, essentially a small-bore (3.72 inches) variation of the 389. A 260-hp 2-bbl. version was the only one initially available, joined in mid-year by a 280-hp 4-bbl. labeled the 326 HO (for "High Output").

A new 3-speed gearbox was the only manual transmission offered with the 326 V-8. The TempesTorque automatic was upgraded, and among its improvements was a new "Park" position. The drive through this transmission was now fully hydraulic—no more "split torque" arrangement.

Reshaped lower control arms in the rear suspension had a greater trailing angle, and the rear tread was widened 1.2 inches. All Tempest brakes for 1963 were self-adjusting, and power assist was optional. Any car with the V-8 had finned iron front brake drums. *Motor Trend* criticized the brakes and rear suspension in its test of a '63 Le Mans convertible, noting especially that the handling was critically sensitive to tire pressures. However, with its 326 V-8 and stick shift, it was easily the quickest Tempest *MT* had ever tested, reaching 60 mph in 9.2 seconds and zipping through the quarter mile in 18 seconds at 85 mph.

All the big Pontiacs received vertically paired headlamps. The new "Coke bottle" shape looked especially impressive on the clean-limbed Grand Prix, which had several exclusive styling touches: a different grille, slimmer roof line, concave rear window, and "invisible" tail lamps.

Missing from the engine lineup were the two familiar high-performance V-8-A versions of the 389. Replacing them were two HO street versions of the 421: a 4-bbl. with 352 hp and a Tri-Power with 370 hp. Along with the 280-hp 326 offered in the Tempest, these were the first Pontiac engines to officially carry the "HO" designation.

Available as an option on any full-size model, the 421 HO engines had 10.75:1 compression ratio, a hot camshaft, stiff valve springs, and valves slightly longer and larger in diameter than those in the 389 engines. The 3.42 axle ratio was mandatory with the 421 HO.

In mid-year came a third 421 street engine. Not an HO, this had a lower 10.25 compression ratio and shared valves and valve springs with several 389 versions. It was rated at 320 hp and delivered its massive 455 foot pounds of torque at only 2800 rpm.

Significant improvements to the big cars were self-adjusting brakes, the replacement of the generator by a Delcotron alternator, a positive crankcase ventilation system, and an optional transistorized ignition system. Improved lubricants and seals allowed the chassis lubrication interval to be 30,000 miles and the oil change interval to be 6,000 miles.

Racing activity proved the durability of the Super Duty 421 racing engine, so the smaller SD 389 was discontinued. With the single 4-bbl. carb mandated by NASCAR rules, the SD 421 was rated at 390 hp; the dual 4-bbl. version for drag racing retained its 405-hp rating.

Pontiac set off a styling revolution with its 1963 full-size models. Vertically paired headlamps, clean lines, and "Coke-bottle" fender shape would be widely copied by competitors.

The 1963 Grand Prix was one of the most stunningly beautiful cars of its own or any other time. The clean lines of this famous coupe mask its true size—it's as big as a Catalina.

Motor Trend tested two '63 Grand Prix coupes. A fully optioned version with the standard 303-hp engine, automatic transmission, and 3.23 axle ratio did 0-60 in 9.9 seconds and the quarter-mile in 18.1 seconds at 80 mph. The other test GP was an enthusiast's dream: 370-hp 421 HO engine, 4-speed close-ratio gearbox, limited-slip differential, and aluminum hub/drum wheels. This magnificent brute shot to 60 mph in 6.6 seconds and turned the quarter-mile in 15.1 seconds at 94 mph.

Pontiac established a new record of 590,107 cars for 1963, finally breaking the old 1955 record. It consolidated its hold on third place by taking 8 percent of all U.S. auto production.

Tempest Triumphant 1964–1966

After three years with its Buick-Olds-Pontiac compacts, GM was confident that the market was changing. Influenced by Ford's Fairlane, GM felt that its compacts should be larger, more powerful, and better appointed, yet more conventional in engineering.

GM's new-sized car, dubbed the "intermediate," appeared in 1964. This A-body corporate machine replaced all the previous B-O-P compacts and also became a new model for Chevrolet: the Chevelle. Only the fact that the three B-O-P divisions chose to retain the established names of their previous compacts obscured the fact that this was a brand-new car.

This change was welcome at Pontiac, for it was painfully clear that the bloom was off the rose; Tempest/Le Mans sales for '63 were down 8.2 percent from '62, despite the fact that Pontiac had a record year. Buick's higher-priced Special/Skylark versions of the same basic car also outsold the Tempest/Le Mans in '62 and '63.

One explanation for the Tempest's sales troubles was the model's technical idiosyncracies. Thus, the big 4-cylinder engine, curved driveshaft, independent rear suspension, and transaxle were discontinued.

Even the body was changed. To reduce noise, the new car had a separate perimeter frame, replacing the previous unibody structure.

The new front suspension was conventional, with large stamped A-arms and coil springs enclosing telescopic dampers. The rear suspension had a rigid axle with coil springs and four trailing links, an exact copy of the arrangement used on the full-size Pontiacs.

Attending to a previous Tempest weakness, brake drum diameter was increased from 9 to 9.5 inches, all drums were heavily finned, and total lining area was increased a dramatic 57 percent to 171 square inches.

The Tempest's 6-cylinder base engine was a variant of the one introduced in 1962 for the Chevy II. With pushrod-operated overhead valves, seven main bearings, hydraulic lifters, non-crossflow porting, small valves, and a single 1-bbl. carburetor, this was an unglamorous workhorse designed for durability and low maintenance. With a bore and stroke of 3.75 x 3.25 inches, it had 215 cubic inches and 140 horsepower.

Optional for the new Tempest were two 326 V-8s: the 326 HO with its 280 hp, and a detuned 250-hp version. Three-speed and 4-speed gearboxes were available with any engine.

The Tempest was an all-new and bigger car for 1964, an "intermediate" instead of a "compact." Handsomer but more conventional in design, it appealed to a wider range of buyers. This is a Le Mans sports coupe.

The automatic transmission was a Buick product designed expressly for the new intermediates. It had a 3-element torque converter, the stator blades of which had a 2-position variable pitch. A sudden opening of the throttle made the blades switch pitch and produce more torque multiplication without necessitating a gear change in the gearbox. This not only improved throttle response, but allowed the use of a simpler 2-speed gearbox instead of a 3-speed one. Buick called this transmission "Super Turbine 300" but Pontiac stuck with the familiar "TempesTorque" name.

The Tempest family was expanded to three lines, which among them had ten models: plain Tempest, a new Tempest Custom, and the top-of-the-line Le Mans, which had distinctive exterior trim including horizontal tail lamps and a black-mesh grille.

Scarcely had the ink dried on the Tempest press releases when Pontiac threw in a strike aimed straight at the heart of the most rabid performance fanatic. It was a special variant of the Tempest, and overnight it became the most sensational model in Pontiac history. The GTO had arrived.

The origins of this mighty motorcar lay in a combination of circumstances. In early 1963 a stern "no racing" edict was handed down by GM corporate headquarters. (GM's board chairman of the time, Frederic G. Donner, was no car enthusiast.) This decree, aimed specifically at Chevrolet and Pontiac, ended Pontiac's official involvement in NASCAR and drag-racing programs.

This state of affairs did not sit well with Estes and DeLorean. Accustomed to the program begun by Knudsen, they felt that the principal reason for Pontiac's satisfying rise to third place in sales was due to its exciting image, and that the identification of Pontiac with performance was a necessary part of this image. With the forced termination of the racing program, something had to be done to counteract the publicity value of the racing programs of Pontiac's market competitors.

A second factor was the obvious temptation to put the 389 V-8 into the new intermediate Tempest. This marrage of big engine/intermediate body is often regarded today as the really new concept pioneered by the GTO, but in retrospect it appears far more evolutionary than revolutionary. After all, the 326 fit into the previous compact Tempest, so why shouldn't the 389 do equally well in the new larger Tempest?

The new concept inherent in the GTO was not the 389 engine, but *which* 389 engine. Estes and DeLorean revived the V-8-A versions last seen in 1962, which were dropped in 1963 due to the emergence of the 421 HO for the big Pontiacs. Reduced to its barest essentials, the GTO was a high-performance 389, heavy-duty driveline and suspension components, special wheels and tires, and discreet identification, all offered as one option package on the Le Mans.

What Pontiac pioneered with this model was the switch in performance emphasis from full-size cars to intermediates. Full-size emphasis was a natural attitude for any manufacturer involved in NASCAR racing, since that organization had a 4000-pound minimum weight limit and a displacement limit of 427 cubic inches. Removed against their will from NASCAR racing, Estes and DeLorean soon realized that a 421 Catalina hardtop no longer needed to be Pontiac's top performance model. They were free to concentrate on the smaller and lighter Tempest. Because of its 3450-pound weight, the GTO could outperform any larger Pontiac—and it had better handling and better fuel economy to boot.

The credit for creation of the GTO is shared among Estes, DeLorean, and Jim Wangers, Pontiac's account executive at its advertising agency of McManus, John, and Adams. Wangers, responsible for much of the creative and provocative Pontiac advertising of the '60s, was a successful drag racer, and was assuredly the loudest blower of Pontiac's publicity horn.

Estes and DeLorean kept very quiet about the GTO during its gestation period. They didn't even inform the Engineering Policy

The most famous model in Pontiac history was the immortal GTO. Introduced in 1964 as an option on the Le Mans, the GTO was the first "supercar." A host of imitators soon sprang up to copy its performance and sales success.

Group, the corporate department with final authority in all engineering matters, until shortly before the car's introduction. They could get away with this stealth since the GTO was a simple car to develop, requiring no new components.

Standard GTO equipment included a 325-hp engine with 4-bbl. carburetor and dual exhaust, 3-speed manual transmission with Hurst floor shifter, heavy-duty clutch, and 3.23 axle ratio. The suspension had stiffer coil springs, stiffer shock absorbers, and a thicker front anti-roll bar. The wheels had a 6-inch rim width and were shod with 7.50 x 14 U.S. Royal Red Line high-performance nylon tires.

This basic GTO package was almost unbelievably cheap—a $296 option on the basic Le Mans, which itself cost $2480 in coupe form. Additional GTO options were a 348-hp Tri-Power engine ($115), a 4-speed gearbox ($188), Safe-T-Track differential, metallic brake linings, heavy-duty radiator, transistorized ignition system, a steering gearbox with 20:1 ratio instead of the standard 24:1, and springs and shocks even stiffer than the normal GTO equipment.

By the proper choice of options a GTO could become anything from a vitamin-packed boulevard cruiser to a dragstrip terror. If a buyer restricted himself solely to performance options, for about $3200 he could have the quickest 2-door sedan in the world.

Where did the GTO name originate? In his biography, DeLorean takes personal credit. "Because the car reminded me of a fast, foreign sports car, I suggested we call it the GTO (after a Ferrari coupe being raced in Europe called the Gran Turismo Omologato)." This bland admission of name-snitching only partially explains the controversy surrounding the GTO.

Pontiac model names were moving in a different direction. Abandoning idyllic Southern California resorts such as Catalina and Ventura, Pontiac was now appropriating racier foreign names like Grand Prix and Le Mans. The sports car fraternity complained that such names were foolish and unethical, since the Pontiac Grand Prix was clearly not a single-seat Grand Prix racing car and no Pontiac had ever appeared in the famous French 24-hour road race at Le Mans.

When the Pontiac GTO was announced, the purists really screamed. Now Pontiac was stealing the name of a specific model from another auto manufacturer. That manufacturer was none other than Ferrari, the most famous name in sports and racing cars, and the specific model was none other than the GTO, a spectacular competition coupe which was a legend in its own time.

Winner of the Manufacturer's Championship in international GT racing three years in a row (1962–1964), the Ferrari GTO was a sensuously shaped aluminum-bodied racing "berlinetta" coupe powered by a 300-hp version of Ferrari's famous 3-liter V-12. Its unusual name, which meant "legalized Grand Touring" in Italian, referred to its acceptance as a genuine production model for purposes of international competition, despite the fact that only 39 GTOs were built by the Ferrari factory.

All of this was a bit much to explain to buyers of a sporty American car, and Estes and DeLorean didn't really try. The end result was that probably 9 out of 10 Pontiac GTO buyers did not know what the letters meant, were not aware that their car was named for a Ferrari, and would not have cared even if they had known.

The GTO was unquestionably very fast. Just *how* fast became difficult to determine. *Car and Driver* was the first magazine to test a GTO, and its version was set up for drag racing: 348-hp engine, 4-speed gearbox, limited-slip differential, and 3.90 axle ratio. The results were astounding: 0 to 60 in 4.6 seconds and 0 to 100 in 11.8 seconds! The top speed was rev-limited to only 115 mph, but the car reached this speed at the end of a quarter-mile in 13.1 seconds. *Road & Track* and *Motor Trend* also tested this very same car and recorded somewhat slower times.

Numerous road tests revealed several facts: the Safe-T-Track differential was absolutely essential, otherwise the car became hopelessly bogged down in wheelspin; the 348-hp version gave a noticeably better performance than the standard 325-hp version; and the axle ratio was a major factor in acceleration. *Car Life*'s test car, for example, which also had the 348-hp engine and 4-speed gearbox but the standard 3.23 axle ratio, turned the quarter-mile in 14.8 seconds at 99 mph, much slower than the *C&D* test car with its 3.90 axle ratio.

A new model for 1964 was the Catalina 2+2. Similar in concept to the original 1962 Grand Prix, it was a specialized version of the Catalina sports coupe fitted with a more powerful engine, floor shift, and individual front seats.

Another new model for 1964 was the Bonneville Brougham. Available only in this Vista body style, it had a vinyl roof and luxurious interior.

To muddy the waters further, the car which recorded those ultra-rapid *C&D* figures was not factory-stock. It was a "Royal Bobcat" GTO, a specially tuned version prepared by Royal Pontiac of Royal Oak, Michigan, a performance-oriented dealership which cooperated heavily with the factory.

However questionable *Car and Driver's* figures, there was no question that the Pontiac GTO was the fastest accelerating 4-place production car in the world.

How about handling? Running their GTO around Daytona racetrack, *Car and Driver* was full of praise. "It was totally forgiving, and always stayed pointed. Its handling starts as understeer at very slow speeds, becomes neutral at moderately fast speeds, and gradually—quite pleasantly, in fact—becomes oversteer when pressed to the limit." Two years later *C&D* would have second thoughts about the handling of the '64 GTO.

Two new models appeared among the big Pontiacs. The 2+2 was a $290.52 option available only on the Catalina sports coupe or convertible. It included front bucket seats, a console, tachometer, heavy-duty 3-speed manual transmission with floor shift, and 283-hp 389 engine. The other new model was the Bonneville Brougham, a special version of the Bonneville Vista 4-door hardtop with a lush Morrokide-and-nylon interior and a padded vinyl top.

The power ratings of the standard 389 engines remained the same as in 1963; however, this year the compression ratio was 10.5:1 rather than the previous 10.25:1, so these are listed as different engines in Appendix II.

Optional on any model was a new Tri-Power 389 with 10.75:1 compression ratio and 330 hp. A new 421 variant appeared, a Tri-

Power with the same camshaft and valves as the 320-hp 421; it was rated at 350 hp.

Two significant accessories appeared for the first time: an electric rear window defroster and a cruise control, which Pontiac called "Electro-Cruise."

Motor Trend tested two '64 Catalinas. One was a 2-door hardtop with a 303-hp engine and a full load of options; it accelerated to 60 mph in 10 seconds and turned the quarter-mile in 17.2 seconds at 80 mph. The other was a stormer: a 2+2 with a mighty 421 HO engine, 4-speed gearbox, 3.42 axle ratio, heavy-duty suspension, and aluminum hub/drum brakes. Virtually duplicating the performance of the previous year's test Bonneville with the same drivetrain, the 2+2 did 0 to 60 in 6.6 seconds and the quarter-mile in 15.7 seconds at 93 mph.

MT was impressed once again by those wonderful aluminum brakes. "They gave stop after grueling stop from speeds as high as 120 mph without appreciable fade or lockup and were always powerful and sure during fast mountain driving. We wouldn't want a Pontiac without these fine brakes on it." This splendid performance was in stark contrast to that of the normal brakes on the other test Catalina, which "soon faded into nothingness under hard use." At a time when American manufacturers were justly criticized for producing overweight cars with poor brakes, it is worth emphasizing that Pontiac continued to offer the best drum brakes in the world for only $122.13.

A 4-door sedan was offered in the Le Mans series for the first time in 1965. The additional length made this intermediate as large as the full-size Chieftains of a decade earlier.

A GTO convertible was the dream of every performance enthusiast in 1965.

The new Tempest spearheaded the division to a soaring new sales record of 715,261. Of this total, Tempest accounted for 235,126 units, a whopping 78.8 percent jump from the previous year's lackluster sales.

The big surprise was the GTO. Only 5,000 units were initially scheduled for production, but eventually 32,450 '64 GTOs were built. This sales performance was spectacular considering that the GTO was available only in 2-door form, had a high-performance V-8 as its only engine, and cost more than other Tempests. Due to its late introduction, it was not even included in Pontiac sales literature; a small booklet finally appeared in January. It was really word-of-mouth advertising and the enthusiastic response of the auto magazines that sold the GTO.

1965

There were two new Tempest models for 1965: a 2-door hardtop for the Custom line, and a 4-door sedan in the Le Mans series. The GTO was still technically an option on the Le Mans to avoid cardiac arrest on the fourteenth floor of the GM building, but Pontiac literature treated it like a separate model.

The big Pontiacs for 1965 looked awkward due to an exaggerated rear fender shape, as shown on this Grand Prix.

The two GTO engines received slight changes. Revised cylinder heads with smoother ports allowed the 4-bbl. version to develop 335 hp. The optional Tri-Power version now had a different camshaft—the same one used in the 421 HO engine—which raised its output to 360 hp.

There were two new Tempest brake options. Metallic linings worked well at high temperatures but were squeaky and erratic until warm, and were recommended only for heavy-duty use. Aluminum drums with bonded iron liners were available for the front brakes. Unlike the celebrated hub/drum units for the big Pontiacs, these Tempest aluminum drums were straightforward replacements for the standard iron drums.

The wheelbase of the full-size Pontiacs was longer by one inch in all series, and all Safari wagons now had wheelbases identical to the other models in their series.

There was a sharp uprating of engines all through the big Pontiac lines, due principally to an across-the-board switch to the larger valves (intake 1.92 inches, exhaust 1.66 inches) previously reserved only for the top-line engines.

A new automatic transmission replaced the Roto Hydra-Matic and Super Hydra-Matic in all full-size models. Consisting of a 3-speed planetary gearbox mounted behind a 4-element torque converter containing variable-pitch stator blades, this water-cooled transmission had been introduced the year before in Cadillacs and Buicks. Cadillac called it "Turbo Hydra-Matic," while Buick called it "Super Turbine 400"; Pontiac adopted Cadillac's name. An excellent transmission, the "Turbo Hydro" soon became famous for its smoothness, rugged construction, high torque multiplication, and rapid shifting action.

The standard 3-speed manual gearbox for the full-size models now had synchromesh on all forward speeds. The lining area on the brakes of the big Pontiacs was increased 8.5 percent to 188.5 square inches, and the front-to-rear proportioning was altered to prevent rear-wheel lockup. Other improvements included an articulated windshield wiper which increased wiped area by 11.5 percent, windshield and rear window bonded to the body rather than inserted into rubber gaskets, curved side window glass, thin tempered glass instead of plastic for convertible rear windows, crossflow radiators, central filler for the fuel tank, and an automatic temperature control for the air conditioning system.

The 2+2 option for the Catalina became a serious performance package. Included in the $418.54 package was the 338-hp 421 engine, 3-speed floor-mounted gearbox with Hurst shifter, 3.42 axle ratio, heavy-duty shocks, stiffer springs, and individual front seats.

Motor Trend's 2+2, with 338-hp engine, 4-speed gearbox, and power brakes, did 0 to 60 mph in 8.1 seconds and the quarter-mile in 16.4 seconds at 88 mph.

With its flair for the dramatic, *Car and Driver* arranged a sensational test: a Pontiac 2+2 matched head-to-head against a Ferrari 330GT 2+2. Both cars were tested for dragstrip acceleration and

Best-looking of the '65 big Pontiacs was the 2+2, which had a sleek new roofline. This model became a serious performer this year with a standard 421 V-8, Hurst shifter, and heavy-duty suspension.

lap times around Bridgehampton Raceway on Long Island by sports car ace Walt Hansgen, who held the lap record at Bridgehampton.

The Pontiac 2+2 was loaded for bear: 376-hp 421 HO engine, 4-speed gearbox, limited-slip differential, and 3.42 axle ratio. The Ferrari had a 300-hp 4-liter engine, 4-speed gearbox with overdrive, limited-slip differential, and standard 4.25 axle ratio. The Pontiac weighed 4155 pounds and the Ferrari 3180 pounds. The Pontiac was prepared by Royal Pontiac, which even sent three mechanics to accompany the car, while the Ferrari was prepared by Luigi Chinetti Motors, the official Ferrari importer for the U.S.

It was perhaps no big surprise that the Ferrari had a much higher top speed—152 to 127 mph—or that the Pontiac had better acceleration, turning the quarter-mile in 13.6 seconds at 106 mph compared to 14.6 seconds at 97 mph for the Italian car. The Pontiac's displacement/weight ratio was far higher than the Ferrari's, which counts for almost everything in drag racing. The real surprise was that the Pontiac's fastest lap around the 2.9 mile racetrack was only a half-second slower than the Ferrari's!

For all its dramatic proof of Pontiac performance, it must be mentioned that the acceleration times turned in by the 2+2 in this test were astonishingly quicker than anything recorded for similar Pontiacs by other publications. Since this car was prepared by Royal Pontiac, its engine had received the same minor but significant modifications—including richer jets and advanced ignition timing—administered to the previous year's hyper-quick GTO tested by *C&D*.

John Z. DeLorean, who succeeded Elliott Estes as Pontiac's general manager on July 1, 1965, proudly displays the division's new lightweight OHC-6 for 1966.

The very notion that a Pontiac was deemed worthy of a racetrack comparison with a Ferrari showed the high esteem that the automotive press held for Pontiac's products. This esteem was underscored when the division once again was awarded the *Motor Trend* "Car of the Year" prize, the third time Pontiac won this accolade.

In 1965 total U.S. auto sales increased by 12 percent over 1964. Pontiac sales kept pace, rising to a new record of 802,000 cars. This easily maintained the division's third place in sales and its 9.1 percent of domestic auto production.

The primary reason for Pontiac's sales gain in 1965 was the sharp increase in Tempest/Le Mans sales by 30.6 percent. Even this, however, was overshadowed by the astonishing sales of the GTO, which jumped an eye-popping 132 percent to 75,352 cars! Fully one-quarter of all Tempest/Le Mans sales were now GTOs! No wonder other manufacturers were scrambling to bring out GTO competitors.

On July 1, Pete Estes left Pontiac to become Chevrolet's general manager, and John DeLorean succeeded him as Pontiac's boss.

1966

Pontiac's major news this year was quite unexpected: a brand-new engine. This overhead-cam six was the first new Pontiac-designed engine since the ill-fated Trophy 4 of 1961. And if that engine is considered merely a tooling variant of the 389 V-8, then this was the first new engine design since the Strato-Streak V-8 of 1955.

Intended for the Tempest, this inline six obtained its displacement of 230 cubic inches from a bore and stroke of 3.875 x 3.25 inches. Its extraordinary design was highlighted by a single overhead camshaft driven by a cogged belt, a separate accessory housing, and automatic hydraulic valve clearance adjustment. It was the first single-ohc engine in a large American car since the 1927 Wills Sainte Claire.

In a technical paper, engine designer Malcolm R. "Mac" McKellar enumerated the advantages of the overhead-cam design: "High rigidity of the overhead cam mechanism, combined with reduction in inertia of moving parts, opens new possibilities in camshaft design: valves can be opened and closed more quickly, higher engine rpm can be achieved without the need for excessively high valve spring loads and without their associated wear problems at low speed. Furthermore, with quick opening and closing of the valves, a low-overlap timing, and the good idle associated therewith, can be achieved."

If an overhead-cam design is so desirable, why is it used so infrequently in the U.S.? In a word, cost; it is easier and cheaper to make a pushrod design. The V-8 cylinder arrangement, so popular in America, would be additionally handicapped by requiring two camshafts, a costly complication.

What made the Pontiac OHC-6 engine possible was a new and cheaper method of driving the camshaft. Instead of chains, gears, or shafting, Pontiac used a cogged timing belt. Made of neoprene reinforced with glass filaments, the belt was one inch wide and weighed only 9.5 ounces. The glass cords were extremely flexible but inextensible; the belt, therefore, did not stretch. The inside toothed surface was coated with nylon fabric impregnated with neoprene, providing excellent wear resistance. This belt had a minimum tensile strength of 3600 pounds yet was subjected to a maximum operating load of only 332 pounds. It engaged three iron sprockets: a 3-inch one on the crankshaft, a 6-inch one on the camshaft, and another 3-inch one for the accessory drive.

The remarkable OHC-6 broke new ground for the American auto industry, particularly in its use of a cogged belt to drive the overhead camshaft. This is the 207-hp version, with 4-bbl. Quadrajet carburetor and dual exhaust manifolds.

Extensive testing over a period of years demonstrated astonishing durability. Not a single belt failed, despite underhood temperatures ranging from -30°F to 250°F and durations in excess of 100,000 miles per belt. None even stretched enough to require a retensioning adjustment. And all this testing was done *without* the production dust covers in place!

Pontiac was the first American manufacturer to use such a belt, but not the originator. Pioneering credit goes to Hans Glas GmBh of Dingolfing, Germany, which introduced a 4-cylinder engine with a belt-driven single ohc in 1961; the Glas company was acquired by BMW in 1966.

Pontiac developed history's first hydraulic "lash" adjuster for an overhead-cam engine. This new device was similar in concept to the familiar hydraulic lifter commonly used in American pushrod engines, and its function was the same: to eliminate valve lash (i.e., to maintain zero valve clearance) while the engine was running.

The end result showed the advantage of the overhead-cam arrangement. Compared to the valve train of the 1965 pushrod six, the total weight of parts driven by the camshaft in the new engine was reduced by 45 percent.

The accessory housing was clever. It was an aluminum casting bolted onto the right side of the engine block, and on which were mounted the distributor, fuel pump, oil pump, and oil filter. The mounting holes were slotted so the housing could be moved up or down to adjust the tension of the timing belt.

The camshaft was mounted in a die-cast aluminum housing which bolted to the top of the iron cylinder head, and was supported by seven permanent bearings. The crankshaft also had seven main bear-

This 1966 Tempest is the sports coupe with the Sprint option, which included the 207-hp engine and 3-speed floor shift.

ings, each of 2.30 inches diameter. The intake valves were the same size as those of Pontiac's V-8 engines—1.92 inch diameter—while the exhaust valves were 1.60 inches in diameter.

This engine was perfectly suited to the Tempest. It weighed no more than the previous pushrod six, and 195 pounds less than Pontiac's lightest V-8.

There were two stages of tune. The base version had 9:1 compression ratio, single 1-bbl. carburetor, and a mild camshaft for 165 hp, while the optional version had 10.5:1 compression ratio, hotter camshaft, 4-bbl. carb, and special exhaust manifolding for 207 hp. A "Sprint" package was offered, consisting of the 207-hp engine, 3-speed gearbox with floor shift, and trim details.

The 4-bbl. carburetor of the 207-hp version was the "Quadrajet,"a recent development of GM's Rochester division. It had small 1.38-inch primary venturis but huge 2.25-inch secondaries, and would become a much-used item on future GM performance cars.

The length of the primary linings in Tempest brakes was reduced from 9.82 to 7.6 inches. This gave a better equalization of forces inside each brake drum, but unfortunately reduced the total lining area by 11.6 percent. A new Tempest brake option was a hub/drum wheel, quite similar to the famous aluminum unit offered on the full-size Pontiacs except that it was made of cast iron.

Other Tempest developments included the handsome 4-door hardtop, and the establishment of the GTO as a separate series. After five years of development the Tempest now offered 16 models in three lines, and was a better all-around automobile than the full-size Pontiac.

Changes were made in many of the lines. Among the big cars, the top-line Bonneville Brougham was expanded to three models as a convertible and 2-door hardtop joined the Vista.

The Bonneville Safari was now a plush version of Pontiac's 3-seat wagon with its rear-facing third seat. Previous Bonneville Safaris had always been the 2-seat version.

The venerable Star Chief series was now called "Star Chief Executive," and included a hardtop coupe in addition to its previous 4-door sedan and Vista models.

Four of the Catalina's seven models were offered with the Ventura trim option, which was identical to the Star Chief Executive.

Like the GTO, the 2+2 now became a separate series, still available only as a convertible or hardtop coupe.

By 1966 the GTO had some serious competitors in the 2-door intermediate-with-a-big-engine class of car, a genre which *Car and*

Driver called "supercars" and *Road & Track* called "musclecars." Oldsmobile fielded its 4-4-2 in late 1964. In 1965 came the Buick Skylark Gran Sport (325-hp 401 V-8) and Chevrolet Chevelle Super Sport (350-hp 327). By 1966 the 4-4-2 had 350 hp, the Skylark Gran Sport 340 hp, and the Chevelle SS396 had 360 hp (a handful even had 375 hp). The Plymouth Belvedere and Dodge Coronet could be had with a 365-hp 426 wedge-head V-8, or even the rare 426 hemi-head racing engine of 425 hp. Ford Motor Co. offered the Ford Fairlane GT and its Mercury clone, the Comet Cyclone GT, with a 330-hp 390 V-8.

To sort out all these supercars *Car and Driver* conducted a 6-car test, leaving out only the Chrysler products. The magazine compared dragstrip performance and lap times around Bridgehampton racetrack, and fitted all the cars with identical tires. The driver was Masten Gregory, an American who had won the 1965 Le Mans in a Ferrari 250LM.

The GTO in this test was a coupe with the 360-hp engine, 4-speed gearbox, metallic brake linings, and the Royal Bobcat tuning kit. At the dragstrip it turned a time of 14.05 seconds at 105.14 mph, the fastest trap speed and second-best elapsed time (behind the Mercury Cyclone). On the racetrack it finished third, behind the Cyclone and 4-4-2.

This comparison test was complicated by the fact that the Ford Fairlane GT and Mercury Comet Cyclone GT were clearly not stock, having been race-prepared by well-known NASCAR racing shops. The magazine's editors took this into account, and in the final rank-

Pontiac's first use of a plastic grille occurred on the 1966 full-size models, such as this Bonneville convertible.

ing placed the GTO third behind the Oldsmobile 4-4-2 and Chevy Chevelle SS396.

C&D criticized the GTO's high noise level and temperamental disposition. "It's hard to start and keep running in the cold; it tends to stall whenever the engine is slowed from high speed; its idle is much too high . . . and the gas mileage at steady turnpike speeds is 11 mpg." Most of these problems were due to the Bobcat kit, with its ignition advance, rich jets, and blocked heat risers. The engine also threw fan belts, the same problem *C&D* encountered with the 2+2 the previous year. Worst of all, the suspension had big problems. "Gregory encountered such massive rear spring windup and resultant axle tramp under heavy braking that he was forced to use both throttle and brake simultaneously while slowing down." Gregory's personal comments were similar. "It tends to float and bounce in corners and the rear axle tramp is awful."

In mid-year a new engine appeared for the GTO. It was called the "Ram Air" option, for it included a functional hood scoop and a tub enclosing the carburetors. The Ram Air 389 engine had a very hot camshaft, with 301 degrees duration on the intake valves and 313 degrees on the exhaust valves. Backing up this camshaft was a single set of very stiff valve springs with dampers, rather than the dual springs used on other GTO engines. The power rating should have been something like 375 hp.

However, there was a problem. Like all GM divisions, Pontiac was under a corporate anti-racing edict, which in its latest form forbade the installation of any engine displacing more than 400 cubic inches in an intermediate-sized car, and also forbade the advertising of weight/power ratios lower than 10 pounds/hp. Since a basic GTO weighed slightly less than 3600 pounds, Pontiac could rate the Ram Air engine no higher than 360 hp—the same rating as the 389 HO engine.

The Ram Air engine was clearly intended for drag racing; included as mandatory options were a 4.33 axle ratio, declutching fan, limited-slip differential, close-ratio 4-speed gearbox, and metallic brake linings. Top speed was rev-limited to about 107 mph, which the car could reach in just a few eyeblinks.

Pontiac ended the 1966 model year with a total production of 831,331 cars. Once again this was a new record, enabling the division to hold third place in sales for the fifth straight year.

"F" Is for "Firebird" 1967–1968

All full-size models for 1967 were heavily restyled. The vertically paired headlamps were now fitted into unattractive recesses, while the split-nose grille was integrated with the bumper.

The Grand Prix, always the recipient of special styling touches, now had disappearing headlights. The four lamps were arranged in horizontal pairs, the only such arrangement on any '67 Pontiac except the Firebird.

A dramatic styling development exclusive to the big Pontiacs was the hidden windshield wipers, tucked away below the upturned trailing edge of the hood. This was not a GM corporate development; it was a Pontiac design. Every other GM division adopted it the following year.

The convertible was no longer available in the Bonneville Brougham line, but a convertible version of the Grand Prix was added.

The familiar 13-year-old name "Star Chief" was consigned to history, as the Star Chief Executive series now became known simply as the Executive. Two Safari station wagons were added to this

"F" Is for "Firebird" 1967–1968

The kindest thing to say about the styling of the 1967 full-size Pontiacs is that it must be considered in the light of the times.

Despite its bulbous styling, the 1967 Grand Prix convertible is much sought after today. It was the first Pontiac model with concealed headlamps, and the only Grand Prix convertible ever offered.

series, identical to the Catalina versions but with fancier interiors and wood-grain exterior paneling.

After just one year with a separate identity, the 2+2 again became an option on the Catalina coupe and convertible.

There were major engine changes in 1967. The classic 389 V-8, the engine which firmly established Pontiac in the performance market and boosted it to third place in sales, was no more. With its bore increased 1⁄16 inch to 4.12 inches, it now displaced 400 cubic inches. In a variety of power ratings from 265 to 333 hp, this new 400 was the standard powerplant for Catalina, Executive, and Bonneville series.

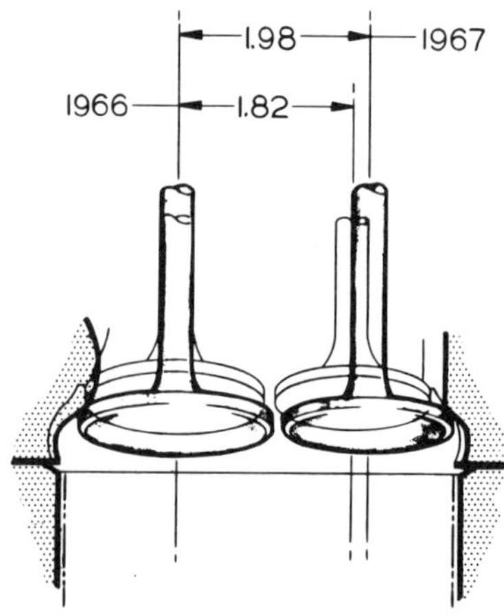

Revised cylinder heads on 1967 V-8 engines allowed larger valves to be fitted to high-performance versions.

The Grand Prix received a special version of the 400, distinguished by different cylinder heads, with repositioned and larger valves: 2.11 inches for the intake and 1.77 inches for the exhaust. (These big valves were also used on GTO engines and the new 428 engines.) The Grand Prix engine was rated at 350 hp @ 5000 rpm with manual transmission and 350 hp at 4800 rpm with automatic.

The big 421 V-8 became the bigger 428 V-8 by a bore increase of 1⁄32 inch to 4.12 inches, meaning that the 400 and 428 V-8s shared a common bore size. Only two versions were offered: 360 hp with 10.5:1 compression ratio and 4-bbl. carburetor, and 376 hp in the HO version with 10.75:1 compression ratio, a hotter cam, and a Quadrajet carburetor in place of the previous Tri-Power arrangement. The 360-hp version was standard on the 2+2, and both versions were optional on any full-size Pontiac.

Many of Pontiac's new engineering developments for 1967 were related to safety, a welcome emphasis. Standard on all models was

The '67 GTO had a thick bright trim strip on its lower body which accentuated the wasp-waisted styling.

Tempest wagons had been available since 1961, but the "Safari" name was first applied in 1967. This Tempest Safari was a separate series, an upmarket version of the same wagon available as a Tempest or Tempest Custom.

a dual master cylinder which gave independent hydraulic circuits for front and rear brakes. The big brake news, however, was the disc brake option. This Bendix system, available only for the front brakes, used a vacuum assist and 11.8-inch vented rotors for the full-size Pontiacs, and smaller rotors for the Tempest.

Should a crash unfortunately occur, a collapsible steering column protected the driver; it was standard equipment on every 1967 model. Another station wagon was added to the intermediate family, the Tempest Safari, which had Morrokide interior, full carpeting, and wood-grain side trim like the full-size Executive wagons.

The basic Tempest engine remained the 165-hp OHC-6. The optional version of this engine was now rated at 215 hp, due to a revised ignition advance curve.

Lucky GTO buyers had a choice of four engines in 1967; all were versions of the new 400 V-8. The standard version had 335 hp, while the 400 HO—also called the "Quadra-Power 400" since it now sported a single Quadrajet in place of the previous Tri-Power carburetion—was rated at 360 hp. The Ram Air engine also switched from Tri-Power to Quadrajet, and was dutifully rated at a conservative 360 hp @ 5400 rpm.

The fourth '67 GTO engine was a tame 255-hp version. Essentially identical to the base Catalina engine and available only with automatic transmission, this was an obvious marketing ploy to entice buyers who wanted the GTO's glamorous image but not its pavement-ripping performance.

A welcome change for the GTO was the switch from TempesTorque to Turbo Hydra-Matic whenever automatic transmission was specified. The rugged and flexible Turbo H-M certainly

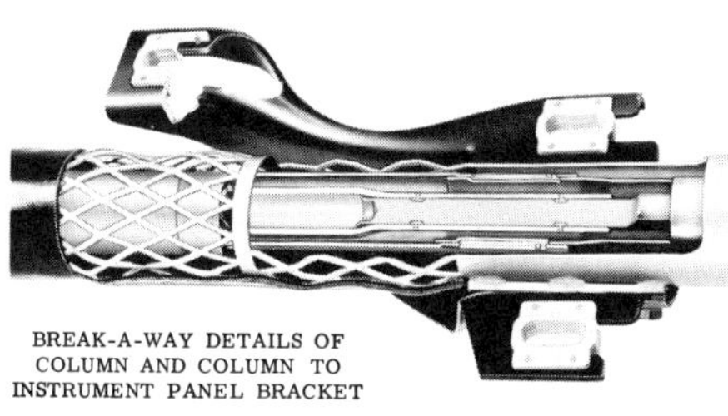

Every 1967 Pontiac had a new collapsible steering column, which absorbed collision energy at a controlled rate.

An industry "first" was Pontiac's introduction of hidden windshield wipers on all 1967 full-size models, improving appearance and aerodynamics.

controlled the GTO's power better than the 2-speed automatic, which was retained for all other Tempest models.

Vacuum-assisted front disc brakes were optional for the Tempest, replacing the previous options of all-iron hub/drum brakes and metallic linings.

Two interesting options for all models were a hood-mounted tachometer—especially popular with GTO and 2 + 2 buyers—and a capacitative-discharge ignition system, available on all engines except the 165-hp OHC-6 and 250-hp 326 V-8.

The most impressive show car Pontiac ever built was the Banshee, intended for introduction at the International Automobile Show in New York in April 1966. A 4-seat coupe, it had a 109-inch wheelbase, all-independent suspension, concealed wipers and headlamps, a one-piece nose section which tilted up for engine accessibility, and a 421 V-8. Mounted on 4-bar links, the unique doors opened by sliding parallel to the car, and also rose slightly to clear curbs. Flip-up roof panels aided entry and exit. In a fit of pique, GM president James Roche ordered this car removed from its display stand before the show opened. It was never seen again, although the Banshee name was revived for a different show car in 1974.

The Firebird did not debut with the rest of the 1967 line since it was not ready in time: this was due to a late decision by GM corporate management. John DeLorean had campaigned long and hard for a Pontiac 2-seat sports car. Many design studies and several prototype cars were made, the most interesting of which was the Banshee show car scheduled for display at the New York International Auto Show in April 1966. Despite considerable pre-show publicity, the 2-door 4-seat coupe with flip-up door panels was yanked from the Pontiac stand just before showtime on the personal orders of GM president James M. Roche, who was under Congressional scrutiny over Corvair-inspired safety issues.

The Firebird was based on the Camaro, Chevrolet's entry in the new "ponycar" field. The Camaro project had begun in August 1964, in a crash program to field a competitor to Ford's spectacularly successful Mustang. Code-named "F-car," the GM ponycar was originally intended only for Chevrolet.

The final decision to give Pontiac a piece of the F-car action was not made until March 1966. Roche and executive vice-president Ed Cole (Chevy's former general manager and one of the most respected executives in GM history) felt they had to give Pontiac *something* after all of DeLorean's efforts to obtain a sporty car, and also because they knew that Ford was going to introduce a pricier Mustang variant—the Mercury Cougar—for the '67 model year. Due to that late decision to field a Pontiac ponycar, the Firebird was not ready until mid-winter. It was formally announced to the press on January 27, 1967, and available at dealers on February 23.

The "Firebird" name was new for Pontiac, but not for GM; it had been used on several corporate show cars of a decade earlier. The most dramatic of these was Firebird I of 1954, which looked like a small rocket ship on wheels and was powered by a gas turbine engine. This was a very good name indeed for a Pontiac. The legendary firebird was an object of worship among certain Indian tribes, and Pontiac, after all, was named for a famous Indian chief.

The Pontiac designers did a masterful job on the F-car body in the limited time available; the Firebird looked different from the Camaro. The split-nose grille looked very clean, utilizing the grille-cum-bumper concept so successful on several previous Pontiacs. Only two body styles were available, coupe and convertible.

The Firebird shared the Camaro's unique body/chassis construction and 108-inch wheelbase. From the cowl rearward was an all-welded unibody structure; the front part of the car was carried on a husky subframe which bolted to the unibody.

The front suspension was a conventional arrangement of ball-jointed unequal A-arms, coil springs, and anti-roll bar, while the solid rear axle was suspended by two single-leaf "mono-plate" semi-elliptic springs. Pontiac engineers were not happy with the tendency of these Chevrolet springs to wind up under heavy torque loadings, and incorporated a radius rod on the right side of the axle on all models except the base Firebird, and a second radius rod on the left side for the most powerful V-8-engined versions.

Coming or going, the first Firebird of 1967 was a handsome automobile. Based on the Chevrolet Camaro, the Firebird quickly established its own identity by using different styling touches and Tempest drivetrains.

Pontiac marketed the Firebird in five versions which differed chiefly in engines, all of which were lifted without change from the Tempest family.

The base model was simply called the Firebird, and it used the 165-hp OHC-6. The Firebird Sprint had the 215-hp OHC-6, stiffer springs, a lower axle ratio, and offered an optional 4-speed gearbox. The Firebird 326 was powered by the 250-hp 326 V-8, while the Firebird H.O. had the 285-hp 326 HO engine.

At the top of the totem pole was the Firebird 400, which was a serious performance car. Standard equipment included very stiff springs with a rate of 135 pounds/inch, and a second radius rod on the axle. Turbo Hydra-Matic was supplied if the automatic transmission were ordered; all lesser Firebirds used the 2-speed TempesTorque. Its engine was the 335-hp GTO engine; however, the curb weight of a Firebird 400 coupe was 3328 pounds. Mindful of that corporate restriction on advertised weight/power ratios, Pontiac carefully rated this engine in the Firebird at only 325 hp @ 4800 rpm.

Even more restrictive was the rating of the optional Ram Air engine, available only on the Firebird 400. Artificially derated even in its 360-hp GTO form, its Firebird rating of 325 hp @ 5200 rpm was laughable.

The Firebird also used Tempest brakes: 9.5-inch iron drums with a total effective lining area of 149.4 square inches. Front-disc brakes with ventilated rotors were optional on any model.

The standard Firebird wheel was the same 14 x 6JK size used on the GTO, shod with either the Firestone "Wide Oval" or its Goodyear "Wide Tread" equivalent in the new low-profile E70 x 14 size. The Firebird 400 received the special Red Line version of the Wide Oval.

The Firebird became the first automobile in history to offer the "Space Saver Spare," a new tire design from B.F. Goodrich. Designed only for emergency use, it was carried in a deflated condition; a pressurized can inflated it. For dubious customers, a standard E70 x 14 tire was a no-cost replacement option.

The prices announced for the Firebird were about $200 higher than the Camaro, but about $200 cheaper than the Cougar: $2,666 for the coupe, $2,903 for the convertible. The best bargain among the options was the front disc brake, only $63.19.

Motor Trend's first two test Firebirds were convertibles, a Sprint with a 4-speed stick shift and a 400 with Turbo Hydra-matic and the 325-hp engine. Both performed creditably, the Sprint turning 0 to

The 1967 Firebird had unusual single-leaf rear springs. Axle torque reaction was controlled by radius rods.

60 in 11.1 seconds and the quarter-mile in 17.8 seconds at 79 mph, while the 400 zipped to 60 mph in 7.5 seconds and the quarter-mile in 15.4 seconds at 92 mph.

Good though these performances were, *MT* pointed out that the Firebird convertible was inordinately heavy. "Our two test cars, both convertibles, were strictly lead sleds compared to the other available body style, the coupe. . . . Sealed containers weighing about 35 pounds apiece—which, we suppose, contain fine old wine and unspecified springs and masses—occupy all four corners of convertible models . . . to damp out body shake."

The bob-weight spring containers on which *MT* poured its scorn were inherited from the Camaro. The curb weight of a basic 6-cylinder Firebird ragtop was 3385 pounds, almost 10 percent more than the equivalent coupe.

MT matched a Firebird against the Mercury Cougar, its "Car of the Year." It preferred the Cougar for "the best compromise between ride and handling," superior comfort, quietness, and 3-speed automatic, but admitted that a Firebird HO was a better-handling car and that a Firebird 400 was much faster.

Road & Track was not thrilled with its test Firebird Sprint; the rear suspension was a special target of criticism. "The independent front suspension is probably as good as anybody's, but the rear is just a shade above the absolute minimum you can find in modern

The two men most responsible for the Firebird's design were Jack Humbert (left), Pontiac's chief designer, and Charles Jordan, executive designer for Chevrolet/ Pontiac.

cars." *R&T* praised the smooth-road handling, but "on anything less than smooth surfaces, all the usual shortcomings of stiff, live-axle rear suspension and limited rear-wheel travel come to light."

Car and Driver's Firebird was a hot one: a 400 convertible with the Ram Air engine, 4-speed gearbox, and 3.90 axle ratio. It was plenty fast: 0 to 60 in 5.8 seconds, the quarter-mile in 14.4 seconds at 100 mph.

Motor Trend tested two Ram Air Firebirds equipped with Royal Pontiac's famous Bobcat kit, which improved performance but voided the factory warranty. One of these carss, with 4-speed gearbox, turned the quarter-mile in 13.99 seconds at 105.01 mph; the other, with Turbo Hydra-Matic, was fractionally slower at 102.85 mph.

It was *Super Stock* magazine which finally matched a hot Firebird head-to-head with a GTO. The F-bird was a 400 with the standard 325-hp engine; the GTO was a '67 coupe with the Ram Air engine, 4-speed gearbox, and 4.33 axle ratio. The Firebird turned twelve dragstrip times which averaged 14.15 seconds at 103 mph, with a best time of 14.03 seconds at 103.156 mph. Despite its more powerful engine and lower gearing, the GTO was a shade slower; its best time was 14.12 seconds at exactly 100 mph.

"The differences would be attributed to the 250 pounds or so difference in weight, the better weight distribution of the Firebird . . . and apparently the reduced frontal area of the small Firebird cut the wind resistance enough to pick up 1 or 2 mph in trap speed. . . ."

"Anyway, that Firebird with a standard GTO engine was quicker out there than the '67 GTO with Ram Air engine. Take it for what it's worth."

What that meant was that the classic GTO, America's supercar champ, was being challenged—and beaten—by a new Pontiac model in its very first year of production. The gradual decline of the GTO, both in performance prowess and in sales, can be traced with pinpoint historical accuracy to the introduction of the Firebird and the decision to equip it with the GTO engines.

The Firebird was an immediate hit in the marketplace. Despite its late introduction it edged out the GTO in total model-year production, 82,560 to 81,722.

Pontiac's total sales delined slightly to 817,826, down 1.6 percent from 1966. However, since total industry sales fell by 11 percent, Pontiac's market share increased to 10.7 percent, the highest it had ever been.

A new horizontal arrangement of the four headlamps and a prominent bumper beak marked the 1968 full-size models like this Executive.

1968

The booming market for intermediate and specialty cars was now dominating Pontiac's attention. Engineering changes included enlargements of intermediate engines, and a revolutionary concept in bumper design for the GTO.

After just one year the Grand Prix convertible was dropped—making it an instant collectible—while the Bonneville Brougham convertible reappeared. A late addition—so late it did not appear in sales brochures—was a 4-door sedan version of the Bonneville, the first-ever Bonneville sedan.

A casualty was the 2+2 option on the Catalina, underscoring the shift in performance models to the smaller intermediates and the new Firebird.

For big-car power, the 428 V-8 came in two forms for 1968: a 375-hp version, and the 428 HO with 390 hp: the most powerful street engine Pontiac had ever produced.

Two models were dropped from the Tempest family: the base station wagon, and the sport coupe version of the GTO. The Tempest's standard engine, the OHC-6, received a longer stroke and now displaced 250 cubic inches. The base version was now rated at 175 hp, while the Sprint version was still rated at 215 hp; both versions had much better low-speed torque.

By boring out the 326 V-8 to 3.875 inches, its displacement was increased to 350 cubic inches. Two versions were optional in any Tempest except the GTO. The mild version had 265 hp; the 350 HO was rated at 320 hp.

The 1968 Grand Prix retained its hidden headlamps and distinctive grille.

Like all Tempests for 1968, this Le Mans 4-door hardtop shows the switch to a horizontal headlamp arrangement, hidden windshield wipers, and a grille much like the Firebird's. All 4-door '68 Tempests had a 116-inch wheelbase; 2-door models had a 112-inch wheelbase.

The GTO had four engines, all 400 V-8s. Standard was a 350-hp version, while the "economy" version now had 265 hp. The 400 HO and 400 Ram Air engines were unchanged from 1967.

Late in the model year came a new and even more potent optional engine for the GTO. Officially released on June 5, 1968, the "Ram Air II" engine was a 400 V-8 with several key changes in the valve train. Most important was a hot new camshaft with 308 degrees duration on the intake valves and 320 degrees on the exhaust valves. The valve lift was very high: .480-inch intake, .475-inch exhaust. Dual valve springs some 13 percent stiffer than those on the Ram Air engine were used. This Ram Air II powerplant was rated at 366 hp @ 5400 rpm, another masterpiece of understatement calculated to avoid apoplectic fits in the GM building.

The most interesting GTO news, however, was about a bumper: the "Endura" nosepiece. Made of an elastomeric material covering a molded urethane shape which was mounted on a steel backing plate, this nosepiece had two enormous advantages over a standard bumper: it could absorb powerful impacts, and it could be formed to match body contours and color. This revolutionary concept originated with designer Warren Fitzgerald in GM corporate styling, then developed by GM's Inland Manufacturing Division in con-

Big news about the 1968 GTO was its body-colored Endura nosepiece, which shrugged off bumps. The GTO was the only Tempest model with concealed headlamps.

Lack of front vent windows is the best clue to distinguish a '68 Firebird from a '67.

junction with Pontiac. The original name for the material was "Indura," which was not changed to "Endura" until shortly before the introduction of the '68 models.

The bumper was primarily responsible for the GTO being named "Car of the Year" by *Motor Trend*, the fourth time Pontiac had won this award.

Traditional multi-leaf rear springs replaced the previous single-leaf springs in the Firebird, and the front vent windows were eliminated. The standard Firebird and the Sprint had the enlarged 250 OHC-6 , while the Firebird 350 and Firebird HO had the new 350 V-8. The standard engine for the Firebird 400 had 330 hp, the optional HO engine (not available in '67) had 335 hp, and this year the Ram Air 400 was rated at 335 hp. The GTO's late-appearing Ram Air II engine was not offered for the Firebird.

Pontiac sales rose to 910,977—another record—and market share increased to 10.9 percent as the division easily held on to third place for the seventh straight year.

High Summer for Specialty Cars 1969–1970

Three new specialty models were introduced in 1969, as Pontiac attempted to cover this fast-growing market.

The first of these was the Grand Prix. Ever since its introduction in 1962, the GP had been a glorified Catalina hardtop coupe. No more. The '69 GP was a brand-new car. Its 118-inch wheelbase was unique among Pontiacs. A "driver's command" seat, covered with expanded Morrokide or genuine leather, faced a wraparound instrument panel. Notable styling features included "hidden" exterior door handles, an electrically heated rear window, and radio antenna wires buried in the windshield, an industry first.

The Grand Prix came in two forms, denoted by letters which Pontiac borrowed from Duesenberg, the greatest American classic. The Model J was powered by a 350-hp 400 V-8 with a floor-shift 3-speed manual gearbox. Optional engines were the regular-fuel 265-hp 400, a 370-hp 428, and the 390-hp 428 HO; optional transmissions were a 4-speed all-synchro manual or Turbo Hydra-Matic. The Model SJ was an option package which included the 370-hp 428 engine, front-disc brakes, a full complement of gauges, fiberglass-belted tires, and "superlift" air-chambered shock absorbers for automatic leveling.

High Summer for Specialty Cars 1969–1970

The 1969 Grand Prix was the last in a long string of Pontiac triumphs for John DeLorean. It was smaller and lighter than its predecessor, yet boasted the longest hood in the industry.

From the rear the '69 Grand Prix exhibits the clean shape and masterful detailing which made it the best-looking Grand Prix since 1963.

Vent windows were deleted from all 1969 full-size Pontiacs, and an Endura center section protected the nose.

All full-size models had wheelbases one inch longer and a front track one inch wider than in '68. All had revised styling with an Endura nosepiece and deletion of the front vent windows. The Bonneville series received a 360-hp 428 as its standard engine, the only powerplant change among the big models. Like the Grand Prix, all the big Pontiacs had a new steel guard beam inside each door.

All Tempest 2-door hardtops and convertibles followed the full-size models by deleting the vent windows. The Sprint version of the OHC-6 now had 230 hp, and the output of the 350 HO engine was raised slightly from 320 to 330 hp.

The optional Ram Air 400 for the GTO—designated L-74—was rated this year at 366 hp @ 5100 rpm, up six hp from '68. The "Ram Air II" now became the L-67 "Ram Air IV" with 370 hp @ 5500 rpm. The 4-hp increase in rating for this powerhouse came from an aluminum intake manifold and an increase in valve lift to .520-inch. The previous 400 HO engine was dropped from the GTO option list.

The two Ram Air engines had functional twin hood scoops; a cable control was added this year to seal off the scoops in rainy weather. The potent Ram Air IV engine had two additional air inlet ducts through the grille which bypassed the radiator, making four cold air inlets in all. This accounted for its "Ram Air IV" designation; there was no official "Ram Air III" engine.

The three 400 engines offered in the Firebird 400 still carried restrictive ratings. The standard F-bird engine was rated at 330 hp, but carried a 350-hp rating in the GTO. The F-bird's 400 HO engine, with a 335-hp rating, was really the GTO's 366-hp L-74 Ram Air engine. And the new L-67 Ram Air IV, rated at 370 hp in the GTO, carried a 345-hp rating in the Firebird. (In a confusing twist of nomenclature, the term "Ram Air" in a '69 Firebird denoted only the optional functional hood scoops, not a specific engine. This led to the use of the *unofficial* term "Ram Air III" for the combination of L-74 engine and functional hood scoops in a Firebird. In a GTO this engine came with functional hood scoops and was simply called the Ram Air engine.)

All '69 Firebirds except the base version had new 7-inch-wide wheels and low-profile F70-14 tires as standard equipment. Turbo Hydra-Matic was now available for all Tempest and Firebird models.

The power front-disc brakes were a new single-piston design which simplified design and maintenance. All power steering units for the Grand Prix and full-size models were a new variable-ratio design which quickened steering response.

In January 1969 came the second of the three memorable specialty models. This was the Judge, a special version of the GTO. Standard were the 366-hp Ram Air engine, 3-speed heavy-duty manual transmission with floor shift, 3.55 axle ratio, and G70-14 fiberglass-belted tires. Optional were the Ram Air IV engine, 4-speed gearbox, Turbo Hydra-Matic, front-disc brakes, a gauge cluster, and hood-mounted tachometer. Available in coupe or convertible form, the Judge was distinguishable from an ordinary GTO by its blackout grille, Rally II wheels, and 5-foot-wide decklid spoiler.

The mighty Judge appeared in mid-1969. A special version of the GTO, the Judge had a standard Ram Air engine, functional hood scoops, and a decklid spoiler.

A revised appearance and two inches of additional length marked the 1969 Firebird. Turbo Hydra-Matic was offered for the first time as a Firebird option.

The first Trans Am appeared in March 1969. A special version of the Firebird aimed at the sports car customer, the T/A was the Firebird equivalent of the GTO Judge.

In March came the third of the specialty models: the Trans Am. This was a super Firebird with the 335-hp engine and Ram Air, 3-speed floor-mounted stick shift, 3.55 axle ratio, and F70-14 fiberglass-belted tires. Available were the usual assortment of performance options, including the Ram Air IV. Available as coupe or convertible, the '69 T/A had a Judge-like rear spoiler and came in only one color: Cameo White with blue stripes.

The Trans Am owed its unusual name to a racing series sponsored by the Sports Car Club of America, the Trans America Challenge Cup. Rules for this Trans Am racing specified a maximum engine displacement of five liters (305 cubic inches), so Pontiac's Trans Am with its big 400 V-8 was not eligible for racing in the series for which it was named. Pontiac investigated this possibility by building a handful of experimental T/A coupes with short-stroke 303-cubic-inch engines, but this version never saw production.

The all-new Grand Prix proved to be an astonishing success, with sales jumping 350 percent from 31,711 in '68 to 112,486 in '69. However, total division sales dropped slightly to 870,528 and the market share to 10.3 percent, still the second-best year in Pontiac history.

In February John DeLorean was promoted to the general managership of Chevrolet. His successor at Pontiac was F. James McDonald, who had been director of manufacturing operations at Chevrolet.

F. James McDonald, who succeeded John DeLorean as Pontiac's general manager in 1969, poses beside the 1970 Bonneville. Grand Prix styling influence is very evident in the frontal appearance.

Introduced in January 1970, the Tempest T-37 was Pontiac's cheapest hardtop. The following year the entire base Tempest series would be named after this coupe.

1970

The excitement with specialty cars continued. The division's biggest ever engine appeared, followed mid-year by a spectacularly restyled Firebird.

The engine array for the full-size models was considerably altered. Standard for Catalina hardtops and the sedan was now a 255-hp 350 V-8, while the familiar 290-hp 400 was the standard powerplant for Catalina wagons, the convertible, and all Executive models. Standard for the Bonneville was a brand-new engine, a 455 V-8. Derived from the 428, the 455 had cylinder dimensions of 4.15 x 4.21 inches. With a 4-bbl. carburetor, this huge but lazy engine developed an effortless 360 hp @ 4300 rpm, with the staggering torque output of 500 foot-pounds @ 2700 rpm! An HO version with 10.25:1 compression ratio was even more powerful: 370 hp @ 4600 rpm. All 428 engines were discontinued.

All Pontiacs, including the intermediates, adopted the Grand Prix's hidden windshield radio antenna.

A sharp marketing realignment struck the Tempest family. The previous Custom S series was discontinued, replaced by a Le Mans Sport series, and the Le Mans convertible was dropped.

In a corporate cost-cutting move that did not sit well with Pontiac engineers, the ingenious and responsive OHC-6 was dropped and replaced with a Chevrolet 250-cubic-inch pushrod six. Rated at 155 hp, this became the standard engine for all Tempest lines except the GTO. The rationale behind this seeming retrograde step was

The largest engine in Pontiac's history appeared in 1970. Rated at 360 hp, this 455 V-8 was standard in the Bonneville. Optional was an HO version rated at 370 hp.

High Summer for Specialty Cars 1969–1970

Except for its Endura nosepiece, the revised front end of the 1970 GTO looked quite like that of the 1970 Firebird.

Introduced in February 1970, the second-generation Firebird was a knockout. The base Firebird with its 6-cylinder engine and the Esprit with its 350 V-8 both had this squeaky-clean body.

that the Sprint version of the OHC-6 could not compete in power output with the much larger optional V-8s, so it ought to be dropped. The cost of manufacturing the base version could then no longer be justified, so it was replaced by the cheaper Chevy engine. The OHC-6 was a very good design indeed, the perfect base engine for the Tempest and especially the Firebird. It's a shame Pontiac never produced a car small enough and light enough for this engine's great weight advantage over a V-8 to be put to proper use.

The tame 265-hp 400 was finally dropped from the GTO's option list, replaced by a husky 360-hp 455.

The truly significant Pontiac for this model year was unveiled in showrooms on February 26: the spectacular new Firebird. Completely redesigned, the new car had its firewall moved rearward three inches, thus lengthening the hood. A high driveline hump separated the front and rear seats, allowing greater suspension travel. Front-disc brakes were standard equipment.

Twin forward-mounted hood scoops identify the Firebird Formula 400 with its 330-hp 400 V-8.

There were four variations of this new car: Firebird, Esprit, Formula 400, and Trans Am. All were coupes; the convertible was dropped. Engines ranged from that 155-hp Chevy six to the L-74 Ram Air 400 (see Appendix II). Automatic transmission was optional on all models—2-speed or Turbo Hydra-Matic with the 400 V-8s.

On the two upper models Pontiac concentrated its performance options and special identification. The Formula 400, identified by its twin air scoops, had a front anti-roll bar 1.125 inches in diameter and a .62-inch rear anti-roll bar; lesser Firebirds had a .94-inch front bar and none at all in the rear.

Rearward-facing shaker scoop, ducktail spoiler, engine vents, air dam and F60-15 tires mark the 1970 Firebird Trans Am, Pontiac's premier road gobbler.

As the Tempest grew larger, Pontiac's need for another compact also grew until it offered the Ventura II. Introduced as a mid-1970 model, it was a clone of the Chevrolet Nova.

The Trans Am was a total performance model. The L-74 Ram Air engine, 4-speed gearbox, power front-disc brakes, and F60-15 high-performance bias-belted tires on 15 x 7 wheels were all standard equipment. So were a 1.25-inch front anti-roll bar, .875-inch rear bar, variable-ratio power steering, limited-slip differential, stiffer springs and shocks, thickly padded small-diameter steering wheel, and complete instrumentation set into an impressive engine-turned panel.

Shortly after the new Firebird's introduction the Ram Air IV engine (now coded LS1 rather than L-67) was offered in the Trans Am, but very few T/As were equipped with this option.

Motor Trend's test Trans Am did 0 to 60 mph in 6.5 seconds and the quarter-mile in 14.5 seconds at 99 mph. *Sports Car Graphic* had equal times, while *Hot Rod*'s times were even quicker: 13.9 seconds at 102 mph for the quarter-mile.

This turned out to be a poor sales year for Pontiac. Production plummeted by almost 200,000 cars and the market share dropped precipitously to 8.1 percent, as the division's 8-year hold on third place was finally broken by a resurgent Plymouth. Most noticeable were the declines of the Grand Prix and GTO: their sales were little more than half their 1969 levels.

The Trans Am sold very slowly, only 697 in 1969 and 3,196 in 1970. To the division's credit it stuck with the Trans Am through its difficult early years when the performance market was waning, and this magnificent car later rewarded management's faith by becoming a popular and profitable model.

For a time Pontiac considered entering factory Firebirds in the Trans America Challenge Cup, a road-racing series for ponycars which imposed a 5-liter (305 cubic inch) displacement limit. A special competition V-8 was developed, marked by huge intake and exhaust ports and nicknamed the "Tunnel Port" 303; this is a proposed production version. The Tunnel Port was never produced; Pontiac eventually dropped its racing plans.

A Changing Market 1971–1973

The decade of the '70s would be a new era of great limitations on the auto industry. It began in 1971 with significant reductions in engine compression ratios, to enable engines to run on the new government-mandated low-lead and unleaded fuels. The U.S. auto industry also initiated a shift from gross to net power ratings. The combined effects of detuned engines and a more conservative rating system dramatically slashed rated engine power outputs.

Pontiac's most important response to this changing market was the Ventura II, its first compact since the 1961–63 Tempest. A facelift of the Chevrolet Nova, the Ventura II had a 111-inch wheelbase and was available as a 2-door or 4-door sedan. Its standard engine was the 145-hp (110 net hp) Chevy 250 six, while a Chevy 307 V-8 with 200 hp (140 net hp) was optional. The Ventura II was a '71½ model, introduced at the Chicago Automobile Show in February and appearing at dealerships a month later.

The Grand Ville was the new top-line series for the full-size Pontiacs, replacing the Bonneville Brougham. Available as a 2-door or 4-door hardtop and a convertible, the Grand Ville had as its standard engine a 4-bbl. 455 rated at 325 hp (230 net hp); there was no optional engine. Standard equipment included Turbo Hydra-Matic, power front disc brakes, and variable-ratio power steering.

Standard in the Bonneville was a 2-bbl. 455 rated at 280 hp (190 net hp); the only optional engine was the Grand Ville's 4-bbl. 455. Grand Ville and Bonneville shared common styling and a new 126-inch wheelbase.

The Executive series was dropped. "Catalina Brougham" was the new name for the previous Ventura trim option on the Catalina; a new name was necessary since the Ventura name was to be transferred to the new compact car. The standard engine on the new Catalina Brougham was a 2-bbl. 400 rated at 265 hp (185 net hp). Optional were the two 455s and a 4-bbl. 400 with 300 hp (200 net hp).

The base series of the big Pontiacs remained the Catalina, with a standard 2-bbl. 350 rated at 250 hp (165 net hp); all the other engines offered in the full-size models were optional. The Catalina and Catalina Brougham had a new 123.5-inch wheelbase, 1.5 inches longer than the previous year.

In the Pontiac sales brochure for 1971 appeared a wonderful rendition of the PBY Catalina in civilian guise, the first advertising tribute Pontiac had ever paid to the famous WWII Navy airplane which shared the Catalina name.

The big station wagons received special attention. In plain trim they were called Safaris and considered part of the Catalina range; in plush form they were called Grand Safaris and serialized as Bonnevilles. All had a revised chassis with a new 127-inch wheelbase and semi-elliptic rear springs, as opposed to coil springs used on previous wagons.

A new name for 1971 was Grand Ville, the top-of-the-line series which replaced the previous Bonneville Brougham. It boasted rich interiors and a standard 455 V-8.

The restyled Grand Prix presented an elegant new face for 1971. The high-intensity single headlamps and vertically barred grille recalled the grand classics of the '30s.

The Grand Prix received a handsome new grille reminiscent of thirties styling. The J version had the 300-hp 400 and a 3-speed manual transmission; the SJ had a 325-hp 455 and Turbo Hydra-Matic.

The time-honored word "Tempest" was expunged from all Pontiac sales literature, as the previous Tempest family had become a rather incoherent group of intermediates. The base series carried the uninformative designation "T-37," while the other three intermediate series retained their names from the previous year.

Intermediate-sized Pontiacs dropped the Tempest name in 1971, with the lowest-priced line simply called T-37.

Base engine for the T-37, Le Mans, and Le Mans Sport lines was the Chevy 250 six rated at 145 hp (110 net hp). Optional on all these cars were the same 350, 400, and even the 455 engines offered in the big Pontiacs. The top engine was a 455 HO version—designated LS5—with 335 gross hp and a whopping 310 net hp. Standard equipment on the Judge and Trans Am, this LS5 powerhouse was not available on any of the big Pontiacs, yet was available as an option in the intermediates!

The Firebird family was expanded, as the Formula 400 now became the Formula 350, 400, or 455, depending upon engine choice. Firebird styling was almost identical to 1970; the best clue to the '71 models was the new slotted air vent behind each front wheel.

In an attempt to inject some excitement into its tamer series, Pontiac offered a Sprint option package for the Ventura II. This was a sporty dress-up kit with blackout grille, 3-speed floor-shift transmission, E78-14 tires, Morrokide upholstery, full carpeting, and a special steering wheel. A similar option was the GT-37 package for any V-8-powered T-37 coupe or hardtop.

Despite the model juggling and the spread of the mighty 455 engine to the intermediates, sales woes continued. A bright spot was the new Ventura II, which sold almost 50,000 units in its first half-year. Yet total production for the division dropped to 536,047 cars, the lowest for the division since 1962. Market share dropped sharply again to 7.4 percent, and the division fell to sixth place in industry sales.

Optional on all 455 V-8 engines in 1972 was a new Delco electronic ignition system with the coil mounted in the distributor cap.

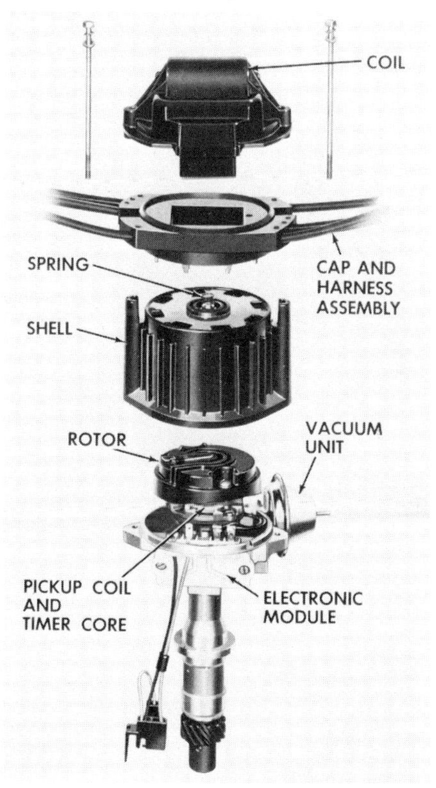

1972

All engines now had induction-hardened exhaust valve seats for greater durability. New spark plugs had a tapered seat with no gaskets, which allowed larger water passages in the cylinder head for better cooling. Revised 2-bbl. carburetors gave better mid-range performance on the lean mixtures required for emission controls. All engines now had net ratings only; the gross ratings were dropped.

The Grand Prix and all full-size models had Turbo Hydra-Matic as standard equipment; no manual transmission of any kind was available, even as an option.

On several models and engines a new Delco unitized ignition system was an option. The voltage regulator was solid-state, the coil was an integral part of the distributor cap, the contact breaker points were replaced by a magnetic pulse system, and there was a built-in rev limiter. It was available on the Grand Prix SJ, Grand Ville, Grand Safari, and all 455 HO engines.

Le Mans became the name of the base intermediate series; the short-lived and uninspired T-37 name was dropped.

Full-size Pontiacs for 1972 had a new energy-absorbing bumper employing urethane blocks inside telescoping steel boxes. Grand Ville and Bonneville styling was similar to this Catalina except that the grille contained vertical bars.

New for 1972, the Luxury Le Mans was Pontiac's top-of-the-line intermediate.

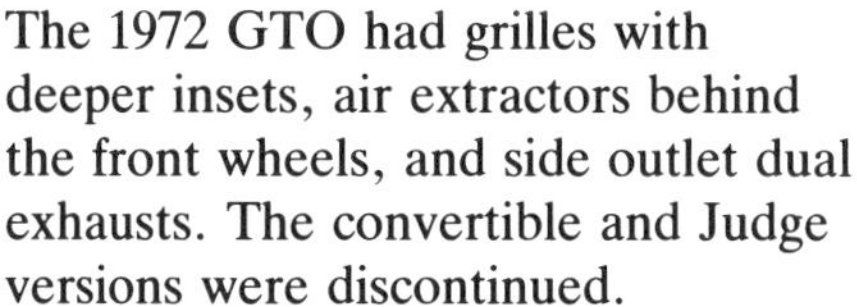
The 1972 GTO had grilles with deeper insets, air extractors behind the front wheels, and side outlet dual exhausts. The convertible and Judge versions were discontinued.

The Sprint option for the 1972 Ventura II was an appearance package which included 3-speed floor shift, custom steering wheel, custom carpets, and exterior identification. The flexible sunroof and mag-type wheels shown here were additional options.

New this year was the Luxury Le Mans. Available only as a 2-door hardtop (112-inch wheelbase) or 4-door hardtop (116-inch wheelbase), this new series combined intermediate size with a plush interior rivaling that of the Grand Ville. The 350 V-8 was standard, and all other Le Mans engines were optional except the 250 six and 455 HO.

The GTO was now an option—code number W62—on the Le Mans coupe and 2-door hardtop, similar to its origins in 1964. The 4-bbl. 400 with dual exhausts was standard equipment, with the 4-bbl. 455 and 455 HO available as options. The muscular Judge was dropped.

The only significant change to the Ventura II was the addition of the Pontiac 350 V-8 to its option list.

Firebirds for 1972 had a honeycomb mesh grille. As in 1971, this twin-scooped Formula was available with a choice of 350, 400, and 455 V-8 engines.

No changes were made to the comprehensive Firebird lineup except that the Trans Am's suspension—stiff rear springs, hefty anti-roll bars, and F60-15 tires on 15 x 7 steel wheels—was now available as a package for any Formula Firebird for $85.

Pontiac's sales doldrums continued. Its market share remained at 7.4 percent as production increased to 638,773 cars, enough to edge out Plymouth for fifth place, but they still trailed Oldsmobile and Buick. Firebird sales were crippled by a strike lasting several months at the sole Camaro/Firebird assembly plant in Norwood, Ohio.

Following the well-trod path to corporate glory, F. James McDonald left Pontiac to become general manager of Chevrolet on October 1, 1972. His successor was Martin J. Caserio, who came to Pontiac from GMC Truck Division.

The 2-inch greater width of the reshaped Grand Prix for 1973 was reflected in the grille, the two halves of which were separated by body-colored sheet metal.

1973

A heavy emphasis on revised mid-size models and a new performance engine marked the 1973 model year.

The all-new Grand Prix was now nearly an intermediate: its wheelbase was reduced 2 inches to 116 inches, yet its overall length went up by 3 inches and its width by 2 inches. The SJ version included GR70-15 steel-belted radial tires in place of the J's G78-15 rubber, an instrument cluster, front and rear anti-roll bars, and stiffer shock absorbers. The SJ's 250-hp 4-bbl. 455 was available as an option for the J version in place of its standard 230-hp 4-bbl. 400, and the new 310-hp SD-455 powerhouse was available for both versions (at least in Pontiac brochures).

The Le Mans family shared the new look of the Grand Prix. The Le Mans was still the base series, available this year only as a 2-door hardtop or 4-door sedan; the previous coupe was dropped. Aside from the Le Mans Safari wagons, this 2-door hardtop and 4-door sedan were the only body styles available in Pontiac's entire intermediate range for '73; all other body styles were discontinued.

The Le Mans Sport line offered only the hardtop, which differed from the Le Mans version by the addition of gill-like non-functional louvers covering the rear quarter windows.

The handsome and functional Endura front end was now gone from the GTO, the machine which had introduced Endura to the world. Except for its blackout grille, the GTO now looked like an ordinary Le Mans.

The intermediate family was completely restyled for 1973 with single headlamps and flowing lines. Le Mans models had simple grille bars, the GTO option had a blackout grille, and the Luxury Le Mans like this coupe had rear fender skirts and prominent vertical bars in the grille.

The high-performance Grand Am was a new intermediate for 1973. Featuring a large flexible beak, its frontal styling was quite different from other Pontiac intermediates.

Brand new was another intermediate, the Grand Am. Available as a sedan and gill-louvered sport coupe, the Grand Am combined, in Pontiac's words, "the feel of a Grand Prix with the response of a GTO." The standard drivetrain was the 2-bbl. 400 teamed with a floor-shifted Turbo Hydra-Matic; a 4-speed manual with floor shift was optional, as were the 4-bbl. 400, 4-bbl. 455, and the new SD-455 for the coupe. Standard equipment included GR70-15 steel-belted radial tires on husky 15 x 7 wide-rim wheels, a 1.125-inch front anti-roll bar, .875-inch rear anti-roll bar, and variable-ratio power steering.

Full instrumentation faced the Grand Am driver from a panel veneered in genuine African mahogany. The individual front seats reclined and even had adjustable lower back supports, and the thickly padded sports steering wheel afforded a firm grip.

Most noticeable about the Grand Am was its nose section, made of a resilient synthetic which shrugged off dents and was painted body color. The synthetic was not Endura, reserved for the Firebird, but a softer material which bent quite easily, even under finger pressure.

The name of hot-selling Ventura II compact was changed to plain "Ventura."

The Ventura line's appeal was greatly enhanced by the addition of a 4-door sedan and a 2-door hatchback to the previous 2-door coupe. All three body styles were available in an upmarket trim form called the Ventura Custom. The Chevy-built 307 V-8 was dropped, with the 250 six and Pontiac's 350 V-8 the only engines offered.

The full-size models were revised and now came in only one size, with a wheelbase of 124 inches and an overall length of 224.8 inches. The Catalina Brougham series, which had combined Bonneville trim with the shorter Catalina size, was therefore discontinued since it was redundant; the Bonneville itself was now the upmarket Catalina. Only three body styles were offered in Catalinas and Bonnevilles: 4-door sedan, 2-door and 4-door hardtops. The Grand Ville series had a convertible but no sedan, and its two hardtops had different rooflines from their less expensive counterparts.

Notable about the lineup of engines for the big cars was the absence of the previous year's 2-bbl. 455. Only four engine variations, in three displacements, supplied all the full-size models—a far cry from the profusion a decade earlier.

The Ventura Sprint for 1973 had a new split-nose grille resembling the GTO and Firebird. Later in the model year it became optional on other Ventura models, and the following year it was standard on all Venturas.

The 1973 Bonneville exhibits its complex grillework; Catalinas had a simpler grille with horizontal bars. All of the big Pontiacs for 1973 had 124-inch wheelbases.

Among the full-size wagons the plainer version was now the "Catalina Safari" rather than "Safari," while the Grand Safari was now serialized as a Grand Ville rather than a Bonneville.

The Endura nose on all Firebirds was reinforced and lengthened by ½ inch to comply with the more stringent federal bumper laws for 1973. All Formula Firebirds, regardless of engine choice, now had twin hood scoops, though this year they were rendered non-functional.

The Trans Am's rear-facing shaker scoop was also sealed off. The T/A was less powerful this year, as its standard engine was now the 250-hp 4-bbl. 455 (same as the Formula 455) rather than the 300-hp 455 HO of the previous year. Optional, however, was the new SD-455 engine.

An optional handling package for the Trans Am substituted GR70-15 steel-belted radials (also used on the Grand Am and the Grand Prix SJ) in place of the T/A's usual F60-15 bias-belted tires. New colors appeared; in addition to its traditional blue and white, the T/A was now available in Buccaneer Red and Brewster Green. The most noticeable T/A option of all was the huge and flamboyant Firebird hood decal, derisively dubbed the "screaming chicken."

The giant hood decal for Trans Ams first appeared in 1973.

The heroic SD-455 engine was one of the great unfulfilled promises in Pontiac history. Under development for two years by the Special Projects Group headed by performance specialist Herb Adams, the SD-455 was designed as a near-racing engine which could nevertheless meet the stiff new emissions laws, be perfectly drivable on the street, and be producible at moderate cost. It bristled with such high-durability features as a stiffened block casting with thicker main bearing webs, 4-bolt main bearing caps, a nitrided crankshaft with rolled fillets, and forged aluminum pistons with special rings. The connecting rods were steel forgings, and each one was shot-peened and magnafluxed. The rod bolts were 7⁄16-inch diameter rather than the 3⁄8-inch bolts found on other Pontiac V-8s. The heavy-duty high-volume oil pump operated at 80 psi. The oil sump was baffled, but with an eye toward racetrack use, the block had casting provisions for a dry sump lubrication system. The special cylinder heads had large ports and seat inserts for the exhaust valves. All valves were swirl-polished. An 800-cfm Quadrajet carburetor sat atop an iron high-rise manifold (aluminum was not used for this manifold since it condensed too much fuel during the cold-start emissions test). Special large-passage exhaust manifolds carried the gases away to 2½-inch-diameter exhaust pipes.

Reviving the name given to its racing engines of a decade earlier, Pontiac called this new engine its Super Duty 455. It was rated at 310 net horsepower at only 4000 rpm, and could turn 6000 rpm in stock form. Yet its compression ratio was only 8.4:1, it could run on 91-octane fuel, and it met all emissions requirements. It was easily the most powerful American production engine of its time.

When introduced at the press previews in July 1972, the SD-455 was announced as a replacement for the previous 455 HO engine. It was to be available as an option for the Firebird Trans Am, Firebird Formula 455, Grand Prix, and all intermediates except the Luxury Le Mans.

The motoring press was pleasantly surprised that any manufacturer would introduce a new high-performance engine at a time when tightening emissions laws, stiffer safety regulations, and escalating insurance premiums were bringing an end to Detroit's golden age of musclecars. *Car and Driver* was positively rapturous over its test Trans Am with the SD-455, which did 0 to 60 in 5.4 seconds, the quarter-mile in 13.8 seconds at 103.6 mph, and had a top speed of 132 mph. And that was with automatic transmission! "The Last of the Fast Cars comes standard with the sort of acceleration that hasn't been seen in years," exulted the editors. "The best compliment

Martin J. Caserio succeeded F. James McDonald as Pontiac's general manager shortly after the 1973 models were introduced.

bestowed on the Firebird is the fact that, even in its own time, it is becoming a collector's item."

Car and Driver could not have known just how much of a collector's item the SD-455 would soon become. New general manager Martin Caserio, who assumed Pontiac's helm after the SD-455 had already been introduced to the press, was reluctant to market this engine. He held up production for many months, relenting only when it was toned down with milder valve timing. In the last few months of the model year it finally went into limited production, rated at 290 hp @ 4000 rpm. Just 252 of them were put into '73 Trans Ams, 43 into Formula 455s, and only one into a Grand Am; none at all went into a GTO or a Grand Prix.

Spurred by an expansion of U.S. auto production by 1.2 million cars, Pontiac's 1973 production jumped to 894,446 cars for its second-best model year in history, bettered only by 1968. The market share jumped to 9.0 percent and the division moved up to fourth place overall, still trailing Oldsmobile. Caserio's confident prediction of Pontiac's permanent return to sales competitiveness and a possible million-car year in 1974 sounded justified.

The Demand for Efficiency 1974–1976

Made confident by the sales success of 1973, Pontiac presented a lineup almost unchanged for 1974.

Uptown versions of the intermediate station wagons appeared with the Luxury Le Mans Safaris. A formal roof option was made available for the Le Mans Sport Coupe, and new rooflines with large quarter windows appeared for Bonneville and Catalina 2-door hardtops. The Firebird had a new sloping nose and black urethane bumpers, requirements to meet '74 federal safety standards.

Full-size Pontiacs had narrower grilles for 1974, as shown by this Catalina. Grand Villes and Bonnevilles had additional vertical grille bars.

The revised face of the Grand Am for 1974 retained its flexible snout, but presented a busy front end with twelve air inlets. This front end was retained the following year.

The most significant change struck the GTO. No longer a Le Mans variant, it became an option—coded WW3—on the Ventura coupe or hatchback. This downsized GTO had a standard 200-hp 4-bbl. 350 V-8 with dual exhaust, 3-speed manual transmission with floor shift, a rearward-facing shaker hood scoop, blackout grille, heavy-duty suspension, 3.-8 axle ratio, and Rally II wheels mounting G70-14 bias-belted tires. Optional were a 4-speed or Turbo Hydra-Matic and FR78-14 steel-belted radials.

This smaller GTO was still a formidable performance car. The Ventura coupe weighed 400 pounds less than a Le Mans coupe, so the '74 GTO with its 200-hp 350 had the same performance as the heavier '73 GTO with its 230-hp 400. However, a clue to its coming demise was the limited option list—no other engine was available.

This GTO engine was offered as the L76 option in any Ventura or Le Mans except the Grand Am and Safaris. With its very low 7.6:1 compression ratio, the 4-bbl. 350 was rated at 170 hp with single exhaust and 200 hp with dual exhaust.

The workhorse 2-bbl. 350 was finally dropped from the Catalina. Already the same car except for interior trim, the Bonneville and Catalina now shared the 2-bbl. 400 as their standard engine.

The 4-bbl. 400 became the Trans Am's standard engine, though the previous 4-bbl. 455 remained an option. The SD-455, with an unchanged 290-hp rating, was now an option only for the Formula 455 and Trans Am Firebirds.

The Demand for Efficiency 1974–1976

Hardly had the Pontiac showrooms received their new '74 models when the roof caved in. Angered by U.S. support for Israel in the "Yom Kippur" war, the nine Arab members of OPEC declared an oil embargo against the U.S. on October 17, 1973. Although non-Arab OPEC members such as Venezuela, Iran, and Indonesia kept up their U.S. shipments and even increased them, the shortages caused by this embargo wrought instant havoc with the U.S. economy.

When the embargo was finally lifted five long months later, the U.S. and the industrialized world faced a new problem: OPEC quadrupled the price of crude petroleum, which caused the price of gasoline to skyrocket.

In such an atmosphere the U.S. auto market contracted sharply. Total domestic production went down by 1.7 million units, and Pontiac's production dropped to 520,216. Still trailing Oldsmobile, Pontiac also fell behind Plymouth for fifth place in sales.

Federal safety standards necessitated a major face-lift for the 1974 Firebird, which included a separate bumper for the first time in Firebird history.

In its last year the once-legendary GTO was demoted to being an option on the compact Ventura instead of the intermediate Le Mans.

Touted as a possible future Firebird, the 1974 Banshee show car had an aerodynamic body on a Firebird chassis. All glass areas were fixed with the exception of small side panels.

All but one of Pontiac's lines showed huge sale losses. Grand Prix production dropped by 35 percent, Le Mans by 44 percent, and the full-size models by a shocking 52 percent. Firebird sales, however, *rose* by 59 percent, suggesting that diehard loyalists would buy the Firebird even if they had to keep it in a garage and ride a bicycle. Of the model year's 73,729 Firebirds, 943 Trans Ams and 58 Formula 455s had the SD-455 engine.

1975

The shattering revelation that America was highly vulnerable to petroleum manipulation by foreign countries caused the most rapid shift in customer preference in the entire history of the American automobile.

While the industry struggled with the overnight demand for fuel efficiency, it was still bound by the tightening emissions and safety laws. To meet these regulations, all '75 Pontiacs were equipped with catalytic converters, which required unleaded fuel, and the fully electronic Delco high energy ignition system. All engines had single exhaust, since federal law stipulated that only one converter was allowed per car.

Pontiac's chief anti-OPEC weapon was its new subcompact Astre. A minor facelift of the Chevrolet Vega, the Astre was available in two body styles: hatchback coupe and 2-door station wagon. With its 97-inch wheelbase, 175.4-inch overall length, and 2600-pound weight, the Astre was the smallest Pontiac yet.

The Astre engine was an aluminum-block overhead-cam 4-cylinder displacing 140 cubic inches, offered in two stages of tune: 78 hp with a 1-bbl. carb, and 87 hp with a 2-bbl. A 3-speed floor-mounted stick shift was standard, with a 4-speed or Turbo Hydra-Matic optional. Front disc brakes and variable-ratio power steering were also standard. The front suspension was conventional, but the rear suspension was elaborate for an economy car: coil springs, four links to control the movement of the solid axle, and an optional anti-roll bar. Three Astre trim levels were offered. The base version had Morrokide upholstery, full nylon carpeting, and A78-13 bias-ply tires on 5-inch wheels. Optional was RTS (Radial Tuned Suspension) which included BR78-13 steel-belted radials on 6-inch wheels, with anti-roll bars front and rear. The Astre GT version

The most intriguing features of the Astre's 4-cylinder engine were its linerless aluminum block, single overhead camshaft, and the tapered screw used to adjust valve clearances.

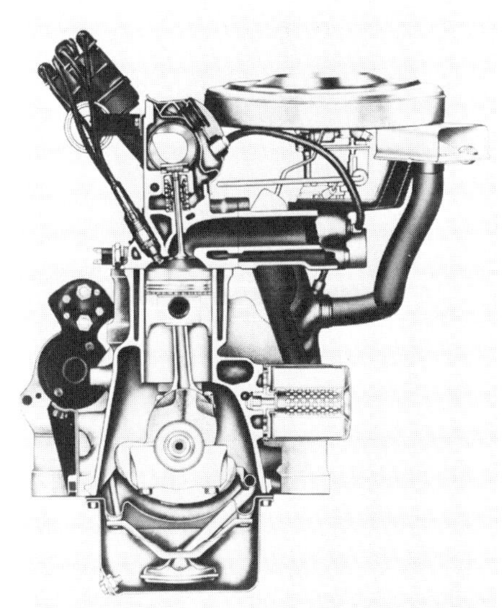

New for 1975 was the Astre, Pontiac's version of the Chevy Vega. This is the top-of-the line SJ hatchback with its standard Rally III wheels.

included the RTS package, 87-hp engine, full instrumentation including a tachometer, special steering wheel, and exterior identification. To the GT's specifications the SJ luxury version added thicker sound insulation and special front bucket seats.

In mid-year the Vega's notchback body style was added to the Astre family, and so was a lower-level "S" trim package.

In the Ventura family a new luxury SJ version was added, which had front bucket seats, a center console, and—in Pontiac's words—"lots of simulated dark flame chestnut accent trim." Translation: fake wood.

A new engine appeared for the Ventura, a 260 V-8 with bore and stroke of 3.50 x 3.385 inches. With 2-bbl. carburetion and 8:1 compression ratio, it was rated at 110 hp. This was an Oldsmobile engine, a small-bore version of the Olds 350 V-8. It marked the first time Pontiac had ever used an Oldsmobile engine.

In a little-noticed change which Pontiac did not publicize at all, a Buick-built 350 V-8 replaced Pontiac's 350 V-8 as an option for the Ventura. Its cylinder dimensions of 3.80 x 3.85 inches differed from the Pontiac's 3.876 x 3.75 inches, and it was a bit more compact with bore centers spaced at 4.24 inches instead of the Pontiac's 4.62 inches.

The high-performance 200-hp 350 4-bbl. was gone from the Ventura line, and with it was also gone that legendary name: the GTO. The Sprint option was still available, but it didn't sprint well anymore; its axle ratio was raised, and it lost both its dual exhaust system and 4-speed gearbox.

The intermediate family had few changes; the new Grand Le Mans was merely a name change for the previous Luxury Le Mans. Emphasizing thriftier engines, the 250 six was now the standard engine for the Grand Le Mans in place of the previous 2-bbl. 350, and the 4-bbl. 455 was no longer available for any model except the Grand Am.

Aerodynamics played a role in the Ventura's face-lift for 1975. The Sprint option included a blackout version of this new grille.

The Grand Le Mans for 1975 was the new name for the previous Luxury Le Mans. It sported an Oldsmobile-like grille, while other Le Mans models had egg-crate grilles.

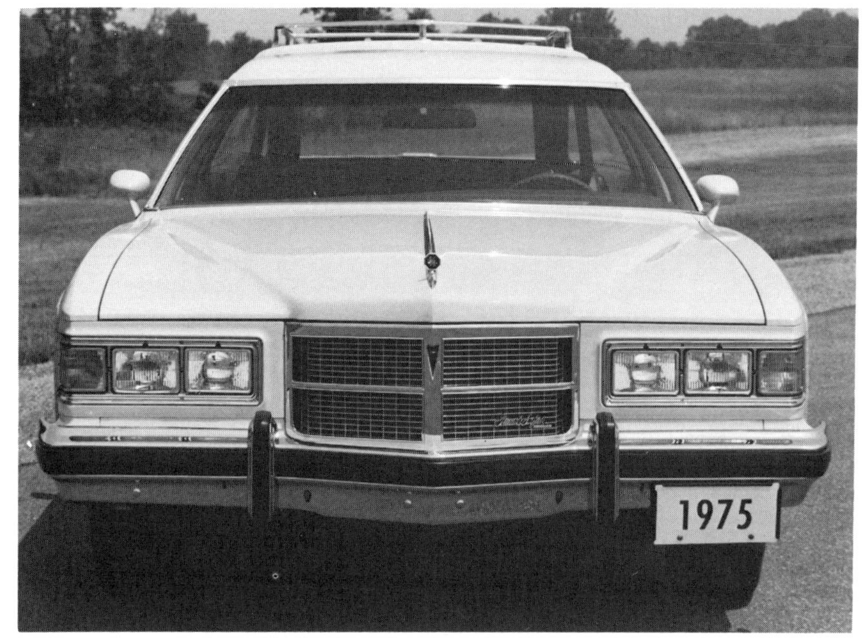

Bonnevilles and the Grand Ville Brougham for 1975 had mesh grilles and were the first Pontiacs to use rectangular dual headlamps. The Catalina had a horizontally barred grille and retained its round headlamps.

The full-size models had their wheelbases shortened a tiny 0.6 inches to 123.4 inches. The Grand Ville's name was expanded to the more snobbish "Grand Ville Brougham," and its formal roofline for 2-door and 4-door hardtops was extended to the Bonneville hardtops. Both the Bonneville sedan and the Catalina 4-door hardtop were dropped, which reduced the full-size lineup to 11 models.

An LJ super-luxury option for the Grand Prix appeared, while the "J" designation for the base-level version was dropped. Grand Prix production must have depleted the supply of genuine African crossfire mahogany, for the '75 GP substituted mere woodgrain vinyl trim.

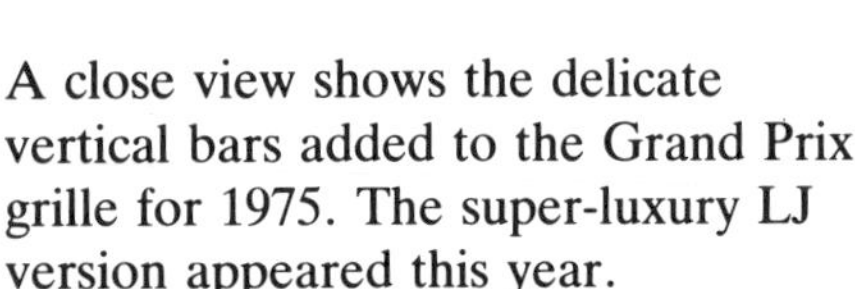
A close view shows the delicate vertical bars added to the Grand Prix grille for 1975. The super-luxury LJ version appeared this year.

The good news for the Firebirds was that they all had 15-inch wheels with steel-belted radials as standard equipment. The bad news was that the 455 engine was no longer available; not just the magnificent SD-455, but *any* 455. The Trans Am's 4-bbl. 400, strangled by a single exhaust and a lower 7.6:1 compression ratio, had its power cut all the way to 185 hp.

Motor Trend bemoaned this loss in its test of a Trans Am. The car did 0 to 60 in 9.8 seconds and the quarter-mile in 16.75 seconds at 85 mph, performance unworthy of a fabled supercar.

Heeding the cries of the faithful, Pontiac announced a 455 HO option for the Trans Am in mid-year. After initial sighs of relief, enthusiasts found that this unfortunately bore scant resemblance to the mighty 455 HO engines of yesteryear. It was nothing more than the same mild 200-hp 4-bbl. 455 offered as an option in full-size Pontiacs, the Grand Am, and the Grand Prix.

Testing a Trans Am with this engine, *Car and Driver* was mightily disappointed. "Once off idle, the station wagon engine you bought under the HO label goes all soft and mannerly, as if it would rather not disturb you with a nudge in the shoulder blades or any commotion as it saunters up through the rev range. . . . You shouldn't consider it High Output at all. That once meant swirl-polished valves, forged pistons, four-bolt main bearings, aluminum manifolds, wild cam grinds, and horsepower ratings manufacturers had to lie about. In 1975, HO means a 200-hp station-wagon engine." The *C&D* test car did 0 to 60 in 7.8 seconds and the quarter-mile in 16.1 seconds at 88.8 mph. Not the stuff of legend, but it was still the fastest 4-seat car made in America.

Engine changes also struck the rest of the Firebird family, as the 2-bbl. 400 was dropped but the 4-bbl. 350 was added. The Esprit's standard engine was now the same 250 six as the base Firebird.

Production of the U.S. auto industry shrank to 6.5 million cars for the 1975 model year. This was a drop of 1.5 million cars from 1974—itself a disastrous year—and the lowest industry total since 1961. Pontiac's production dropped to 525,413 cars, but its market share increased to 8.02 percent and it regained fourth position in industry sales. The Firebird again showed astonishing strength, its sales rising 14 percent to 84,063 cars in the teeth of the oil crisis.

On October 1, Martin Caserio was made a vice-president of GM in charge of a newly formed electrical components group which included Delco, AC, and Packard Cable. His successor as Pontiac's general manager was Alex C. Mair, previously head of GMC truck and bus division.

Alex C. Mair succeeded Martin Caserio as Pontiac's general manager shortly after the introduction of the 1976 models.

1976

The nation's bicentennial was also Pontiac's semicentennial. To celebrate its 50th anniversary the division introduced another subcompact.

The new Sunbird was Pontiac's version of a corporate small sporty car introduced simultaneously as the Chevrolet Monza, Olds-

The first Pontiac Sunbird rolls off the assembly line at South Gate, California. A modified version of the Chevrolet Monza, the Sunbird was introduced in 1976.

mobile Starfire, and Buick Skyhawk the year before; the Monza garnered *Motor Trend*'s "Car of the Year" laurels. In its Monza form this car was powered by the Vega's 4-cylinder engine, with a new 262-cubic-inch version of Chevy's small-block V-8 as an option; the Skyhawk and Starfire versions used a new 231 V-6 from Buick.

This subcompact was initially available only as a 2-door hatchback, but in mid-'75 a notchback version of the Monza appeared. This notchback was the body style used for the Sunbird.

Standard Sunbird powerplant was the Vega/Astre 1-bbl. overhead-cam four, now down to 70 hp; optional were the 87-hp 2-bbl. four and the Buick V-6 with 2-bbl. carburetion and 105 hp.

In addition to the usual assortment of transmissions, the Sunbird offered a brand-new all-synchromesh 5-speed gearbox. This splendid new transmission was also an option on the Astre, Ventura, and Le Mans Sport Coupe.

Unlike the Astre, the Sunbird's coil-sprung rear axle was located longitudinally by two trailing links and transversely by a Panhard rod. Axle torque reactions were controlled by a very long torque arm which ran from the front of the differential to a mounting point near the rear of the transmission.

The rear suspension of the Sunbird was notable for its very long torque arm, which controlled axle torque reactions.

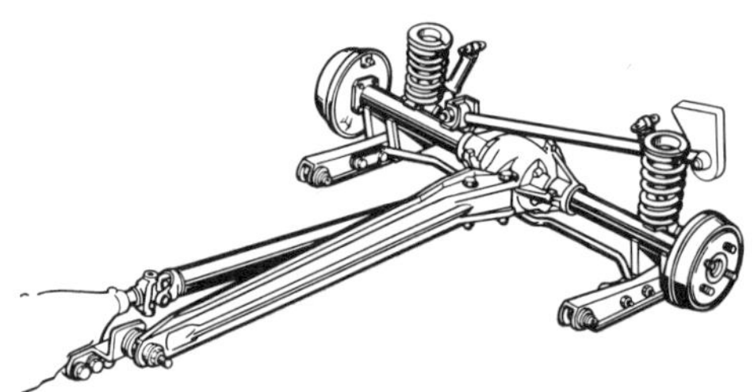

The rest of the small Pontiacs showed few changes. The Astre SJ was now called the Astre Custom, while the mid-range Custom line of the Ventura was dropped.

In the intermediate group, the news was the demise of the Grand Am. Only three years old, this big-engined performance/luxury model now seemed inappropriate to the new age of fuel efficiency.

The Olds-built 260 V-8 now became an option for any Le Mans (except station wagons), while the 200-hp 4-bbl. 455—available in '75 only in the Grand Am—was now offered with any intermediate.

The Le Mans Sport Coupe was the only intermediate available with the new 5-speed transmission, and then only with the 260 V-8.

Face-lifts for 1976: the Ventura showed little change, while the Grand Le Mans displays its new rectangular twin headlamps.

This is the special limited-edition version of the 1976 Grand Prix honoring Pontiac's fiftieth anniversary, with tinted removable roof panels and a special hood ornament. A total of 4,807 such commemorative Grand Prixs were produced.

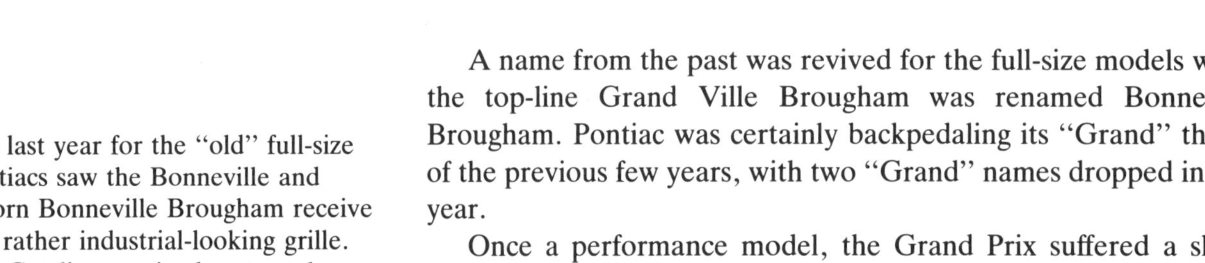

A name from the past was revived for the full-size models when the top-line Grand Ville Brougham was renamed Bonneville Brougham. Pontiac was certainly backpedaling its "Grand" theme of the previous few years, with two "Grand" names dropped in one year.

Once a performance model, the Grand Prix suffered a sharp power cut as the 2-bbl. 350 V-8 became standard in place of the previous 4-bbl. 400, becoming the first-ever GP without a 4-bbl. carburetor. Perkier performance was available in the SJ version, but even it was downgraded with a 4-bbl. 400 replacing the previous 4-bbl. 455.

The only engine change for the Firebirds was the 2-bbl. 350 again becoming the standard engine for the Formula; the previous 4-bbl. 350 now became a California-only engine. Due to California's tight emissions laws, Firebird enthusiasts in the Golden State had slim pickings this year; the 2-bbl. 350 and 4-bbl. 455 were not available at all, nor were the 250 six if mated to the 3-speed manual transmission or the 4-bbl. 400 with the 4-speed.

The last year for the "old" full-size Pontiacs saw the Bonneville and reborn Bonneville Brougham receive this rather industrial-looking grille. The Catalina received rectangular headlamps.

Bumpers for all 1976 Firebirds were body-colored and integrated into the body contours. The traditional twin hood scoops identify this Formula, which additionally has the Formula Appearance Package—black rocker panels with "Formula" graphics.

The first Black Special Edition Trans Am appeared in 1976, with its black-on-black exterior/interior, gold accents, and T-top roof.

After the terrible sales years in 1974 and 1975, U.S. auto production bounced back in 1976 to 8 million units, and Pontiac sales recovered strongly to 721,614 cars for a 8.90 percent market share. The division nevertheless slipped back to fifth place, just 16,000 units behind Buick and some 150,000 cars behind third-place Oldsmobile.

The most interesting point about Pontiac's sales were the models showing increases. The heavy hitters were the Firebird, again, the sales of which were up by 32 percent to 110,775, and the Grand Prix, which was up by an incredible 263 percent to 228,091! For the first time in history the Firebirds outsold the entire Le Mans range and the Grand Prix outsold the entire range of full-size models.

The Downsized Era Begins 1977–1979

As a watershed year in Pontiac history, 1977 saw the introduction of the long-awaited smaller full-size models and two brand-new engines.

The downsized big cars were the first significant effort in GM's long-range five-billion-dollar response to the demand for better fuel economy. All previous steps were really stopgap measures utilizing equipment GM already had on hand when the fuel crisis erupted in 1973. Since then the federal government had promulgated its CAFE (Corporate Average Fuel Economy) standards, which stipulated that the average fuel economy of a manufacturer's full range of automobiles must rise in progressive steps until it reached the eventual goal of 27.5 miles per gallon by 1985. The only way that manufacturers could meet such ambitious economy levels while still meeting the emissions laws was to reduce the size and weight of their cars and power them with smaller engines. Since GM's big cars obtained the least fuel economy, it was appropriate that the massive corporate downsizing program begin with them.

The differences in size were startling. The 1977 Pontiac full-size 4-door sedan was 12.2 inches shorter, 3.9 inches narrower, and 0.3 inches lower than its 1976 counterpart. It rode on a 115.9-inch wheel-

The all-new downsized big Pontiacs debuted in 1977. The Catalina looked cleaner than the Bonneville due to simpler trim and exposed rear wheels.

base, shorter by 7.5 inches. Weight reductions ranged from 805 pounds for the Catalina sedan to a whopping 969 pounds for the Grand Safari wagon. The station wagons now had the same wheelbase as the sedans and reverted to a 4-link rear suspension with coil springs.

This remarkable shrinkage brought the big Pontiacs down to a size previously called "intermediate." In fact, compared to the 1977 Le Mans, the new Catalina had a wheelbase 0.1-inch *shorter*, was 143 pounds *lighter*, and was only 2.3 inches longer!

Despite the substantial reductions in size and weight, the new body had generous interior dimensions. Head room, leg room, and knee room were all fractionally greater than the previous body, and the trunk was 1.15 cubic feet larger. Only hip room suffered, being four inches narrower.

The new Pontiac engines were the first from the division since the OHC-6 of 1966.

They were an inline 4-cylinder and a V-8. Under project managers Tom Davis (V-8), John Sawruck (4-cylinder), and chief engineer Stephen Malone, the designs shared common cylinder dimensions of 4-inch bore and 3-inch stroke, resulting in displacements of 150.8 cubic inches (2.5 liters) for the four and 301.6 cubic inches (5 liters) for the V-8. They also shared common pistons, piston rings, wrist pins, connecting rods, and rod bearings. They did not, however, have the same bore centerline spacing, and thus the cylinder heads were not interchangeable. The valves were different, as was the porting; the V-8 had crossflow porting, while the L-4 had its intake and exhaust ports on the left side.

Pontiac's two new engines for 1977 pose for a family portrait. The 2.5-liter "Iron Duke" four (left) and the 5-liter V-8 shared a number of interchangeable parts.

Since these engines were designed to meet emission and fuel economy requirements, the emphasis was placed on durability, low weight, high torque at low rpm, flexibility, and accurate control of fuel mixture. High rotational speed was not important, so simple pushrod valve gear was used. The five main bearings of the 151 L-4 were 2.30 inches in diameter, while those of the 301 V-8 were no less than 3 inches in diameter—the same size as those in the larger 350 and 400 V-8s.

Considerable attention was paid to weight control; the 301 V-8 weighed only 452 pounds, some 120 pounds less than Pontiac's 350 V-8.

Each engine came in only one form for 1977: 88 hp for the L-4, and 135 hp for the V-8.

Both new engines saw widespread duty in their first year. Coded LX6, the L-4 became the standard engine for all Sunbirds and the Astre hatchback and wagon; it was optional on the Astre coupe and all Venturas. Coded L27, the 301 V-8 became Pontiac's big-car workhorse as standard equipment in the Bonneville, Bonneville Brougham, Grand Prix, Grand Prix LJ, Grand Le Mans, and all Safari wagons except the Astre. It was optional on the Ventura, Catalina, Le Mans, Firebird, and Firebird Esprit.

These engines were part of a massive GM engine rationalization program. Four engines used in '76 Pontiacs disappeared in '77: the

The last minor face-lift for the intermediate body introduced in 1973 left the 1977 Le Mans looking almost indistinguishable from its predecessors.

The Downsized Era Begins 1977–1979

The mildly revised Grand Prix for 1977 remained Pontiac's most popular model and set an all-time Grand Prix sales record.

Chevy 250 L-6, the Olds 260 V-8, the Buick 350 V-8, and Pontiac's own 455 V-8. New faces in the engine lineup were the Olds 350 V-8 (L34) and Olds 403 V-8 (L80); later in the model year these were joined by the Chevy 350 V-8 (LM1) and the new Chevy 305 V-8 (LG3). Amid all these changes, the only familiar engines returning for duty were the Chevy 140 OHC-4, Buick's 231 V-6, and Pontiac's own 350 and 400 V-8s.

One of the reasons for so many engines was that some of them would not meet California state emissions standards or the new federal high-altitude emissions regulations. In fact, this was true of all the Pontiac-built V-8s. The Olds 350 and 403 V-8s were substituted for the Pontiac 301, 350, and 400 engines in those circumstances. Pontiac promotional literature circumvented this awkwardness by referring to the 350 V-8s collectively as its "5.7-liter V-8" and the 400/403 engines as its "6.6-liter V-8."

The 231 V-6 became the standard engine for the new Catalina. All the full-size models had a revised turbo Hydra-Matic which weighed 80 pounds less than the previous version.

The 151 L-4 became Sunbird's new standard engine, with the 231 V-6 and 140 OHC-4 as options. New was the Sunbird Formula, a package which included body trim, Rally wheels, full instrumentation, and RTS suspension. The 151 L-4 also became the standard engine for the Astre hatchback and wagon, and an option for the coupe; the OHC-4 remained the standard engine for the coupe and was an option for the other Astres. All OHC-4 engines this year had 2-bbl. carburetion.

The Firebird family received rectangular dual headlamps and smaller engines for 1977.

The Ventura received a handsome new nose and the 231 V-6. The 151 L-4 was an option only on the base-level coupe and sedan.

The 231 V-6 was also the standard engine for all Le Mans models except the station wagons, which had the 301 V-8. Optional for Ventura and Le Mans were an assortment of V-8s.

The Firebirds received a handsome restyled nose with quad rectangular headlamps. There were some nifty new appearance options, including side-splitter exhaust pipes, cast aluminum wheels, and a "T-top" version of the Trans Am with removable roof panels.

Performance cars or not, the Firebirds also had to take the bitter medicine of smaller engines. The 231 V-6 became standard for Firebird and Esprit, with the 301 V-8 standard for the Formula. The Trans Am's standard engine remained the L78 4-bbl. 400, though down 5 hp from the previous year. A new engine appeared to replace the discontinued 455: the T/A 400. This had a higher compression ratio than the L78 (8.0:1 instead of 7.6:1), a longer-duration camshaft, and was rated at 200 hp. Not available in California, it was optional only on the Formula and Trans Am.

Two special Firebird appearance packages deserve mention. The Sky Bird was a special Esprit that was a symphony in blue—two-tone blue exterior, blue velour interior, even blue grille and blue aluminum wheels. The Black Special Edition Trans Am was finished in black with gold trim.

Engine realignment also struck the Grand Prix, where the 301 V-8 became standard for the base model and the LJ. The SJ retained its standard L78 400, but lost its optional 455. Like the Trans Am, the Grand Prix offered an optional T-top with removable roof panels.

The massive shakeup of engines, plus the introduction of a whole new lineup of big cars, might have seemed quite enough for Pontiac to digest in one year; however, Alex Mair badly wanted to wrest the coveted third spot in sales away from Oldsmobile. In mid-year he came out with all guns blazing, introducing three new models.

The Sunbird Sport Hatch was a 2+2 hatchback, which finally allowed Pontiac to offer this body style of the subcompact. It had the same powertrain as the Sunbird coupe: standard 151 L-4 (coded LX6, but called in Pontiac literature the "Iron Duke"), optional 231 V-6.

The Can Am was a special performance version of the Le Mans Sport Coupe. Rather like a 1977 version of the GTO, this hot car

A mid-year addition to the 1977 line was the Can Am, a high-performance version of the Le Mans which recalled past GTO glory.

A formal front end and luxurious interior marked the Phoenix, introduced in mid-1977. An uptown version of the Ventura, the Phoenix was the first Pontiac to employ rectangular single headlamps.

was named for the Canadian-American Challenge Cup, a series of professional road races. Standard equipment included the 200-hp T/A 400 engine (California: 185-hp Olds 403), full instrumentation, RTS Rally suspension, GR70-15 steel-belted radials on white-painted Rally II wheels, power brakes, variable-ratio power steering, automatic transmission, and only one paint color: Cameo White.

The Phoenix was essentially a plushed-up Ventura with a different "formal" nose. Named for the legendary bird which is consumed by fire but rises recreated from its own ashes, the Phoenix was available as a 2-door or 4-door sedan (no hatchback) and had the same powertrain options as the Ventura with the exception of the 301 V-8. It was obvious that Pontiac was trying to establish a separate image for the Phoenix, yet equally obvious that it was little more than a Ventura LJ with a different nose and name. The logic of this marketing move did not become clear until the '78 Pontiac lineup appeared.

Motor Trend put 24,000 miles on a Sunbird with a 231 V-6 and 5-speed gearbox. They liked the car's size, appearance, interior appointments, fuel economy, and high-speed cruising ability, but disliked a host of minor annoyances: heavy clutch, stiff gearshift, lumpy engine, uncomfortable seats, rapid tire wear, brake juddering, road noise, broken air conditioning, and lack of footwell ventilation. *MT* had "mixed emotions" and looked forward to "the next edition."

The auto industry's recovery continued apace. Pontiac's production increased to 847,129 and its market penetration to 9.3 percent, barely edging out Buick for fourth place. Sales of the new full-sized models were gratifyingly strong at just over 200,000, up 47.5 percent from '76. Firebird production was up 40.6 percent to 155,736, outselling the entire Le Mans line by more than 2:1. The Grand Prix improved on its previous year's spectacular effort by 26.5 percent, handily outselling the entire full-size array to remain Pontiac's best-selling model.

Despite such a good year, Mair must have despaired of ever catching Oldsmobile, which had a better one. Paced by soaring Cutlass sales, Oldsmobile's 1977 production climbed to 1,116,818 cars, the first time in history that any GM division other than Chevrolet had sold more than one million cars.

1978

The second year of the downsizing era affected two Pontiac lines: the Le Mans intermediates and the Grand Prix. The new intermediates were also introduced elsewhere in GM as the Chevrolet Malibu, Oldsmobile Cutlass, and Buick Century.

The downsized 1978 Le Mans was especially attractive in 2-door form.

Introduced at the 1978 New York Auto Show, the Trans Am Type K show car combined sports car driving pleasure with station wagon utility. The front was standard Trans Am, but folding rear seats and glass gullwing hatches provided voluminous cargo room. Pontiac contemplated producing this car, but costs proved to be too high.

Compared to its predecessor, the new Le Mans was 13.5 inches shorter, 5 inches narrower, and 0.9 inches taller. The 108.1-inch wheelbase was 7.9 inches shorter, and it was 624 pounds lighter. Yet it had greater head room, leg room, and knee room.

The new car had a perimeter frame and suspension system quite similar to the previous Le Mans. Body styles were 4-door sedan, 2-door coupe, and 4-door 2-seat station wagon.

A surprise for 1978 was the return of the Grand Am, last seen in 1975. Standard equipment included a 301 V-8, heavy-duty suspension, and full instrumentation.

A controversial feature of the new sedan was its fixed windows on the rear doors. GM cited better weather sealing, increased interior room, lower cost, and the wide use of air conditioning as justification for these unopenable windows, but they ran into strong sales resistance.

In addition to the previous Le Mans and Grand Le Mans names, there was a surprising third series: a rebirth of the Grand Am. Carrying a distinctive grille, it was offered only as a coupe or sedan.

The Buick 231 V-6 remained the standard powerplant for the Le Mans and Grand Le Mans. However, it was not quite the same engine used previously. For even firing impulses, a V-6 with a 3-throw crankshaft should have 120° between its cylinder banks. The Buick V-6 had 90°, since it was manufactured with V-8 tooling to save money. This resulted in uneven firing impulses, causing vibrations especially noticeable at low engine speeds. A redesign of the crankshaft for 1978 provided offset crankpins with six throws, giving even firing impulses. This new even-firing V-6 had the same displacement and 105-hp rating as the earlier version, but was coded LD5 instead of LD7.

With its accent on performance, the Grand Am's standard engine was the L27 301 V-8 with 2-bbl. carburetion and 140 hp. Optional was a new 4-bbl. version of this engine, designated L37 and rated at 150 hp. Automatic transmission was standard, with a 4-speed gearbox optional.

The all-new Grand Prix for 1978 was based on the Le Mans coupe. A 231 V-6 was standard, making this the smallest and smallest-engined Grand Prix yet.

Since its inception, the Grand Prix had established a special identity through unique styling, underscored since 1969 by a unique wheelbase. The new 1978 Grand Prix, however, had a 108.1-inch wheelbase; it was obvious that its basic structure was that of the new downsized Le Mans coupe. Pontiac tried to mask this cost-cutting move by fitting modified exterior body panels, a different grille, and a half-vinyl roof with formal quarter windows.

Judged purely as an automobile, the new Grand Prix was undoubtedly a superior car to its predecessor. Shorn of 16.9 inches and 750 pounds, it was far more nimble, livelier, economical, and easier to park.

Downsized engines powered this smaller Grand Prix. The base GP had the 231 V-6, the LJ had the 2-bbl. 301, and the SJ had the new 4-bbl. 301; the Chevy 305 substituted for the Pontiac 301 in California and high-altitude areas. No 350 or 400 engines were available.

The full-size Pontiacs saw some shuffling of optional engines, due chiefly to the discontinuance of Pontiac's 350 V-8. In its place was the L77 Buick 4-bbl. 350 rated at 155 hp. Standard engines remained the 231 V-6 (in its new LD5 form) for the Catalina and the 301 V-8 for the Bonneville.

The Astre was dropped, and to cover this void the Sunbird range was extended to three models by adding a less expensive base Coupe to the Sport Coupe and Sport Hatch. Standard Sunbird power remained the Iron Duke 151 L-4, with the 231 V-6 and 305 V-8 as options; the 140 OHC-4 was dropped.

The whole Ventura range was also discontinued. Once called a "compact," the Ventura was now larger than the new Le Mans "intermediates," and a positive giant compared to the Sunbird. So Pontiac created a new model from the same car by loading it with luxury features and giving it a new name: Phoenix. Introduced in mid-'77, the Phoenix now fit comfortably into the marketing slot between the Le Mans and Catalina/Bonneville.

The LD5 231 V-6 was the standard Phoenix engine, backed by the optional Iron Duke four, 305 V-8, and Chevy LM1 350 V-8. The 2-door hatchback body style was too useful to die with the Ventura name, so it became a third Phoenix model for 1978. An upmarket LJ version of the Phoenix also appeared, available only as a coupe or sedan.

Engines dropped entirely from the Firebird option list were the 301, the discontinued L76 Pontiac 350, and the Olds L34 350. The Olds L80 403 remained a California substitution for the Trans Am's

An egg-crate grille and exposed rear wheels marked the 1978 Catalina, while the Bonneville had a heavier appearance.

L78 400. Last year's performance engine, the W72 T/A 400, was not only still available but surprisingly had 20 more hp; it was now rated at 220 hp, a real powerhouse by 1978 standards.

Press reaction to the downsized intermediates was positive. "The consensus of the staff was the the Grand Le Mans is a *very* trim car," observed *Motor Trend*. "The car has a well-balanced look that is, in a word, modern." Performance of the *MT* test car, fitted with the optional 305 V-8 and automatic transmission, was quite good considering its astronomically high 2.29 axle ratio: 0 to 60 mph in 11.3 seconds, the quarter-mile in 17.8 seconds at 75 mph. It obtained a creditable 21.2 mpg fuel economy.

Pontiac remained in fourth place in sales as its production increased slightly to 877,749 cars. This was 9.82 percent of domestic auto production, the division's greatest market penetration since the halcyon days of 1969. The downsized Grand Prix ran into consumer resistance as its sales fell 24 percent, but this was offset by a spurt in Sunbird sales. Those of the new Le Mans shot up a gratifying 52 percent, while the Firebird continued its dizzying climb with a 20 percent sales increase.

Alex Mair left Pontiac at the end of the 1978 model year and was succeeded by Robert C. Stempel, who came from GM corporate headquarters where he had been special assistant to the president.

Robert C. Stempel succeeded Alex Mair as Pontiac's general manager in 1978. Like Elliott Estes and F. James McDonald before him, Stempel eventually became president of General Motors.

1979

GM continued its massive trimming program by introducing much smaller versions of its three most luxurious coupes: the Cadillac Eldorado, Buick Riviera, and Oldsmobile Toronado. All shared a common front-wheel-drive package, though powered by different engines.

This activity did not involve Pontiac. In mid-year a revolutionary front-drive compact was introduced—the Phoenix—but as Pontiac insisted, this was a 1980 model, thus it will be discussed in the following chapter. The only other model change all year was the discontinuance of the rear-drive Phoenix upon the introduction of the front-drive version.

The biggest engine news was a redesigned variant of the 151 L-4 Iron Duke. Bore and stroke were unchanged, but the intake manifold was now made of aluminum and heated by water, and total

Face-lift for 1979: Grand Prix.

engine weight was reduced by 35 pounds. A new crossflow cylinder head had intake ports on the right side and exhaust ports on the left. Coded LX8, this new version was rated at 90 hp. The previous 85-hp "sideflow" version was retained for California use and recoded from LX6 to LS6. Both versions were offered only in the Sunbird; the Iron Duke was no longer available in the Phoenix.

All 1979 Firebirds had a revised front end with separate nacelles for the four headlamps and a larger bumper incorporating the air intakes.

Pontiac produced 7500 copies of this Tenth Annivesary Limited Edition Trans Am in 1979 to celebrate the tenth anniverary of the Trans Am's introduction. All were finished in silver and black, and powered with a 400 V-8 with 4-speed or a 403 V-8 with automatic transmission. Standard equipment included a T-top roof, electric windows and door locks, 4-wheel disc brakes, and "Turbo" aluminum wheels. One was chosen to be the pace car for the 1979 Daytona 500 NASCAR race, and Bob Stempel, Pontiac's general manager (left), poses with Bill France, founder and president of NASCAR.

Another new engine variant was a 4-bbl. version of the Chevrolet 305 V-8, coded LG4 and rated at 155 hp. This replaced the 2-bbl. LG3 version as an option in all members of the Le Mans intermediate family and the Grand Prix, while the LG3 remained an option for the Phoenix, Firebird, and Sunbird.

Amid all the changes, however, one fact stood out: the L78 400 had been dropped completely. Only the W72 high-performance version of the 400 remained as an option for the Firebirds. Pontiac-built V-8s were becoming scarce indeed; the 350 and 455 were both gone, and now the 400 was close to extinction. Once the producer of some of the most thunderously powerful automotive engines ever built by General Motors, Pontiac's new role in corporate engine development was becoming clear: it would become the supplier to all the other divisions of the two engines introduced in 1977—the 151 L-4 and the 301 V-8—and in turn receive from those divisions any other engines it needed.

The Sunbird, a distinctly slow seller in its first two years, was turning into a hit—almost 100,000 were produced this year. Grand Prix production declined sharply, but Firebird production increased once again and broke through the 200,000 level for the first time. In a situation which would have been considered preposterous a decade earlier, the Firebird was now the best-selling Pontiac model of all.

At the end of the model year Pontiac had produced 817,000 vehicles for a market share of 8.88 percent. Oldsmobile again had a million-car year, so Pontiac remained in fourth place in industry sales.

Front Drive for the Eighties 1980–1983

The most revolutionary automobile yet in Pontiac history made its debut on April 19, 1979. Surpassing even the 1961 Tempest in innovation, this new model had front-wheel drive, a choice of two transverse engines, and a body and chassis different from any previous Pontiac. Named the Phoenix, this new car was introduced as a 1980 model and superseded the rear-drive model of the same name.

The new Phoenix had its genesis in the Chevrolet division in the dark days following the Arab oil embargo of 1973. Pontiac evinced an early interest in this design, joined by Buick and Oldsmobile in 1976. As it finally came to fruition, the Chevrolet front-drive compact became a corporate project and bore the designation "X-body."

The X-body compact had five different configurations apportioned among the four GM divisions; Pontiac had two of these body styles, offering the Phoenix as a 4-door hatchback and a formal-roof coupe.

From any angle, the 1980 Phoenix 2-door was a handsome car. It had the interior room of the older rear-wheel-drive Phoenix but was 600 pounds lighter.

All X-cars shared a common wheelbase of 104.9 inches. The front suspension used MacPherson struts—the first on any Pontiac—and coil springs, while the rear suspension had a lightweight axle with a single trailing link on each side, a Panhard rod for lateral location, and coil springs. Front and rear anti-roll bars were standard, as were ventilated-rotor front-disc brakes, rack-and-pinion steering, and 13-inch wheels fitted with glass-belted radial tires. Optional were power assists for the brakes and steering, and alloy wheels with steel-belted radials.

The standard Phoenix engine was the Iron Duke with its 1979 improvements, but mounted transversely, with its "front" to the right. The water pump was moved to the side of the block, and a belt from this pump drove the compressor for the optional air conditioning. Its distributor was relocated farther to the rear, and a thermostatically controlled electric fan pulled air through the radiator. None of these changes affected power output, but they were sufficient enough to cause this transverse version to be designated by a new LW9 code. The LX8 longitudinal version was still retained for the Sunbird, but the LS6 "sideflow" version was dropped.

The second Phoenix engine was a new overhead-valve V-6 manufactured by Chevrolet. Designed specifically for the X-car, this compact V-6—coded LE2—had 60° between its cylinder banks. It had four main bearings of 2.5-inch diameter, and all major castings were of iron. With a bore and stroke of 3.50 x 3.00 inches, it displaced 173.2 cubic inches (2.8 liters) and developed 115 hp with 8.5:1 compression ratio and 2-bbl. carburetor.

Backing up these engines were two new transmissions. A 4-speed all-synchromesh manual was standard, employing the first cable-shifting mechanism ever used on a GM car. This gearbox was located directly "behind" the engine (actually, to the left of the engine) and transmitted its output directly to a differential/final drive unit with which it shared a common casing and lubricant. The optional automatic transmission had its torque converter attached to the rear of the crankshaft in a conventional manner, but the planetary gearbox was located parallel to the engine; a chain transmitted power from the converter to the gearbox.

The payoff from this compact propulsion package was a car that had the interior room of the previous Phoenix yet was 600 pounds lighter.

Pontiac offered the new Phoenix in two series, base and LJ. There was also an SJ option package which included Rally RTS suspension, blackout grille and window frames, lower body accent color, sport mirrors, bucket seats, and Rally wheels.

The motoring press greeted the X-cars with open arms. "Malibu-sized interiors nestled within Monza-sized exteriors," wrote *Car and*

Besides being the first Pontiac with front-wheel drive and a transverse engine, the 1980 Phoenix was also the first Pontiac with strut-type front suspension and rack-and-pinion steering.

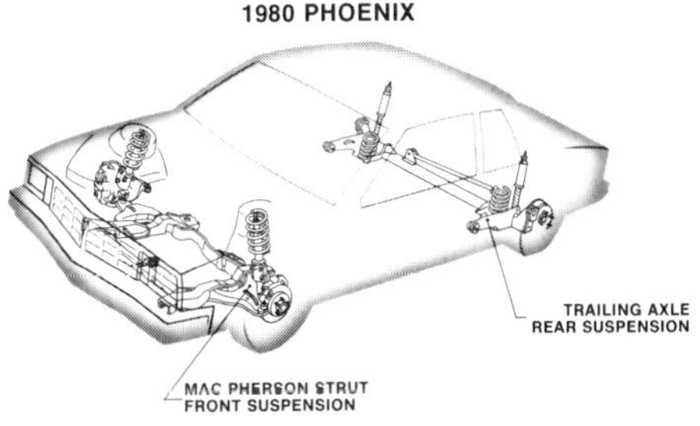

This 4-door Phoenix hatchback has the SJ option, which included two-tone paint, Rally wheels, stiffer suspension, larger tires, and power steering.

Driver enthusiastically. "What the folks at GM were doing while you were waiting in line at the gas station." "The dawning of a new era at GM," noted *Road & Track*. "GM has made a statement that will cause distress in competitors' boardrooms from Dearborn to Turin," observed *Motor Trend*.

Several points in particular were praised: the absorbent ride, the low noise level, and performance. *R&T*'s Citation with a V-6 and manual transmission zipped to 60 mph in 9.6 seconds and turned the quarter-mile in 17.8 seconds; *C&D*'s test Citation was even quicker. Handling was exemplary, especially with the stiffer suspension in the Phoenix SJ.

When the rest of the 1980 Pontiacs made their debut there were four new engines.

The first of these was a diesel V-8, an option only on the Bonneville Brougham and full-size station wagons. Manufactured by Oldsmobile, this was a dieselized version of the Olds 350 V-8. Designated LF9, it developed 125 hp compared to 160 hp in its L34 gasoline form. This engine cost an extra $790 and added a staggering 386 pounds of weight to a Bonneville Brougham compared to its standard 265 V-8, but boosted the big car's DOT city mileage figure to 24 miles per gallon.

A huge hood decal, asymmetrical hood bulge, and "Turbo" aluminum wheels identify the 1980 Turbo Trans Am; one was selected to pace the 1980 Indianapolis 500.

The second engine was a Chevrolet V-6 displacing 229 cubic inches. Coded LC3, it became the base engine for the 49-state Le Mans and Grand Le Mans, while the previous Buick V-6 was used for these models in California.

The third new engine was a Pontiac design, a small-bore version of the 301 V-8. With its bore and stroke of 3.75 x 3.00 inches, it displaced 265 cubic inches—coincidentally, the same cylinder dimensions as the epochal 1955 Chevrolet V-8. Coded LS5, the 120-hp 265 V-8 became the standard engine for the Bonneville Brougham, and an option for the Catalina, Bonneville, Grand Prix, Le Mans, Grand Le Mans, base Firebird, and Esprit.

The last new engine was spectacular: a 210-hp turbocharged 301 V-8. In fact, this was the only turbo V-8 available anywhere in the world. An AiResearch turbine-compressor unit mounted downstream of the Quadrajet carburetor generated the boost, limited by a waste gate to 9 psi. To avoid troubles a low compression ratio of 7.5:1 was combined with a Buick-developed electronic sensor which automatically retarded spark advance upon detecting detonation. The block, crankshaft, pistons, wrist pins, and main bearing caps were all strengthened.

This turbo 301, coded LU8, was an option for the Formula and Trans Am Firebirds. It replaced the W72 400 V-8, which was discontinued as Pontiac finally finished its long and memorable line of big V-8 engines.

The Turbo Trans Am was moderately quick: 0 to 60 in 8.2 seconds, the quarter-mile in 16.7 seconds at 86 mph. The boost came in at such a low rpm it could hardly be felt, and increased gradually to full value at 3500 rpm. The engine felt and acted like a normally aspirated engine of larger displacement, and the instrument panel was devoid of a boost gauge. As *Car and Driver* noted, "You'd swear Pontiac was trying to keep its turbocharger a secret."

The 4-speed manual transmission was dropped from the entire Firebird range. The only manual transmission offered was the 3-speed, and then only with the standard 231 V-6 in the base Firebird and Esprit.

There were many other engine changes in the Firebird family. The L37 4-bbl. 301 became the new standard engine in the Formula and Trans Am. Among the optional engines, new models were the LS5 265 V-8 for the base Firebird and Esprit, a high-output 170-hp W72 version of the L37 301 for the Formula and Trans Am, and the LG4 4-bbl. Chevy 305 for California versions. Dropped entirely from the Firebirds—in fact, from all Pontiacs—were the L27 2-bbl.

Heart of the 210-hp turbo 301 V-8 of 1980 was the turbine-compressor unit, shown here with the turbine housing cut open. The diaphragm-operated rod controls the position of the turbine's waste gate.

The 1980 Grand Am received a minor face-lift and a much more powerful engine. It was available only as this handsome coupe, and only with automatic transmission.

301, the LG3 2-bbl. 305, the LM1 350, the L78 400, and the L80 403.

Optional for the Formula and Trans Am were rear-wheel disc brakes, first offered in 1979. A new "Yellow Bird" package was offered for the Esprit.

The Sunbird family grew smaller, and the Astre-derived Sport Safari wagon was finally discontinued. Engine choices for the remaining Sunbirds were simplified to the LX8 151 and LD5 231. For California use a new version of the LX8 with electronic fuel control appeared, which developed the same 90 hp as the standard LX8. The 5-speed gearbox was regrettably discontinued.

All intermediate models returned except the 4-door sedan version of the Grand Am. The base engine for the Le Mans and Grand Le Mans was switched from the LD5 V-6 to the Chevrolet LC3 V-6. The L37 301 remained an option—with the Chevy LG4 305 for California—and was joined by the new LS5 265.

The Grand Am's standard—and only—engine became the new high-output W72 version of the L37 4-bbl. 301 V-8. Automatic transmission was now standard; no manual transmission was available.

In 1979 *Car and Driver* had tested a Grand Am sedan, equipped with its optional L37 150-hp engine, head-to-head against a BMW 528i. It concluded that the German sedan was clearly superior, but not nearly by the margin one might expect in view of its far greater price. One year later *C&D* tried a 1980 Grand Am coupe and found no reason to change its opinion.

The Grand Prix presented a more classic appearance this year with a vertically barred grille. The LJ's standard engine was now the same LD5 V-6 as the base Grand Prix, while the SJ got the new W72 version of the L37 301. All optional engines remained the same as in 1979, but all manual transmissions were deleted.

The full-size Catalina/Bonneville models were subtly but thoroughly rebodied in quest of lower aerodynamic drag and increased

The modified Grand Prix for 1980 was back to vertical grille bars again, while the subtly reshaped full-size models had a new grille shared by Bonnevilles and Catalinas.

interior room. The cowl height was raised one inch, and the hood given a steeper slope. The headlamps were flush-fitted, the bumper edges smoothly integrated into the body shape, and the front wheel wells no longer had flares. The roof was raised 1.8 inches and given a formal squared-off shape, while the deck lid was also raised and the trunk made more rectangular in shape. The end result was a body on which every single panel had been changed, but so unobtrusively that they were unnoticeable unless 1979 and 1980 models were parked side by side.

All in all, 1980 was a landmark year in Pontiac history. It witnessed the division's first front-wheel-drive car, its first diesel engine, and its first turbocharged engine. However, it was a disastrous year for the automotive industry. Soaring interest rates deterred auto financing, while gasoline and auto prices rose sharply due to high inflation. New-car sales plummeted to 73.6 percent of the 1979 level.

Pontiac's output fell 24 percent to 620,023, and its product mix changed drastically. Full-size Catalina/Bonneville models fell off sharply with a staggering 59 percent sales drop, while the Grand Prix and Le Mans were also big losers. Even the high-flying Firebird, after seven consecutive years of dazzling sales increases, was shot out of the sky with a dizzying 49 percent drop. Pontiac's best-seller was now the frugal and inexpensive Sunbird, the sales of which jumped 92 percent to 187,979. The Phoenix also proved to be a hot seller with 125,539 units in its first full model year. Overall, Pontiac slipped to fifth place in industry sales.

In August 1980 Bob Stempel was assigned to Adam Opel AG, GM's German subsidiary. His replacement as Pontiac's general manager was William E. Hoglund.

William E. Hoglund succeeded Bob Stempel as Pontiac's general manager in 1980.

1981

A reskinned Grand Prix was the only new model introduced at the start of the model year. Like the full-size models the year before, this restyling was subtle but thorough, and smoothed out the body to such an extent that the car's wind drag coefficient dropped from .55 to .44. The performance SJ version was discontinued, but there was a new super-luxury version, the Grand Prix Brougham.

The standard engine for all Grand Prix variants was the LD5 231 V-6. Like all 1981 Pontiac gasoline engines it was equipped with Computer Command Control, GM's electronic governing system. Optional on all GP models were the LS5 265 V-8 and the LF9 350 diesel V-8. No other engines were necessary, as Computer Command Control enabled engines to meet both federal and California emissions standards.

Car and Driver tested a Grand Prix LJ with its optional diesel engine, and came away less than impressed. The car was abysmally slow: 0 to 60 in 19.3 seconds, the quarter-mile in 21.5 seconds at 64 mph. Top speed was a laughable 88 mph. The EPA fuel economy rating of 27 mpg hardly justified the additional $695 charge for the diesel engine, let alone the disappointing performance.

All full-size models now used the LD5 V-6 as their standard engine, with the LS5 V-8 and LF9 diesel optional. Standard on the Safari wagons, however, was LV2, a 145-hp 4-bbl. 307 V-8 from Oldsmobile. It would prove to be as short-lived as the previous year's Chevrolet LC3 V-6.

The reshaped Grand Prix had a distinct wedge profile in 1981. The high-performance SJ version was discontinued, but a super-luxury Brougham version appeared.

In the Le Mans family, the Grand Am was dropped—again. Though a noble effort to produce an American car with European driving characteristics, the Grand Am apparently tended to confuse traditional Pontiac buyers who preferred the familiar and more prestigious Grand Prix.

A modified grille changed the look of the Phoenix. The same engines were offered as in 1980, but toned down a bit in power; the LW9 Iron Duke four now had 84 hp instead of 90, while the LE2 V-6 dropped from 115 to 110 hp.

All standard engines for the Firebird family remained the same except for the Formula, where the LS5 265 replaced the previous L37 301—a loss of 30 hp. Optional engines also remained the same except for the loss of the W72 high-output version of the L37 301, an engine which vanished completely this year. The LU8 turbo 301 dropped slightly in power to 200 hp.

The 4-speed manual transmission made a welcome return to the Firebirds for '81. Unfortunately, it was available only in the Formula and Trans Am, and then only paired with the LG4 305 V-8.

Something important was missing from 1981 Pontiac sales literature: the Sunbird, the division's best-selling car line. It was due for replacement in mid-year by a new subcompact, the GM J-car. So strong, however, was the demand for the Sunbird that Pontiac kept it in production until the end of the 1980 calendar year, but did not advertise it. The Sunbird could not be kept in production any longer since it was built in the same plant in Lordstown, Ohio, which was retooling to build the J-car. The new J-car, however, was

Early in the 1981 calendar year Pontiac introduced the T1000, the smallest and lightest Pontiac model yet made. The T1000 replaced the Sunbird, which was discontinued in December 1980.

not due until May of 1981. Between the end of Sunbird production and the debut of the J-car, therefore, yawned a gap of many months—too many, Pontiac management felt, at a time when customers were clamoring for economy cars.

Into this marketing breach Pontiac threw the only true econocar GM had: the Chevrolet Chevette, which Pontiac called the T1000. The "T" designation harked back to the Chevette's design origins when it was coded GM's "T-car," while the "1000" signified that this was Pontiac's lowest-priced car in a planned lineup of number-designated models.

Pontiac offered the T1000 in 2-door and 4-door hatchback forms. The coupe had a wheelbase of 94.3 inches and an overall length of 161.9 inches, while the 4-door had a 97.1-inch wheelbase and a 164.7-inch length; in all other basic dimensions the two models were identical.

With its 2100-pound weight, the T1000 was the smallest, lightest, and thriftiest Pontiac ever. Its engine, coded L17, was a 4-cylinder overhead-cam unit displacing 1.6 liters (98 cubic inches) and rated at 66 hp.

The T1000 was not an advanced small car in 1981. With its solid rear axle, rear-wheel drive, small engine, and stiff springing, the car was slow and rode harshly. Its virtues, however, were obvious: clean styling, hatchback utility, simplicity, handiness, low price, ease of service, and excellent fuel economy. The design was certainly a proven one; the same basic car was in production in Brazil (GM Chevette), Germany (Opel Kadett), Japan (Isuzu Gemini), and Britain (Vauxhall Chevette).

Few auto introductions in American history were as eagerly awaited as that of the GM J-car. This was the high-tech front-drive small car aimed straight at the Japanese invasion.

"J-day" was May 14, 1981. The car was initially available in four body styles: 4-door sedan, 2-door notchback coupe, 2-door hatchback, and 4-door station wagon. There were three nameplates: Chevrolet Cavalier, Pontiac J2000, and Cadillac Cimarron. The Cavalier and J2000 offered all four body styles, while the Cimarron was available only as a sedan. Buick and Oldsmobile were slated to receive their J-cars for the 1982 model year.

The J-car was smaller than the X-car, with which it shared basic design concepts and many parts. Wheelbase was 101.2 inches and overall length 169.4 inches. Only one engine was available: a Chevrolet pushrod 4-cylinder design, designated L46. With bore and stroke of 3.50 x 2.91 inches, the L46 displaced 112 cubic inches

Introduced in May 1981 as a 1982 model, the J2000 was a high-tech import fighter. Front-wheel drive, rack-and-pinion steering, strut front suspension, and trailing-arm rear suspension were all similar to concepts pioneered by the Phoenix.

(1,840 cc); it was rated at 85 hp with its 2-bbl. carburetor and 9:1 compression ratio. The bore size was the same as the LE2 173 V-6, and the L46 shared pistons, wrist pins, connecting rod bolts, and some valve train components with that engine.

Two transmissions were available for the J2000, a 4-speed manual and a 3-speed automatic; both were modified X-car devices. The MacPherson strut front suspension was conventional, but the steering had an unusual high-mounted rack which allowed a short steering column devoid of universal joints. Like the X-car, the rear suspension had an axle tube, trailing arms, and coil springs. The axle tube, however, was moved much closer to the arm pivot points, which allowed it to act as a supplementary spring when it twisted; GM dubbed this a "double-crank rear axle" which gave a "semi-independent rear suspension." The rear coil springs were cleverly given a severe conical taper so that the coils nested within each other when the spring was compressed, thus conserving space. More space was saved since the double-crank rear axle did not require a Panhard rod for transverse location. Ventilated-rotor front disc brakes were standard equipment.

Pontiac marketed its four J2000 models in three trim levels: base (all models), plush LE (coupe and sedan), and sporty SE (hatchback only). Options included larger wheels and tires, and a Rally handling package.

GM was surprised when the automotive press greeted the J-cars with something less than the ebullient enthusiasm given the X-cars two years before. Although the handling and steering were universally praised, as was the excellent sound insulation, the problem was the car's weight and its anemic engine. Pontiac claimed a curb weight of 2439 pounds for the J2000 hatchback, but it actually weighed 2630 pounds, which badly overmatched the engine. *Road & Track*: "The Great Disappointment: starting the engine and driving away . . . (the engine's) displacement is only 1.8 liters and, quite simply, that just isn't enough." The *R&T* test car turned 0 to 60 mph in 16.3 seconds, the quarter-mile in 20.6 seconds at 67.5 mph; the magazine noted that only six of the previous 77 cars it had tested were slower in acceleration, and all six were diesels.

The 22-mpg fuel economy was another great disappointment. *Motor Trend*: "There were far too many downshifts into 2nd and even 1st gear to maintain momentum on slight upgrades, too much lag between throttle application and engine response, and subpar fuel mileage."

Despite all the press reservations, the general public took to the J-cars with enthusiasm. In the very short model year after the mid-May introduction, Pontiac sold 48,306 J2000s. The T1000—also with an abbreviated model year—was a success with sales of 70,194. Phoenix sales were unchanged from 1980, while Le Mans and full-size sales were up substantially. Grand Prix sales doubled to 147,705. The only losing model was the Firebird, sales of which dropped 34 percent to 70,899 for the lowest Firebird total since 1973. In all, the division produced 648,852 cars in its seven lines for 1981, retaining fifth place in industry sales with 9.1 percent of domestic auto production.

The 2-door hatchback was the sportiest of the four J2000 body styles, while the wagon was the roomiest.

1982

A year of upheavals, 1982 would witness the demise of two of Pontiac's traditional model names, balanced by the midyear introduction of two new models. Fuel injection would appear on a Pontiac for the first time since 1958, while all V-8s and turbocharging would be terminated.

The big surprise at the start of the model year was the absence of Pontiac's oldest model name: Catalina. Dating back to 1950, it had been in longer continuous use than any other model name in the entire U.S. auto industry except for Cadillac's Coupe de Ville and Fleetwood names.

The Catalina name was discontinued because the car itself was discontinued. Despite selling very well, the big Pontiacs were victims of the federal government's CAFE requirements. In 1981 GM had a CAFE of 22.9 mpg, exceeding the mandated 22.0 mpg by a scant 0.9 mpg. For 1982 the CAFE demand jumped to 24.0 mpg, which GM could not meet unless it emphasized smaller cars. Several larger models were therefore axed, the full-size Pontiacs among them.

Missing also was the Le Mans name. In a marketing sleight of hand, the previous Le Mans was now named the Bonneville G. This "recontented Bonneville," as Pontiac called it, was available as a 4-door sedan and a station wagon in two trim levels, Bonneville G and Bonneville G Brougham. Standard engine was the LD5 231 V-6, with the LF9 350 diesel V-8 and a new LC4 252 V-6 from Buick as options.

All Catalina and Bonneville full-size models were discontinued in 1981, but the Bonneville name replaced the Le Mans name on the intermediate range. This is a 1982 Bonneville G sedan; other versions offered were a plush Brougham and a wagon.

This marketing ploy certainly allowed Pontiac to advertise that the "recontented" Bonneville was much more efficient than its full-size predecessor, but anyone could see it was last year's Le Mans with a new grille. Why bother with a name change?

The reason was that a new front-drive model was due to debut in January. Shorter than a Le Mans, longer than a Phoenix, this would become Pontiac's new "intermediate." If the Le Mans name for the old intermediate were retained, Pontiac would then have a confusing marketing array with two "intermediates" and no "full-size" model. By applying the full-size Bonneville name to the old intermediate, the way was cleared for the new front-drive car to fit in as an intermediate.

The T1000 received a redesigned cylinder head which raised the compression ratio to 9.2:1. The 3-speed automatic for the littlest Pontiac now had a lockup torque converter, while a lightweight Borg-Warner 5-speed gearbox became an option for the 2-door hatchback.

New for the Grand Prix was the Landau Package, another one of those silly options of chintzy glitter which so afflict American luxury cars; this one had opera lights and plusher seats. The standard GP powerplant remained the faithful LD5 V-6, while the new LC4 252 V-6 joined the LF9 diesel as an option.

The standard Iron Duke engine in the Phoenix now sported an electronic fuel injection system. Called throttle-body injection (TBI), this new Rochester system injected the fuel into a "throttle body" located where the carburetor would normally be, and employed a computer and electronic sensors to determine the proper amount of fuel. Though not offering as precise a control over the distribution of the fuel as a typical European port injection system, TBI was much cheaper since it did not require a separate injection nozzle for each cylinder.

With TBI, the Iron Duke's output jumped from 84 to 90 hp. Designated LR8, this injected engine would become the standard engine for the new 6000 and Firebird as well as the Phoenix.

Remaining as an option for the Phoenix was the 110-hp LE2 173 V-6. It was joined by the hopped-up version of this engine which Chevrolet had introduced the year before for the Citation X-11. Coded LH7, this 135-hp engine had higher compression, higher-lift cam, larger exhaust valves, low-restriction exhaust system, and a larger air filter.

Pontiac offered the LH7 engine only as part of a complete package, the Phoenix SJ, which became a serious performance car. In-

In mid-1982 the 6000 appeared, Pontiac's version of the corporate A-car. Essentially a rebodied Phoenix, the 6000 was available as a 2-door or 4-door sedan.

cluded with the LH7 were a 4-speed gearbox, aluminum wheels, 205/70R13 steel-belted radials, power brakes (front disc, rear drum), power steering, stiffer springs, thicker anti-roll bars, full instrumentation, bucket seats, sport steering wheel, front air dam, body side moldings, decklid spoiler, sport mirrors, and 2-tone paint.

Taking all the press criticism to heart, GM initiated a program of running changes to improve J-car performance. By the end of the 1981 calendar year, the power was up to 88 hp, throttle response was quicker, lower axle ratios enhanced acceleration, and the automatic transmission had higher torque multiplication. Finally, at the introduction of the Buick Skyhawk and Oldsmobile Firenza J-cars in early 1982, came an optional long-stroke version of the Chevy pushrod engine. Designated LQ5, this 90-hp engine displaced 121.2 cubic inches (1990 cc) with its cylinder dimensions of 3.50 x 3.15 inches. Torque was up by 11 percent over the L46, from 100 to 111 foot-pounds. Initially available only for the Skyhawk and Firenza, the LQ5 was offered for the J2000 by the start of the '83 model year.

Welcome as the 2-liter engine was, it was not enough for Pontiac. At the Firenza/Skyhawk introduction a second optional J-car engine was announced, available only for the Skyhawk and J2000. Designed by Opel and already in use in Germany, Brazil, and Australia, this inline 4-cylinder had a belt-driven single overhead camshaft and made extensive use of aluminum alloy. Designated LH8, it displaced 109.6 cubic inches (1796 cc) from its cylinder dimensions of 3.34 x 3.13 inches. With 9:1 compression ratio and TBI, it was rated at 84 hp; at 271 pounds, it weighed 29 pounds less than the L46.

Backing up the LH8 engine was a new 5-speed gearbox from Isuzu, GM's Japanese affiliate. Pontiac even offered it in two forms: a close-ratio performance version and a wide-ratio economy version.

In January 1982 GM unveiled a significant new family of front-drive sedans and two spectacular sports models. The sedan family was the A-body cars: Chevrolet Celebrity, Pontiac 6000, Oldsmobile Cutlass Ciera, and Buick Century. Mechanical derivatives of the X-cars, the A-cars had a new wedge-shaped body. Each division contributed an engine. Pontiac's LR8 injected Iron Duke was the basic powerplant for all A-cars, while a new diesel V-6 from Oldsmobile was optional in all. The Celebrity and 6000 had an optional LE2 V-6 from Chevrolet, while the Cutlass Ciera and Century shared an optional new V-6 from Buick. The A-car was six inches longer than the X-car, allowing a larger engine compartment to accommodate the two new 90° V-6 engines.

Though introduced as intermediates, it was clear that these were the full-size GM cars of the future. As the public grew to accept the changing size of automobiles, the perception of what constituted a full-size GM car would eventually be an A-car—or so GM hoped. As that happened, the older rear-drive G-body intermediates would either be dropped entirely or plushed up and sold as oversize luxury models.

Pontiac originally intended to call its A-car the A6000, but at the last minute dropped the alphabetical prefix, as it would soon do to the J2000 and T1000. There were two series, the 6000 and up-market 6000LE.

Optional for the 6000 was a new engine, a 4.3-liter diesel V-6 from Oldsmobile. Coded LT7, this 85-hp engine had cylinder heads and intake manifold of aluminum. Its most unusual features were that its cylinder banks were set at 90°, and that it had the same bore and stroke as the LT9 350 diesel V-8; it therefore shared pistons, valve train components, and tooling with the V-8.

Downsized and completely reshaped, the spectacular 1982 Firebird was the first Pontiac to have concealed headlamps since the 1969 GTO.

All three major American auto magazines specifically singled out the 6000 as the best of the A-cars. *Road & Track* felt "the overall design award has to go to the Pontiac 6000" and applauded body designer Terry Henline for "subduing the brightwork." *Motor Trend* said that the 6000 had "success written all over it." *Car and Driver* did not like the styling and thought the engines needed a dose of vitamins, but was full of praise for the optional Y99 Rally handling package.

Introduced at the same time as the A-body family were the third-generation F-body cars, the Chevrolet Camaro and Pontiac Firebird. The new Firebird was commendably smaller and lighter than its predecessor. The 101-inch wheelbase was 7.2 inches shorter, while the overall length was 7.8 inches shorter. It was also .6 inches narrower and .5 inches lower.

Over the smaller chassis was draped the most handsome coupe body ever made in the U.S., a hatchback in which the hatch was a single complex piece of glass.

The new F-body was a dazzling monument to the 6-year effort of GM's advanced design studios in conjunction with the Chevrolet and Pontiac styling studios. In Pontiac's case this was Studio Two, headed by John Schinella.

The new Firebird was the most aerodynamically perfect American production car yet made. With its concealed headlamps, rearward-tilted grille, smooth hatchback, and steeply raked, flush-fitted windshield, the Firebird had an aerodynamic drag coefficient of .330. The Trans Am version, which added a front air dam and decklid spoiler, brought the drag coefficient down to .309.

The Firebird was now offered in three trim levels: Firebird, Firebird S/E, and Trans Am. The standard engine for the base Firebird was a surprise: the Iron Duke. Fitted with TBI it developed the same 90 hp as in the Phoenix and 6000, but since it was mounted longitudinally it had a new LQ9 code. Standard on the S/E was the familiar 173 V-6, carrying the new engine code LC1 instead of LE2 since it was also longitudinally mounted. Standard on the Trans Am was the Chevy-built LG4 305 V-8, a holdover from the '81 Formula Firebird. A 4-speed manual transmission was standard in all Firebirds, regardless of engine choice, with a lockup-clutch Turbo Hydra-Matic optional.

A new optional engine was available only for the Trans Am, and then only with automatic transmission and the WS6 handling package. Coded LU5, this was the Chevy 305 V-8 with twin throttle-

All 1982 Firebirds had a glass hatchback. Decklid spoiler and air vent behind the front wheel identify this as a Trans Am. The wheel covers were standard on the Trans Am, optional on other Firebirds.

body injection. Each of the two TBI injectors was mounted close to a cylinder bank but fed the opposite bank through a ram-tuned manifold; GM dubbed this its "cross-fire" injection arrangement. With twin TBI and 9.5:1 compression ratio, the LU5 put out 165 hp @ 4200 rpm. Since the turbocharged 301 had been discontinued, this was the hottest engine Pontiac was able to offer.

Under the sleek Firebird body were some major changes to the running gear. The front suspension had a modified MacPherson strut arrangement with the coil springs mounted separately on large fabricated A-arms, and a front anti-roll bar was standard. The solid rear axle was retained, but coil springs were now used, with two trailing links, a Panhard rod, and a long torque arm locating the axle. The new Firebird's front track was narrower than in '81, but the rear track was wider.

There were three levels of Firebird suspension, offering various combinations of tire size, wheel size, anti-roll bar diameter, and spring stiffness. The level III suspension was part of the WS6 performance package, which also included a limited-slip differential, 4-wheel disc brakes, and quick-ratio steering. This WS6 package was optional on the S/E and Trans Am, and mandatory with the LU5 twin-TBI V-8.

At 2864 pounds, the curb weight of the base Firebird was a satisfying 521 pounds less than the previous year's equivalent model. Much of that commendable reduction, however, was due to the light weight of the 4-cylinder base engine. The high-performance version, a Trans Am with the injected V-8, WS6 suspension and mandatory automatic transmission, weighed 3350 pounds, about 350 pounds less than an '81 Turbo Trans Am.

All these improvements raised the handling to new heights; the Trans Am could reach .83g in lateral acceleration.

There was only one fly in this ointment: lack of straight-line performance. The culprits were the engines—they were simply not very powerful. Bunkie Knudsen and John DeLorean would have snorted in derision at the idea of a 4-cylinder engine in Pontiac's premier performance model. A Trans Am with the injected V-8 took 9 seconds to accelerate to 60 mph, strained through the quarter-mile in 17 seconds at 80 mph, and had a top speed of 115 mph.

Despite the lackluster speed, the new Firebird rekindled the love affair between enthusiasts and Firebirds. Rather startling was the market preference for the Trans Am. Almost 60 percent of '82 Firebirds were Trans Ams, and most were ordered with the optional WS6 handling package. This unexpected demand caused such a shortage of rear-disc brake assemblies that Pontiac hastily introduced an alternate WS7 package which substituted rear drum brakes for the discs.

Some last-minute corporate rethinking resulted in yet another Pontiac model being introduced quite late in the model year. Sales of fuel-efficient models were going so well that GM decided it could reinstate the popular Pontiac full-size line without running afoul of CAFE requirements. Accordingly, full-sized Pontiacs were imported from Canada—where they had never ceased production—and called by their traditional Canadian name, Parisienne. Two trim levels were offered, Parisienne and Parisienne Brougham, with three body styles: sedan, coupe, and station wagon. The engines were familiar: standard LD5 231 V-6, optional LG4 305 V-8 and LF9 diesel 350 V-8. These were joined by L39, a 267 V-8 built by GM of Canada.

This year turned out to be a disastrous one for the U.S. auto industry. Domestic production slumped from 7.1 to 5.7 million units, the lowest industry total since 1961. This condition was caused partly by fierce import competition—2.8 million units—but mostly by economic uncertainty, with the national unemployment rate exceeding 10 percent and interest rates still high. Pontiac's production declined 21 percent to 510,422 cars, holding fifth place in the industry.

Discontinued after the 1981 model year, the full-size Pontiac made an unexpected reappearance in 1983 bearing the name "Parisienne."

1983

Pontiac wasted little time responding to criticisms that the third-generation Firebird was short on performance; available at the start of the '83 model year were a new optional engine and a 5-speed transmission.

The engine was predictable; coded LL1, it was a longitudinal adaptation of the transverse LH7 high-output 173 V-6 available in the Phoenix, and rated at the same 135 hp.

The 5-speed all-synchromesh gearbox was a delight, and could withstand the torque output of Pontiac's most powerful V-8. The exact gearbox ratios depended upon the engine to which it was mated, but fourth gear was always 1:1 direct drive and fifth was a very high overdrive ratio.

The new engine and gearbox were both standard equipment on the 1983 Firebird S/E. The S/E's previous engine, the mild-mannered LC1 V-6, became an option for the base Firebird.

The 5-speed gearbox was also standard in the Trans Am, and optional for $125 in the base Firebird; however, it was *not* available mated to the optional LU5 injected V-8, which must have been a disappointment to many Trans Am fans.

In mid-year came their salvation as a firebreathing new engine appeared. A variation of the 305 V-8 with a high-lift camshaft, 9.5:1

Six lamps up front were the immediate visual clue to the 1983 6000 STE, the most lavishly equipped and most expensive standard model in Pontiac history.

compression ratio, and a freer exhaust system, it developed 190 hp @ 4800 rpm. Coded L69, this engine rather surprisingly used a 4-bbl. carburetor rather than the twin-TBI system of the LU5. It was available only for the Trans Am, and only with the 5-speed gearbox and WS6 suspension; this combination turned a Trans Am into a Trans Am HO. The L69/5-speed gearbox/WS6 package cost $913, exactly the same as the LU5/4-speed automatic/WS6 combination.

The new L69 engine and 5-speed gearbox finally put some steam back into Trans Am performance. *Road & Track*'s test car did 0 to 60 in 7.9 seconds, 0 to 100 in 24.9 seconds, the quarter-mile in 16.1 seconds at 85 mph, and had a top speed of 125 mph.

Also making a memorable debut was the 6000 STE, a new version of the 6000 for sophisticated enthusiasts. Intended to battle high-tech European luxury/performance sedans, the STE's list of standard equipment was incredibly comprehensive: LH7 high-output V-6, automatic transmission, heavy-duty suspension, automatic height adjustment through electronically controlled air shock absorbers at the rear, aluminum wheels, 195/70R14 Goodyear Eagle GT radials, quick-ratio power steering, air conditioning, tinted power windows, power door locks, an elaborate sound system, reclining front seats, folding rear seat armrest, tilt steering wheel, cruise control, special instrumentation, heavy-duty battery and alternator. The only options offered at all were a leather interior ($545) and a glass sunroof ($295).

The price for all this lavishness was high: $13,986, making it by far the most expensive model Pontiac had ever produced.

The auto press heaped praise on the STE. *Car and Driver*: "The 6000 STE is my hands-down favorite 1983-model American car . . . a superb package . . . within a gnat's eyelash of being a 100-percent perfect American car." *Road & Track* compared an STE to a Dodge 600 ES and Buick Century T-type. "The Pontiac emerged as an easy winner by nature of its excellent engine performance, good handling, nice style and detailing, and a minimum of aggravating characteristics." *Motor Trend*'s performance figures were typical: 0 to 60 in 10.2 seconds, the quarter-mile in 17.57 seconds at 80.3 mph, and a top speed of 108 mph. Though production of the STE would be limited to 8,000 units for the 1983 model year, it was another entry in Pontiac's impressive high-performance stable.

Dropping its letter prefix, the J2000 became the 2000 for 1983. The standard drivetrain was now the LH8 overhead-cam 1.8-liter engine and 5-speed gearbox. Optional was the 2-liter pushrod engine, now with TBI instead of carburetion. Still coded LQ5, it now

Phoenix for 1983: the standard Phoenix and the LJ had a revised lighting arrangement and horizontal grille bars, while the SJ, with its high-output V-6, had a blackout grille and black trim.

had 9.3:1 compression ratio and was rated at 88 hp. On the 2000SE hatchback, the previously optional Rally suspension became standard.

The big news in the 2000 series was the unexpected appearance of a convertible. Built to SE specifications, it revived the Sunbird name. At its steep $11,669 base price, the 2000 Sunbird was the second most expensive Pontiac after the 6000 STE.

The little T1000 also lost its letter prefix and became the 1000. During the last several months of the '82 model year a 1.8-liter Isuzu-built diesel engine was optionally available in this smallest Pontiac, developing 51 hp and coded LJ5; it did not prove to be popular and was dropped at the start of the '83 model year.

Other changes throughout the vast Pontiac marketing array were minor. The power output of the standard LR8 Iron Duke in the Phoenix was raised from 90 to 94 hp, and the muscular SJ version was now available as a 4-door hatchback as well as a 2-door coupe. The Bonneville (no longer Bonneville G) and Grand Prix were unchanged except for the substitution of the evergreen Chevy LG4 305 V-8 in place of the Buick-built LC4 252 V-6 on the option list. The Parisienne series was simplified by dropping the coupe and the Canadian-built L39 V-8.

The U.S. auto industry recovered somewhat from 1982's disaster, with production rising 12.8 percent to 6.5 million cars. Pontiac did not fare so well, with its production dropping slightly from 1982's level but still holding fifth place in industry sales.

Pontiac's Pride

1984–1988

After years of speculation in the automotive press, the Fiero finally appeared for 1984. The most dramatic car in Pontiac's history, it was the division's first 2-seat sports car and (discounting early turn-of-the-century cars) the first mid-engined production car in American automotive history.

The Fiero—"proud" in Italian—was a compact coupe designated the 2M4, signifying a 2-seater with a mid-placed 4-cylinder engine. Its dimensions were tiny for an American car: 93.4-inch wheelbase, height of 46.9 inches, length of 13.4 feet, and a curb weight of 2459 pounds. The powertrain was straight from the X-cars and A-cars: the transverse LR8 Iron Duke 2.5-liter 4-cylinder engine, 4-speed manual or 3-speed automatic transmission, strut suspension with coil springs, and disc brakes. Instead of being mounted at the front of the car, however, it was mounted at the rear and was equipped with nonsteering wheels. It was the packageability of this proven

The revolutionary 1984 Fiero was Pontiac's first 2-seat sports car, the first Pontiac with a plastic body, and GM's first mid-engine production car. Powered by the fuel-injected Iron Duke 4-cylinder engine, it had good performance and excellent fuel economy.

Backbone of the Fiero was an all-welded space frame composed of 280 stampings of galvanized and high-strength steels.

drivetrain that made the Fiero possible and endowed it with many of its virtues, such as moderate cost, independent rear suspension, and 4-wheel disc brakes. Unequal-length A-arms were used for the front suspension.

Even more arresting than the basic mechanical packaging of the Fiero or its exciting wedge-shaped styling was its construction concept. The basic structure was a space frame, an all-welded affair of six major modules and 280 individual stampings. Made largely of galvanized and high-strength steels, the complete frame weighed almost 600 pounds and contained 4300 spot welds.

To this frame were bolted the plastic outer body panels, which carried no loads. Three different types of plastic were used. The horizontal panels, designed for stiffness, were made from sheet molding compound, a mixture of polyester resin, glass filaments, and a filler. The bumper fascias, made to take abuse, were reaction-injection-molded (RIM) plastic, a flexible polyurethane. The rest of the panels were made of RIM strengthened with additional fiberglass, and could shrug off minor dents and dings. Pontiac applied the name "Enduraflex" to all these panels, regardless of their polymer compound.

One of the traditional problems with fiberglass bodies has been the poor fit of body panels. Pontiac solved this problem with a new method for determining the precise location of each panel. At each of the 39 mounting points was a small epoxy-filled pad on a steel backing plate. After the completion of its assembly welding, the space frame was inserted into a huge Gilman "mill-and-drill" machine. This structure, after dimensionally gauging the frame with electromechanical probes, used 39 cutting heads which descended upon the pads, milling each to precisely the right height and drilling a hole in precisely the right spot. By holding a tolerance of .5 mm on the location of each hole, Pontiac assured that every body panel fit on every Fiero frame in exactly the same way.

The Fiero was sold in three trim levels: coupe, sport coupe, and SE. The difference between the first two was principally the gearbox: wide-ratio in the base coupe, close-ratio in the sport coupe. Both these versions had 13-inch steel wheels with 185/80R13 radials; "turbo finned" 13-inch cast aluminum wheels were optional for $195. The SE coupe included a WS6 handling package, consisting of a stiffer suspension, 14-inch "Hi-Tech" cast aluminum wheels with a distinctive 5-bladed spoke pattern, and low-profile 215/60R14 Goodyear Eagle GT radials. This WS6 package was available for the sport

The Sunbird name was revived in 1983 for this 2000 convertible, and applied to all 2000 models in 1984.

coupe for $459, and proved to be so popular that Pontiac ran short of the spiffy Hi-Tech wheels in mid-year. The SE also included such niceties as tinted glass, deck lid luggage carrier, console, better instrumentation, and more comfortable seats. Available only on the SE were special fleece-covered seats with suede trim.

Fiero production began with red and white as the only available body colors, joined by black and silver late in the model year.

With only 92 hp from the Iron Duke, the Fiero was certainly no challenge to Corvettes and Porsches in straight-line performance. Various road tests showed 0 to 60 mph in 11.5 seconds, the quarter-mile in 18.2 seconds at 73 mph, and a top speed of 105 mph; however, the SE version with its WS6 suspension could generate formidable cornering power, and the sophisticated chassis was clearly capable of handling far more power than the asthmatic Iron Duke could generate. A big power jump from an adaptation of the 173 V-6 was obviously in the Fiero's future.

The 2000 family were now all called 2000 Sunbirds, the name previously applied only to the convertible. The top-level series was now called S/E instead of SE, a seemingly innocuous revision which really designated a tremendous change: a turbocharged fuel-injected engine.

Designated LA5, the turbo engine was a thoroughly worked-over version of the 1.8-liter OHC-4. It had a new fuel injection system which delivered the fuel right to each intake port in typical

European fashion: Pontiac called it Multi-Port Fuel Injection (MPFI) to distinguish it from the simpler TBI system used on its LR8, LQ9, LH8, and LQ5 engines.

Air was pumped into the LA5 engine by an AiResearch T2 turbine-compressor unit which delivered a maximum boost of 10 psi. This was a high boost pressure for a street engine, made possible by an elaborate electronic system which controlled the injection, ignition, and even the turbo boost.

So prodded, the LA5 engine churned out a frantic 150 hp @ 5600 rpm, a staggering 79 percent increase over the 84 hp of the unblown LH8 version. This was a specific power output of 1.36 hp/cubic inch, easily the highest figure in the American auto industry.

To nail all this power to the ground the Sunbird S/E came equppped with heavy-duty suspension, power steering, 14 x 6 Hi-Tech aluminum wheels like the Fiero SE's, 205/60R14 steel-belted radials, and special instrumentation. A 4-speed manual transmission was standard, with 3-speed automatic optional. Unfortunately the slick 5-speed gearbox of lesser Sunbirds was not available, because it could not take the turbo engine's output.

To top it all off, Pontiac offered the turbo engine—complete with all the items listed above—as an option package for any other Sunbird model except the station wagons! The price for this turbo package was $1546 for the base 2000 Sunbird, $1508 for the LE models.

Despite a balky shift linkage, *Road & Track*'s test Sunbird S/E hatchback did 0 to 60 mph in 9.9 seconds and the quarter-mile in 17.2 seconds at 79.5 mph—much faster than a Fiero. *Car and Driver*'s sedan was even quicker: 0 to 60 in 8.3 seconds, the quarter-mile in 16.3 seconds at 82 mph. *R&T* praised the surprisingly quick throttle response, but thought the engine was peaky and lacked low-speed punch. The 4-speed gearbox was a real handicap, since it was slow-shifting and had wide ratios, not at all helpful to a peaky engine. Neither magazine cared for the considerable torque steer.

Introduced in 1984, this injected and turbocharged version of the 1.8-liter overhead-cam engine developed 150 hp and endowed the 2000 Sunbird S/E with blistering performance.

The changes throughout the rest of Pontiac's vast array of models for '84 were relatively minor.

A new Sport package was available for the 1000. Called option Y90, it cost $464 and included aluminum wheels, stiffer suspension, larger front anti-roll bar, rear anti-roll bar, decklid spoiler, stripes, sport mirrors, and special steering wheel. Mandatory with this package were P175/70R13 steel-belted radials for an additional $119.04.

The Phoenix family had nomenclature changes, as the hot SJ and luxurious LJ versions were redesignated SE and LE. The Grand

Prix also underwent the same redesignation, as the LJ became the LE. Yet another LE series appeared in the Bonnevilles, inserted between the standard Bonneville and the Brougham. The Bonneville wagon was dropped, replaced by a new 6000 wagon. There was no change in the big Parisienne, which was included in the full-line sales brochure for the first time.

The 6000 STE received a revised instrument panel with a new analog tachometer and digital speedometer; rear-disc brakes were now standard.

The LU5 305 V-8 with its twin-TBI injection was dropped from the Firebird family, rendered superfluous by the high-output L69 carbureted engine. The L69 was still available only in the Trans Am, but could now be mated to the 4-speed automatic as well as the 5-speed manual transmission.

New for the Trans Am was the Aero Package. Costing $199, this included smooth wheel covers and extensions for the rocker panels and extremities of the body. The reshaped front end actually blocked all forward-facing air inlets and made the engine a "bottom breather." These changes reduced the car's drag coefficient to .299, the lowest yet for any American production automobile.

The Recaro Special Edition Trans Am was a very exclusive model. This included Recaro's finest bucket seats upholstered in leather, the Aero Package, split folding rear seats, luxury door paneling, leather-wrapped steering wheel, leather-covered shift

An optional Aero package—shown here with all its components except the wheel covers—reduced the 1984 Trans Am's drag coefficient to .299.

knob and parking brake handle, a superior sound system, T-top removable glass roof panels, and gold-anodized 15 x 7 Hi-Tech aluminum wheels. Mandatory with the Recaro option was the deep-breathing L69 engine for $530, and either the WS6 handling package (215/65R15 steel-belted radials, heavy-duty suspension, 4-wheel disc brakes, and limited-slip differential, all for $408) or WY6 handling package (same as WS6 except for deletion of the limited-slip differential). All this added some $4,000 to the Trans Am's list price of $11,113.

Pontiac's 1984 array illustrated how very complex and expensive modern automotive manufacturing and marketing had become. There were now nine separate car series, built from seven completely different structures (the Phoenix and 6000 shared a common basis, as did the Bonneville and Grand Prix). There were nine different-sized engines: four inline fours, three V-6s, and two V-8s. If one included differences of tune and counted the Iron Duke and 173 V-6 twice since they were made in both longitudinal and transverse versions, Pontiac offered 15 different engines. Of these, one was turbocharged, two were diesels, five had gasoline fuel injection, and seven were transversely mounted. There were surely a few long-time Pontiac employees who remembered the good old days of a quarter-century earlier, when all of Pontiac's models were minor variations of the same car in two wheelbase lengths, and just one V 8 engine in different stages of tune powered them all.

On January 10 the heavily publicized reorganization of General Motors took effect. Pontiac was joined with Chevrolet and GM of Canada into one major division—commonly called CPC—while Buick, Oldsmobile, and Cadillac became another division (BOC). Bill Hoglund remained Pontiac's general manager.

On July 1 Hoglund was promoted to corporate management at GM headquarters, and seven months later was named to head GM's Saturn small-car project. Replacing him as Pontiac's general manager was Harvard-educated J. Michael Losh, who had a background in finance and had been managing director of GM of Mexico.

This proved to be the great recovery year for the American auto industry, as production soared to 8.7 million units. Pontiac production jumped to 827,576 cars and 9.5 percent market share, one of the best years in the division's history. The Fiero's sales success was phenomenal; in its very first year it sold 136,840 units, surpassing all other Pontiac models except the Sunbird. Pontiac remained in fifth place in industry sales, however, as both Oldsmobile and Buick set new sales records.

J. Michael Losh succeeded Bill Hoglund as Pontiac's general manager in 1984.

With its standard 140-hp fuel-injected V-6 and WS6 handling package, the 1985 Fiero GT became a serious sports car.

1985

Expected and eagerly awaited, the biggest change this year was the inclusion of a V-6 for the Fiero. Improving on the expected, Pontiac introduced a whole new version of the Fiero with an uprated V-6 as its centerpiece.

The new Fiero GT looked quite different from other versions, especially from the front. Its aerodynamic outer body panels were those from the 1984 Indianapolis pace car, duplicates of which were available in the latter part of the 1984 model year.

The GT's V-6 was a new version of the 173 V-6 that used the HO cylinder heads and camshaft combined with port fuel injection, a new intake manifold, and revised exhaust system. Coded L44, it developed 140 hp and 170 foot-pounds of torque, the latter a satisfying 17 percent increase over the torque output of the carbureted HO version. It was standard in the Fiero GT and optional in other Fiero models, in which case they bore the designation "2M6" instead of "2M4."

The L44 V-6 transformed the Fiero. It chopped 3 seconds off the 0 to 60 time (now 8.3 seconds), 2 seconds off the quarter-mile time (16.3 seconds @ 85 mph), and added 15 mph to the top speed (120 mph). For a list price of just over $11,000—half the price of a Corvette—the Fiero GT was now firmly into performance-car territory.

The WS6 handling package—standard on the GT—was revised with a half-inch greater suspension travel in front, rear spring rates 10 percent stiffer, revalved shock absorbers, and reduced rear-end roll steer.

Car and Driver expressed disappointment: while lauding the engine, it complained about the lack of a 5-speed gearbox, the suspension's inability to cope with a bumpy road, the "drugged" steering, which lacked proper feel yet transmitted road shocks, and the large turning circle. "The upshot is that the Fiero is not yet ready to take its place among the world's better road cars." *Road & Track*, however, was ecstatic. It considered the handling and steering characteristics annoyances, not problems. "The debate is over. . . . It's a world-class sports car." *Motor Trend* compared a Fiero GT head-to-head with Toyota's new MR2 mid-engined 2-seater. "We'd probably choose the Pontiac Fiero. The silky smooth engine won our hearts (though we hope they'll give us a 5-speed soon) and we personally prefer the way it looks."

The injected V-6 also made a difference to two other Pontiac performers: the 6000 STE, where it replaced the previous carbureted HO version as standard equipment, and the Firebird, where it was standard on the SE version. In transverse form for the front-drive

Standard equipment for the Trans Am in 1985 was the Aero package; optional equipment included a 210-hp injected version of the 305 V-8.

STE it was coded LB6, while in longitudinal form for the rear-drive Firebird it was designated LB8; both these versions had lower compression and less power than the Fiero's L44.

New for the Trans Am was an optional multi-port injected version of the 305 V-8. Designated LB9, it developed 210 hp and was Pontiac's most powerful engine. Unfortunately it was available only with automatic transmission. For those who wanted a hot V-8 with a 5-speed gearbox, the 190-hp carbureted L69 was still offered; both these engines were exclusive to the Trans Am.

The previously optional Aero package was modified and made standard equipment on the Trans Am.

Available only for the Trans Am as part of its WS6 suspension package was a Hi-Tech wheel in a new 16- x 8-inch size, fitted with huge P245/50VR16 Goodyear "gatorback" Eagle GT radials. The upgraded WS6 package this year also included gas-pressurized shock absorbers and very large anti-roll bars as well as the usual rear-disc brakes and limited-slip differential.

Third time lucky? Pontiac revived the Grand Am name once again in 1985 for this coupe, its version of the GM N-car. Optional equipment included a Buick-built 3-liter injected V-6.

The 1000, Sunbird, Grand Prix, Bonneville, and Parisienne were basically unchanged from '84, while the 6000 was improved by the availability of a 4-speed automatic transmission and the LB6 port-injected V-6.

The Phoenix was discontinued. In its place was a new model, one of GM's corporate N-body cars which were derived from the J-cars. Others were Buick's Somerset Regal and Oldsmobile's Calais; reviving a twice-discontinued name, Pontiac's N-car was the Grand Am.

Available only as a coupe in two trim levels (standard and LE), the Grand Am was touted as a complete driver's car—as had its two predecessors. Slightly longer than a J-car, the Grand Am had a wheelbase of 103.4 inches and an overall length of 177.5 inches, nicely fitting in between the Sunbird and 6000. The standard powerplant was the ever-faithful 2.5-liter Iron Duke in its latest "Tech IV" guise, designated L68 though it developed the same 92 hp @ 4400 rpm as the LR8 version in the 6000 and Fiero. A 5-speed manual transmission was standard, with 3-speed automatic optional. Also optional was a new engine for Pontiac, a 3-liter V-6 built by Buick. Designated LN7, this V-6 had multiport fuel injection and 125 hp. Automatic transmission was standard with this V-6; no manual transmission was available at all, which tended to mitigate the "driver's car" image. An optional Y99 handling package included the same 14-inch Hi-Tech aluminum wheels and P215/60R14 Goodyear Eagle GT radials available on the Fiero.

Motor Trend put a V-6 Grand Am with the Y99 suspension through its paces against a VW Scirocco and Honda Prelude, and concluded that Pontiac still had some work to do before building a proper driver's coupe. The Grand Am's tires were praised, but its mushy steering, poor instrumentation, and lack of a manual transmission were criticized.

Despite *Motor Trend*'s reservations, the Grand Am was an instant hit with a production of 82,542 for the model year. This was a boon, as sales of every other Pontiac specialty model declined. Sales of the mainline 6000 showed a strong increase, but the surprising model was the big Parisienne whose sales exceeded 82,000—not bad for a model that had been temporarily discontinued a few years before.

The Grand Am SE was a new series for 1986, marked by aerodynamic body panels, fog lamps, flush-mounted composite headlamps, and monochromatic paint. All Grand Ams this year were available as 4-door sedans as well as the coupe.

1986

A major expansion of the Grand Am family was Pontiac's headliner for the new model year. A high-performance SE series was added, and a 4-door sedan body became available in all three Grand Am series.

The SE was distinguished from other Grand Ams by several strong styling touches. Composite headlamps and neutral-density tail lamps presented a cleaner appearance, a wraparound aerodynamic package reduced wind drag, fog lamps were standard, and monochromatic paint—including the bumpers and grille—lent a businesslike, no-nonsense look.

Underneath the SE's sleek skin was a comprehensive package of speed and luxury items. Standard equipment included the Y99 suspension, 14-inch aluminum wheels with P215/60R14 radial tires, the 3-liter V-6 with automatic transmission, power steering, power door locks, power front-disc brakes, cruise control, Delco AM/FM stereo with four speakers, full set of analog gauges, liquid crystal driver information center, interior releases for the fuel filler door and decklid, 4-way adjustable driver's seat, tilt steering wheel, variable-cycle windshield wipers, and a leather accent group. In concept the Grand Am SE was therefore very like the 6000 STE sedan—a fully equipped package for the serious but sophisticated driver—but was slightly smaller in size, lower in price, and available as a coupe as well as sedan.

The Sunbird family was revised. The premier performance version was the new Sunbird GT, which had the LA5 turbo engine, 4-speed gearbox, heavy-duty suspension, and Hi-Tech 14-inch aluminum wheels with P215/60R14 Goodyear Eagle GT radials as standard equipment. Available in every Sunbird body style except the wagon, the GT boasted hidden headlamps, black-accented fender flares, and distinctive trim; all other Sunbirds had unchanged styling from 1985. The SE (no longer S/E) version now had the LH8 engine and 5-speed gearbox as standard, although the turbo engine was available as an option. The Sunbird remained the only Pontiac available as a convertible, offered in both the SE and GT series.

Though there were no mechanical changes to the Fiero, the aero bodywork—standard on the GT—was now also considered standard on the SE. However, the SE could be ordered without it, in which case the car's retail price was $9,995; the aero body added another $600.

The restyled Fiero GT for 1986 had a fastback shape and optional deck spoiler. The 15-inch diamond-spoke aluminum wheels were exclusive to this model.

Sunbird GT was the new name in 1986 for the turbocharged version of Pontiac's J-car. The GT had new styling with hidden headlamps; all other Sunbird models had unchanged 1985 styling.

All other '86 Pontiacs carried on unchanged. The 1000, now in its second decade (counting its original Chevette form), was still selling well, as were the Grand Prix, Bonneville, and the big Parisienne. It was clear that Pontiac would continue to offer these older rear-drive models so long as they continued to sell, but also clear that the next redesign of them would incorporate front-wheel drive.

Sales showed a strong recovery as Pontiac had its best-selling model year since 1979. Though still trailing Oldsmobile and Buick (barely), Pontiac was the only GM division which did not show a sales decline from 1985. The 6000 was a strong seller, up 26 percent, but a surprise was the Grand Am. Pontiac historically had trouble with cars carrying the Grand Am name, but this latest version was a runaway success; its sales were up by an astonishing 132 percent over 1985.

1987

Thirty years after the first Bonneville appeared, a spectacular new Bonneville became Pontiac's big-car leader. It replaced the Parisienne as well as the previous Bonneville, both of which were discontinued.

The new Bonneville had a longer wheelbase and a wider stance than its predecesssor, but was 1½ inches shorter. The interior room was cavernous, due primarily to the compact new front-wheel-drive propulsion package.

Power for the Bonneville was provided by the faithful Buick-built 231 V-6, now equipped with electronic sequential fuel injection and delivering 150 hp. Due to its transverse positioning, this engine carried a new LG3 code—the same code which had designated a Chevrolet-built 305 V-8 a decade earlier. A notable durability feature was the use of stainless steel in the exhaust manifold and exhaust pipe. A 4-speed Turbo Hydramatic was standard equipment.

All four wheels were independently suspended with MacPherson struts, and anti-roll bars were fitted front and rear. Power front-disc brakes were standard, as was power rack-and-pinion steering.

This chassis sophistication was matched by the striking new body. Tall glass area and a sharply sloping hoodline aided visibility, flush-mounted composite headlamps and wraparound tail lamps cut wind resistance, and a sporting stance was imparted by the fully exposed wheels highlighted by subtle fender flares. Working within the constraints of GM's H-body program, John Schinella and his team at Pontiac's Design Studio Two had created another styling triumph, a handsome and original design which bore no obvious resemblance to its corporate sister cars, the Buick LeSabre and Oldsmobile Delta 88.

Star of the 1987 line was the all-new Bonneville sedan, featuring front-wheel drive, all-independent suspension, and aerodynamic styling. This is the SE version with its standard fog lamps, 15-inch "tri-port" aluminum wheels, and Y99 suspension package.

The new Bonneville was offered in three versions. The base-level version was not plain at all: reflecting increasing customer demand for amenities once deemed luxuries, it included tinted glass and air conditioning as standard equipment! The axle ratio was a high 2.73, enhancing fuel economy. Options included the Y99 Rally Tuned suspension with thicker anti-roll bars, quicker-ratio steering, stiffer struts, and Goodyear Eagle GT tires on 15-inch alloy wheels. The upmarket Bonneville LE added electric window lifts, richer interior detailing, 55/45 reclining seats with front and rear armrests, body side molding, and 14-inch diamond-spoke alloy wheels. Most exciting of the Bonneville trio was the performance-oriented SE, which included as standard equipment the Y99 suspension package, a 2.97 axle ratio, dual exhaust, fog lamps, full analog instrumentation, floor shift, and leather-wrapped steering wheel. This handsome and competent new Bonneville was the most interesting big sedan in America.

In the Firebird family a new Formula replaced the previous SE version, and a power-packed GTA option was added to the Trans Am. The Tech IV 4-cylinder economotor was thankfully banished from this series, as the base Firebird now had the 2.8-liter V-6 and 5-speed gearbox as standard equipment; optional was the LG4 4-bbl. 305 V-8. Reviving a famous Firebird name, the Formula offered the LG4/5-speed combination as standard, coupled with the WS6 performance suspension package that included massive 245/50VR16 tires on 16-inch alloy wheels. Optional were the LB9 injected 305 V-8 (downrated a bit this year to 205 hp) and B2L, an injected 350 (5.7-liter) V-8. This latter engine was a real powerhouse, essentially

The 1987 Firebird GTA was an option on the Trans Am. Standard equipment included a monochromatic color treatment, gold-anodized cross-lace aluminum wheels, and a 210-hp fuel-injected 5.7-liter V-8.

Sunbird SE for 1987 received semi-hidden headlamps, a standard 5-speed gearbox, and an enlarged 2-liter engine.

the same as the Corvette's 230-hp engine; perhaps for insurance purposes, Pontiac carefully downrated it to 210 hp. Due to its torque output, the B2L engine was available only with automatic transmission.

The Trans Am visually differed from the Formula and base Firebird by aerodynamic panels, fog lamps, and hood louvers. Its drive-train combinations were the same as the Formula's, but its suspension was the Y99 Rally Tuned version with 15-inch aluminum wheels; the WS6 package was optional. The new GTA was an all-out performance version of the Trans Am with the B2L 350 V-8, WS6 suspension, 4-wheel disc brakes, and a lushly trimmed interior with new articulated bucket seats.

Motor Trend tested a Formula with the 5-speed and injected 305 V-8, and found it a "delight to drive." Much of that delight came from its quickness: 0 to 60 in 7.7 seconds, the quarter-mile in 16.9 seconds at 87.6 mph. Top speed was not tested, but the Formula's standard 3.45 axle ratio would limit it to about 125 mph. Equipped with its taller 3.27 axle ratio, *MT*'s test GTA reached 141.5 mph and was even quicker in acceleration: 0 to 60 in 6.89 seconds, the quarter-mile in 15.35 seconds at 91.6 mph.

The Sunbird's overhead-cam 4-cylinder was enlarged to 2 liters (121 cubic inches) and now produced 96 hp in atmospheric form (coded LT2) and 165 hp in turbocharged (LT3) form. A stout new 5-speed manual gearbox, built by GM's Muncie division under license from Getrag of Germany, was teamed with the turbo engine in the Sunbird GT. In mid-year this LT3/5-speed combination also appeared as an option for the Grand Am, and transformed that capable but mild-mannered tourer into a feisty stormer. *Motor Trend* found 0-60 in 8.8 seconds and applauded the quick throttle response, but noted considerable torque steer.

The Getrag/Muncie 5-speed gearbox improved two more lines. Curing a long-standing complaint from sports car enthusiasts, it finally became available with the V-6 in the Fiero, replacing the 4-speed as standard equipment. It did not quite replace the automatic as the standard transmission in the 6000 STE, but was available as a credit option. Pontiac now offered a 5-speed in every line except the Bonneville, Grand Prix, and the big ex-Parisienne Safari wagon. Indeed, it was the 4-speed manual which was now a rare transmission, available only in the 1000.

Few changes were made to the Grand Prix and 1000, as both were slated for replacement the following year.

Several significant technical advances benefited a number of Pontiac models. "Direct Ignition" employed a notched reluctor ring mounted on the engine flywheel to signal the proper firing time for each cylinder to the engine's computer, which then triggered the

All Fieros except the GT sported this new nose for 1987, and had 5-speed gearboxes as standard equipment.

appropriate coil; there were two coils, each firing two cylinders. This system totally eliminated the distributor, improving ignition reliability and timing accuracy. It was standard equipment on all Tech IV 2.5-liter 4-cylinder engines (Fiero, 6000, Grand Am) as well as the 6000 STE's 2.8-liter V-6.

For many years, a multiplicity of drive belts was the bane of automotive engines with a number of accessories. Pontiac attacked this problem in 1987 by redesigning and relocating the accessories so they could all be driven by a single "serpentine" belt, greatly improving serviceability. It was a feature of the Tech IV engine in the Fiero and 6000 (but not in the Grand Am), and also of the Sunbird's new 2-liter engine.

Available only for the Grand Am, and then only if mated to a 5-speed gearbox, was a special version of the Tech IV. This had a pair of counter-rotating balance weights located in the sump, greatly reducing the typical vibration of a large 4-cylinder engine. This, of course, necessitated a redesigned sump and the addition of a drive gear to the crankshaft, so Pontiac engineers utilized this opportunity to also redesign the oil pump and even the oil filter, which was located *inside* the sump! Access to the filter was provided by a large removable plate on the sump. This new balanceshaft version of the Tech IV surprisingly retained the L68 designation used since 1985 for the Grand Am's engine; LR8 remained the code for the version used in the Fiero and 6000.

1988

The division's revamped product mix for 1988 began a few months early when the Le Mans was unveiled at dealers on June 11, 1987. As a replacement for the 1000, the Le Mans revived a famous Pontiac name. It was truly an international automobile, an Opel Kadett design built by GM's Korean affiliate, Daewoo Motors. Pontiac was the exclusive beneficiary of this arrangement; no other GM division received a version of the Le Mans.

The new econocar came in three body styles: 4-door sedan, 2- door hatchback, and 2-door coupe. An upmarket SE trim level was available only for the sedan, while the coupe was offered only as a stripped "value leader" version. Though approximately the

Built in Korea to a German design, the 1988 Le Mans finally gave Pontiac a sophisticated entry in the econocar field.

same exterior size as the superseded 1000, the Le Mans was much roomier inside, and far more sophisticated. A 1.6-liter overhead-cam 4-cylinder transversely mounted engine with throttle-body injection put its 74 hp to the front wheels through a 5-speed gearbox (4-speed in the value leader coupe). The independent front suspension used MacPherson struts, while the semi-independent rear suspension had a torsion beam axle and coil springs. Rack-and-pinion steering and automatic transmission were options. Reflecting the increased desire for amenities even in econocars, included in the standard equipment were a tachometer, tinted glass, defoggers for rear and side windows, and reclining front bucket seats.

When the full 1988 line appeared on October 1, the principal changes were improvements to the entire family of engines, including several new ones. The Fiero received a redesigned suspension system and there was an additional Bonneville model, but the really significant models—an all-new Grand Prix and a 4-wheel-drive version of the 6000 STE—were scheduled for mid-year introduction.

Causing genuine excitement was an historic new engine built by Oldsmobile. Called the "Quad-4" and coded LD2, this inline 4-cylinder powerplant boasted twin overhead camshafts, aluminum cylinder head, four valves per cylinder, electronic port injection, direct ignition, and complex manifolding. Such advanced features enabled it to develop 150 hp from only 2.3 liters (141 cubic inches) of displacement. This was a prodigious specific power output of 1.06 hp/cubic inch, easily the highest figure for any American atmospheric-induction engine. Compared to the similarly sized Tech IV, the Quad-4 developed 63 percent more power yet had 7 percent less displacement. This was the first engine offered by Pontiac which had either double overhead camshafts or four valves per cylinder, and was the first GM engine with these features since Chevrolet's limited-production Cosworth-Vega engine of the early seventies.

America's most advanced engine was the Quad-4, introduced in 1988 as an option for the Grand Am. Double overhead camshafts, four-valve combustion chambers, lightweight construction, electronic fuel injection, and distributorless direct ignition enabled this powerplant to produce 150 hp from only 2.3 liters of displacement.

Like the Tech IV, the Quad-4 used a single "serpentine" belt to drive its accessories. Its direct ignition system had the two coils mounted in a die-cast cover directly above the spark plugs, an arrangement Pontiac called "Integrated Direct Ignition." In a seemingly retrograde step, the two camshafts were driven by a double roller chain rather than a toothed belt.

In its introductory year the Quad-4 was offered by Pontiac only as an option for Grand Am models, but it was certain that this advanced and potent powerplant would see more widespread use in the future.

The Buick-built 231 V-6, whose origins dated back a quarter-century, received a thorough redesign for 1988. Since it was originally designed to be manufactured with V-8 tooling, it had 90 degrees between its cylinder banks instead of the ideal 120 degrees. Despite the adoption of an even-firing crankshaft in 1978, this engine still had an inherent vibration which became more apparent when it was adapted for front-wheel-drive in the 1987 Bonneville. To eliminate this vibration a balance shaft was placed between the cylinder banks, making it the first such V-6 (along with Ford's similar V-6, also introduced this year) in American automotive history. The cylinder bores were respaced in the engine block to eliminate a slight off-center condition relative to the crankpins, with the result that lighter pistons could be used. Other improvements were relocated injector nozzles, larger-diameter exhaust manifold, larger-capacity air intake system, and a revised electronic control module. Compared to the previous LG3 version, the net result of all these improvements was a 10 percent increase in power to 165 hp, an increase in torque, and a sharp reduction in carbon monoxide and unburned hydrocarbon emissions. Called the "3800 V-6" and coded LN3, this new variant of the 231 V-6 became standard in the Bonneville SE and new SSE; the previous LG3 version remained standard in the Bonneville LE.

Detail modifications improved the rest of Pontiac's engines. All versions of the Tech IV now used the balance shafts, as well as new stronger connecting rods and lighter pistons. The L44 transverse V-6 of the Fiero and the LB8 longitudinal version used in the base Firebird had a new crankshaft with improved balancing and an advanced "Multec" (multiple technology) fuel injector nozzle. All V-8 engines had a single serpentine accessory belt, stronger head gaskets, and the Multec injectors. The Firebird's LG4 carbureted 5-liter V-8 was replaced by a new LO3 5-liter V-8 which had throttle-body injection and developed 170 hp. Thus it came to pass that, with one exception, every single Pontiac engine from the little 1.6-

liter L73 four in the Le Mans to the mighty B2L V-8 in the Firebird GTA now had fuel injection; the sole holdout with a carburetor was the mild-mannered LV2 V-8 available only in the Safari station wagon.

The base model Bonneville was dropped, while a new top-level SSE model was added to the LE and SE. The SSE was a serious attempt to build a full-size American sedan with much of the appeal of the great European road cars, an extension into a larger car of the same philosophy behind the 6000 STE and Grand Am. Aero bodywork panels, fog lamps, and different tail lamps distinguished it from other Bonnevilles. The new 3800 V-6 provided power, while stopping was aided by standard ABS anti-lock braking system. Included in the long list of standard features were electronic ride control, variable-ratio power steering, anti-roll bars, headlamp washers, and 16-inch body-colored "Aero Lite" cast aluminum wheels shod with low-profile Goodyear P215/60R16 Eagle GT+4 all-season radials. Inside, the most noticeable features were full analog instrumentation and a leather-wrapped steering wheel with the dubious feature of radio controls in its center.

No longer did the Fiero have to make do with its Chevette front suspension and X-car rear suspension. In its fifth year it received a redesigned arrangement with longer control arms and a thicker anti-roll bar in front, and a new tri-link system at the rear. Combined with the elimination of the steering damper, the result was lighter steering action, a smoother ride, and more accurate wheel location.

The new Fiero Formula, a replacement for the previous SE, had the V-6 engine and WS6 suspension of the GT but the notchback body of the Fiero Coupe.

Top Bonneville for '88 was the new SSE, marked by aero body extensions, 16-inch body-colored alloy wheels, and a new balance-shaft version of the 3.8-liter V-6.

In the Firebird family, the top-ranked GTA was now considered a separate model rather than an option on the Trans Am. Its standard B2L 5.7-liter V-8—still available only with the 4-speed automatic—was uprated a bit to 225 hp. The new LO3 throttle-body injected 5-liter V-8 became the standard powerplant for the Trans Am and Formula, with the LB9 port-injected 5-liter V-8 and the B2L 5.7-liter V-8 as options.

There were no cosmetic changes to the Grand Am, but the SE version now had the LT3 2-liter turbo engine as standard equipment. Optional on all three Grand Am versions was the new Quad-4 engine. By contrast, the Sunbirds had no mechanical changes, but the coupes and convertibles had a redesigned aft end with new tail lamps, rear window, decklid, and quarter panels.

Pontiac's big star for '88 was an all-new Grand Prix, introduced in mid-year. This was Pontiac's version of the highly touted GM10 line, available in 1988 only as coupes; the GP's sister cars were the Buick Regal and Oldsmobile Cutlass Supreme. The sleek new GP body had a drag coefficient of .287, lowest in the entire American auto industry. Lower, wider, shorter and lighter than its predecessor, it had greater interior room due to that now-familiar space-saving phenomenon: front-wheel drive. Indeed, less than a decade after the first front-wheel-drive Pontiac, the 1980 Phoenix, the front-wheel-drive revolution had advanced so far that the only traditional front engine/rear drive Pontiacs remaining were the Firebirds and the Safari. Front suspension of the new GP utilized MacPherson struts with tapered coil springs; the independent rear suspension was a new design with three links and a strut locating each wheel, the spinging action provided by a Corvette-like fiberglass monoleaf spring mounted transversely. Power-assisted 4-wheel disc brakes, vented in front, were standard equipment.

Power for the sleek new GP was provided by the LB6 2.8-liter V-6 shared with the 6000 STE. A 5-speed Muncie-Getrag gearbox was standard, with a 4-speed automatic optional.

The new GP was sold in the usual three Pontiac trim levels: base, luxurious LE, and sporty SE. The SE had monochromatic paint, aero body moldings, fog lamps, Y99 suspensions, and color-keyed aluminum wheels with Goodyear P215/65R15 Eagle GT+4 all-weather radials.

Car and Driver bubbled with enthusiasm for the new GP, stating that it "should go far to reestablish the Grand Prix at the leading edge of distinctive transportation." The only disappointment expressed was the lack of power; figures of 0 to 60 in 9.5 seconds, the quarter-mile in 16.8 seconds, and a top speed of 119 mph were "not good enough. This car deserves more engine." Should Pontiac agree with *C&D*, the solution is obvious: make the Bonneville's 3800 V-6 available as an option.

While echoing the sentiments of *Car and Driver* about the desirability of more power, *Motor Trend* liked the new Grand Prix enough to award it the "Car of the Year" prize. *MT*'s greatest praise was given to the Grand Prix's styling and handling, especially the SE version. "Its strikingly sculpted sheetmetal endows this top-of-the-line Grand Prix with . . . a degree of pure flash not seen in any of its GM10 counterparts. Its fully independent suspension tuned to Y99 specifications puts the Grand Prix SE on par with the finest European touring machines when it comes to matching compliance with control." This was the fifth time Pontiac had won *Motor Trend*'s coveted award.

All-new for 1988, the Grand Prix was transformed into a supersleek road car. Based on the corporate GM10 front-drive platform, the split grille and sloping Sunbird-like hood gave it strong Pontiac identity—personal luxury with Pontiac excitement.

On March 1, 1988, the stunning and unexpected announcement came that Pontiac would cease production of the Fiero at the end of the 1988 model year. At a press conference Pontiac general manager Michael Losh said, "Times have changed, and the market has changed. The Fiero no longer seems to fit the market." Though sales of the Fiero after 1984 never reached those of its introductory year, termination seems a harsh sentence for a sports model which regularly outsold GM's other 2-seat sports car, the Corvette. The problem, at least in part, stemmed from the lack of proper definition of the Fiero's marketing niche. As a mid-engined 2-seater, the Fiero's natural market was the sports car enthusiast, to whom a powerful engine and driving pleasure are of paramount importance. Yet Pontiac initially equipped it solely with a 4-cylinder engine and insisted on describing it as a "commuter car," as if it were intended to be a low-priced utility vehicle. Even after the availability of the V-6 in 1985, enthusiasts had to wait another two years to get a 5-speed gearbox, and until 1988 to get a decent suspension. Two things might have saved the Fiero: turbocharging and a convertible. Both were available on the Sunbird, which *did* start life as a utility car. It's a shame Pontiac did not use its considerable expertise in these fields to improve its most interesting model.

Slated for introduction late in the model year was a model even more dramatic than the aerodynamic front-wheel-drive Grand Prix: a 6000 STE with full-time four-wheel drive. Powered by a 3.1-liter V-6, this would be Pontiac's response to such sophisticated European four-wheel drive cars as the Audi Quattro and Lancia Delta HF, commonly considered to be the forerunners of the great road cars of the future.

Pontiac management perceived the future of the division in a high-tech high-performance image, and already offered more interesting models than any other manufacturer. Despite the demise of the Fiero, exciting models like the sleek new Grand Prix and four-wheel drive 6000 STE reaffirmed the commitment to that vision, and furthered Pontiac's claim as the most advanced and forward-thinking automaker in America.

Appendices

Appendix I. **MODEL SPECIFICATIONS**

Notes

1. All linear dimensions in inches.
2. Engine numbers locate engine in Appendix II.
3. All specifications shown are for 4-door sedans or 4-door hardtops unless the series did not include a 4-door body style.

Abbreviations and Definitions

Series: Pontiac's designation. It is the difference in these designations that determines different series, not the difference in model names.

Curb weight: weight in pounds of base-level model (no options) with all fluids and ½ tank of fuel.

3M, 4M, 5M: 3-speed, 4-speed, and 5-speed manual transmissions.

2A, 3A, 4A: 2-speed, 3-speed, 4-speed automatic transmissions.

Brakes: only standard brakes are indicated.

Axle ratio: only the ratio fitted with the standard engine and standard transmission is shown.

C: coil springs.

DRHM: Dual-Range Hydra-Matic

HM: Hydra-Matic

MS: MacPherson strut suspension.

RA: rigid axle

SA: swing axle independent suspension.

SE: semi-elliptic leaf spring.

SHM: Super Hydra-Matic

SLA: short and long arm independent suspension.

TA: trailing arm.

THM: Turbo Hydra-Matic

Year	Series	Model	Dimensions					Track		Suspension		Transmission		Brakes		Axle Ratio	Engines	
			Curb Wt.	Wheel Base	Length	Width	Height	Front	Rear	Front	Rear	Std.	Opt.	Front	Rear		Std.	Opt.
1946	46-25	Torpedo Six	3412	119	204.5	75.8	66	58	61.5	SLA, C	RA, SE	3M	—	drum	drum	4.1	1	3
↓	46-27	Torpedo Eight	3472	↓	↓	↓	↓	↓	↓	↓	↓	↓	↓	↓	↓	↓	2	4
↓	46-26	Streamliner Six	3612	122	210.3	76.8	65.3	↓	↓	↓	↓	↓	↓	↓	↓	4.3	1	3
↓	46-28	Streamliner Eight	3672	↓	↓	↓	↓	↓	↓	↓	↓	↓	↓	↓	↓	↓	2	4
1947	47-25	Torpedo Six	3400	119	204.5	75.8	66	↓	↓	↓	↓	↓	↓	↓	↓	4.1	1	3
↓	47-27	Torpedo Eight	3460	↓	↓	↓	↓	↓	↓	↓	↓	↓	↓	↓	↓	↓	2	4
↓	47-26	Streamliner Six	3605	122	210.3	76.8	65.3	↓	↓	↓	↓	↓	↓	↓	↓	4.3	1	3
↓	47-28	Streamliner Eight	3663	↓	↓	↓	↓	↓	↓	↓	↓	↓	↓	↓	↓	↓	2	4
1948	48-25	Torpedo Six	3430	119	204.5	75.8	66	↓	↓	↓	↓	↓	HM	↓	↓	4.1	5	3
↓	48-27	Torpedo Eight	3490	↓	↓	↓	↓	↓	↓	↓	↓	↓	↓	↓	↓	↓	6	4
↓	48-26	Streamliner Six	3639	122	210.3	76.8	65.3	↓	↓	↓	↓	↓	↓	↓	↓	4.3	5	3
↓	48-28	Streamliner Eight	3699	↓	↓	↓	↓	↓	↓	↓	↓	↓	↓	↓	↓	↓	6	4
1949	49-25	Six	3425	120	202.5	75.8	63.3	↓	59	↓	↓	↓	↓	↓	↓	4.1	5	3
↓	49-27	Eight	3510	↓	↓	↓	↓	↓	↓	↓	↓	↓	↓	↓	↓	↓	6	4
1950	50-25	Six	3435	↓	↓	↓	↓	↓	↓	↓	↓	↓	↓	↓	↓	↓	5	3
↓	50-27	Eight	3520	↓	↓	↓	↓	↓	↓	↓	↓	↓	↓	↓	↓	3.9	7	8

Appendix I. (continued)

Year	Series	Model	Dimensions					Track		Suspension		Transmission		Brakes		Axle Ratio	Engines	
			Curb Wt.	Wheel Base	Length	Width	Height	Front	Rear	Front	Rear	Std.	Opt.	Front	Rear		Std.	Opt.
1951	51-25	Six	3432	120	202.5	75.7	63.3	58.2	59	SLA, C	RA, SE	3M	HM	drum	drum	4.1	9	10
↓	51-27	Eight	3520	↓	↓	↓	↓	↓	↓	↓	↓	↓	↓	↓	↓	3.9	11	12
1952	52-25	Six	3440	↓	↓	↓	↓	↓	↓	↓	↓	↓	DRHM	↓	↓	4.1	13	14
↓	52-27	Eight	3525	↓	↓	↓	↓	↓	↓	↓	↓	↓	↓	↓	↓	3.9	15	16
1953	53-25	Six	3531	122	202.7	76.6	↓	58.5	↓	↓	↓	↓	↓	↓	↓	4.1	17	18
↓	53-27	Eight	3606	↓	↓	↓	↓	↓	↓	↓	↓	↓	↓	↓	↓	3.9	15	16
1954	54-25	Six	3541	↓	↓	↓	63.2	↓	↓	↓	↓	↓	↓	↓	↓	4.1	17	18
↓	54-27	Eight	3601	↓	↓	↓	↓	↓	↓	↓	↓	↓	↓	↓	↓	3.9	19	20
↓	54-28	Star Chief	3686	124	213.7	↓	↓	↓	↓	↓	↓	↓	↓	↓	↓	↓	↓	↓
1955	55-27	Chieftain	3661	122	203.2	75.4	60.5	58.7	↓	↓	↓	↓	↓	↓	↓	3.64	22	21,23
↓	55-28	Star Chief	3706	124	210.2	↓	↓	↓	↓	↓	↓	↓	↓	↓	↓	↓	↓	↓
1956	56-27	Chieftain	3646	122	205.6	75.1	↓	↓	↓	↓	↓	↓	↓	↓	↓	↓	24	25,26 27
↓	56-28	Star Chief	3711	124	212.6	↓	↓	↓	↓	↓	↓	↓	↓	↓	↓	↓	25	26,27
1957	57-27	Chieftain	3710	122	206.8	75.2	60.1	59	59.4	↓	↓	↓	↓	↓	↓	3.42	28	30,32 33
↓	↓	Super Chief	3735	↓	↓	↓	↓	↓	↓	↓	↓	↓	↓	↓	↓	↓	29	31,32 33
↓	↓	Safari	3995	↓	207.7	↓	60.7	↓	↓	↓	↓	↓	↓	↓	↓	3.64	29	31
↓	57-28	Star Chief	3780	124	213.8	↓	60.1	↓	↓	↓	↓	↓	↓	↓	↓	3.42	29	31,32 33
↓	↓	Bonneville	4225	↓	↓	↓	58.6	↓	↓	↓	↓	↓	↓	↓	↓	3.23	34	—
1958	58-27	Chieftain	3735	122	210.5	77.4	57.0	58.8	↓	↓	RA, C	↓	↓	↓	↓	3.42	35	37-42
↓	↓	Safari	4025	↓	↓	↓	58.7	↓	↓	↓	↓	↓	↓	↓	↓	3.64	↓	↓
↓	58-28	Super Chief	3770	124	215.5	77.4	57.0	↓	↓	↓	↓	↓	↓	↓	↓	3.42	↓	↓
↓	↓	Star Chief	3825	↓	↓	↓	↓	↓	↓	↓	↓	↓	↓	↓	↓	↓	36	38-42
↓	58-25	Bonneville	3740	122	211.7	77.4	55.6	↓	↓	↓	↓	↓	↓	↓	↓	↓	↓	↓
1959	59-21	Catalina	4103	↓	213.7	80.7	56.4	63.7	64	↓	↓	↓	SHM	↓	↓	3.23	43	45-50
↓	59-24	Star Chief	4153	124	220.7	↓	↓	↓	↓	↓	↓	↓	↓	↓	↓	↓	↓	↓
↓	59-27	Bonneville Safari	4512	122	214.3	↓	56.3	↓	↓	↓	↓	↓	↓	↓	↓	↓	44	46-50
↓	59-28	Bonneville	4233	124	220.7	↓	54.6	↓	↓	↓	↓	↓	↓	↓	↓	↓	↓	↓
1960	60-21	Catalina	4119	122	213.7	↓	56.4	64	↓	↓	↓	↓	HM	↓	↓	↓	50	51,52 54-58
↓	60-23	Ventura	4174	↓	↓	↓	54.6	↓	↓	↓	↓	↓	↓	↓	↓	↓	↓	↓
↓	60-24	Star Chief	4179	124	220.7	↓	56.6	↓	↓	↓	↓	↓	↓	↓	↓	↓	↓	↓

Appendix I. (continued)

Year	Series	Model	Dimensions					Track		Suspension		Transmission		Brakes		Axle Ratio	Engines	
			Curb Wt.	Wheel Base	Length	Width	Height	Front	Rear	Front	Rear	Std.	Opt.	Front	Rear		Std.	Opt.
1960	60-27	Bonneville Safari	4544	122	213.7	80.7	56.3	64	64	SLA, C	RA, C	3M	HM	drum	drum	3.23	52	51,53 55-58
↓	60-28	Bonneville	4249	124	220.7	↓	54.8	↓	↓	↓	↓	↓	↓	↓	↓	↓	↓	↓
1961	61-23	Catalina	3910	119	210	78.2	55.8	62.5	62.5	↓	↓	↓	HM,4M	↓	↓	↓	50	52, 57-61
↓	61-25	Ventura	3980	↓	↓	↓	↓	↓	↓	↓	↓	↓	↓	↓	↓	↓	↓	
↓	61-26	Star Chief	4025	123	217	↓	↓	↓	↓	↓	↓	↓	↓	↓	↓	↓	↓	52,54 55-59
↓	61-27	Bonneville Safari	4333	119	209.7	↓	57	↓	↓	↓	↓	↓	↓	↓	↓	↓	52	55-59
↓	61-28	Bonneville	4080	123	217	↓	55.8	↓	↓	↓	↓	↓	↓	↓	↓	↓	↓	↓
↓	61-21	Tempest	2914	112	189.3	72.2	53.5	56.8	56.8	↓	SA, C	↓	2A	↓	↓	3.55	62	63-67
1962	62-23	Catalina	3950	120	211.6	78.6	55.9	62.5	62.5	↓	RA, C	↓	HM,4M	↓	↓	3.23	50	52, 55-60
↓	62-26	Star Chief	4060	123	218.6	↓	↓	↓	↓	↓	↓	↓	↓	↓	↓	↓	↓	52, 54-60
↓	62-27	Bonneville Safari	4404	119	212.3	↓	57	↓	↓	↓	↓	↓	↓	↓	↓	↓	52	55-59
↓	62-28	Bonneville	4190	123	218.6	↓	55.9	↓	↓	↓	↓	↓	↓	↓	↓	↓	↓	↓
↓	62-29	Grand Prix	4020	120	211.6	↓	54.5	↓	↓	↓	↓	↓	↓	↓	↓	3.42	55	56-59
↓	62-21	Tempest	2930	112	189.3	72.2	53.6	56.8	56.8	↓	SA, C	↓	2A,4M	↓	↓	3.31	62	63,65 68-71
1963	63-21	Tempest	2985	↓	194.3	74.2	54	57.3	58	↓	↓	↓	↓	↓	↓	3.30	68	63,65 69,72 73
↓	63-22	Le Mans	3015	↓	↓	↓	53.6	↓	↓	↓	↓	↓	↓	↓	↓	↓	↓	
↓	63-23	Catalina	3948	120 ↓	212 ↓	78.7	55.2	62.5	64	↓	RA, C	↓	HM,4M	↓	↓	3.23	50	52,55 59,60 74-77
↓	63-26	Star Chief	4078	123	219	↓	↓	↓	↓	↓	↓	↓	↓	↓	↓	↓	↓	52,54 55,59 74-77
↓	63-28	Bonneville	4178	↓	↓	↓	54.4	↓	↓	↓	↓	↓	↓	↓	↓	↓	52	55,59 74-77
↓	63-29	Grand Prix	4108	120	212	↓	54.1	↓	↓	↓	↓	↓	↓	↓	↓	3.42	55	59, 74-77
1964	64-20	Tempest	3125	115	203	73.3	54	58	58	↓	↓	↓	2A,4M	↓	↓	3.08	78	79,80
↓	64-21	Tempest Custom	3145	↓	↓	↓	↓	↓	↓	↓	↓	↓	↓	↓	↓	↓	↓	↓
↓	64-22	Tempest Le Mans	3150	↓	↓	↓	↓	↓	↓	↓	↓	↓	↓	↓	↓	↓	↓	79-82
↓	64-23	Catalina	3963	120	213	79.2	55.8	63	64	↓	↓	↓	HM,4M	↓	↓	3.23	83	59,71, 84-90
↓	64-26	Star Chief	4078	123	220	↓	↓	↓	↓	↓	↓	↓	↓	↓	↓	↓	↓	59,77, 85-90

Year	Series	Model	Dimensions					Track		Suspension		Transmission		Brakes		Axle Ratio	Engines	
			Curb Wt.	Wheel Base	Length	Width	Height	Front	Rear	Front	Rear	Std.	Opt.	Front	Rear		Std.	Opt.
1964	64–28	Bonneville	4188	123	220	79.2	55.2	63	64	SLA, C	RA, C	3M	HM,4M	drum	drum	3.23	87	59,77, 86,88 89,90
↓	64–29	Grand Prix	4123	120	213	↓	54.6	↓	↓	↓	↓	↓	↓	↓	↓	↓	↓	
1965	233	Tempest	3120	115	206.1	73.1	54	58	58	↓	↓	↓	2A,4M	↓	↓	3.08	78	91,92
↓	235	Tempest Custom	3146	↓	↓	↓	↓	↓	↓	↓	↓	↓	↓	↓	↓	↓	↓	↓
↓	237	Le Mans	3178	↓	↓	↓	↓	↓	↓	↓	↓	↓	↓	↓	↓	↓	↓	91-94
↓	252	Catalina	3973	121	214.6	79.6	55.2	63	64	↓	↓	↓	THM, 4M	↓	↓	3.23	95	96-102
↓	256	Star Chief	4059	124	221.7	↓	↓	↓	↓	↓	↓	↓	↓	↓	↓	↓	↓	
↓	262	Bonneville	4194	↓	↓	↓	54.3	↓	↓	↓	↓	↓	↓	↓	↓	↓	98	95,97 99-102
↓	266	Grand Prix	4110	121	214.6	↓	53.9	↓	↓	↓	↓	↓	↓	↓	↓	↓	↓	
1966	233	Tempest	3234	115	206.4	74.4	54.4	58	59	↓	↓	↓	2A,4M	↓	↓	3.08	103	91,92 104
↓	235	Tempest Custom	3259	↓	↓	↓	↓	↓	↓	↓	↓	↓	↓	↓	↓	↓	↓	↓
↓	237	Le Mans	3354	↓	↓	↓	54.8	↓	↓	↓	↓	↓	↓	↓	↓	↓	↓	↓
↓	242	GTO	3618	↓	↓	↓	54.2	↓	↓	↓	↓	↓	↓	↓	↓	3.55	93	94
↓	252	Catalina	3988	121	214.8	79.7	55.3	63	64	↓	↓	↓	THM, 4M	↓	↓	3.23	95	96-98 100-102
↓	256	Star Chief Executive	4070	124	221.8	↓	↓	↓	↓	↓	↓	↓	↓	↓	↓	↓	↓	
↓	254	2 + 2	4206	121	214.8	↓	54.1	↓	↓	↓	↓	↓	↓	↓	↓	3.42	100	101, 102
↓	262	Bonneville	4202	124	221.8	↓	54.3	↓	↓	↓	↓	↓	↓	↓	↓	3.23	98	97, 100-102
↓	266	Grand Prix	4120	121	214.8	↓	53.9	↓	↓	↓	↓	↓	↓	↓	↓	↓	↓	
1967	223	Firebird	3093	108 ↓	188.8 ↓	72.6 ↓	51.5 ↓	59 ↓	60 ↓	↓	RA, SE ↓	↓	2A, THM, 4M	↓	↓	3.08	103	91,92 105, 106
↓	233	Tempest	3287	115	206.6	74.4	55	58	59	↓	RA, C	↓	2A,4M	↓	↓	↓	↓	91, 92, 105
↓	235	Tempest Custom	3304	↓	↓	↓	↓	↓	↓	↓	↓	↓	↓	↓	↓	↓	↓	↓
↓	237	Le Mans	3418	↓	↓	74.7	↓	↓	↓	↓	↓	↓	↓	↓	↓	↓	↓	↓
↓	239	Tempest Safari	3664	↓	203.4	74.4	55.4	↓	↓	↓	↓	↓	↓	↓	↓	3.36	↓	91, 105
↓	242	GTO	3673	↓	206.6 ↓	74.7 ↓	53.7 ↓	↓	↓	↓	↓	↓	THM, 4M	↓	↓	3.55 ↓	108 ↓	107, 109, 110
↓	252	Catalina	4024	121	215.6	79.7	55.3	63	64	↓	↓	↓	↓	↓	↓	3.23	111	112-114, 117, 118
↓	256	Executive	4154	124	222.6	↓	55.6	↓	↓	↓	↓	↓	↓	↓	↓	↓	↓	

Appendix I. (continued)

Year	Series	Model	Dimensions					Track		Suspension		Transmission		Brakes		Axle Ratio	Engines	
			Curb Wt.	Wheel Base	Length	Width	Height	Front	Rear	Front	Rear	Std.	Opt.	Front	Rear		Std.	Opt.
1967	262	Bonneville	4309	124	222.6	79.4	54.6	63	64	SLA, C	RA, C	3M	THM, 4M	drum	drum	3.23	114	111, 113, 117, 118
↓	266	Grand Prix	4204	121	215.6	↓	↓	↓	↓	↓	↓	↓	↓	↓	↓	↓	115	111, 116, 117, 118
1968	223	Firebird	3112	108.1	188.8	72.8	50	60	60	↓	RA, SE	↓	2A,4M THM	↓	↓	3.08	119	108, 120-122, 125, 126
↓	233	Tempest	3463	116	204.7	74.8	52.5	↓	↓	↓	RA, C	↓	↓	↓	↓	3.23	↓	120-122
↓	235	Tempest Custom	3493	↓	↓	↓	↓	↓	↓	↓	↓	↓	↓	↓	↓	↓	↓	↓
↓	237	Le Mans	3605	↓	↓	↓	52.3	↓	↓	↓	↓	↓	↓	↓	↓	↓	↓	↓
↓	239	Tempest Safari	3800	↓	211	↓	54.4	↓	↓	↓	↓	↓	↓	↓	↓	↓	↓	121
↓	242	GTO	3666	112	200.7	↓	52.2	↓	↓	↓	↓	↓	4M, THM	↓	↓	3.55	123	109-111, 124
↓	252	Catalina	4041	121	216.5	79.8	55.3	63	64	↓	↓	↓	↓	↓	↓	3.23	112	111, 127-129
↓	256	Executive	4162	124	223.5	↓	55.6	↓	↓	↓	↓	↓	↓	↓	↓	↓	↓	
↓	262	Bonneville	4322	↓	↓	↓	↓	↓	↓	↓	↓	↓	↓	↓	↓	↓	127	111, 128, 129
↓	266	Grand Prix	4217	121	216.3	↓	54.6	↓	↓	↓	↓	↓	↓	↓	↓	↓	115	
1969	233	Firebird	3120	108.1	191	73.9	49.6	60	60	↓	RA, SE	↓	4M,2A THM	↓	↓	3.23	119	120, 121, 125, 126, 130, 131, 133
↓	233	Tempest	3379	116	205.5	75.8	52.7	61	↓	↓	RA, C	↓	↓	↓	↓	↓	↓	120, 121, 130, 132
↓	235	Custom S	3391	↓	↓	↓	↓	↓	↓	↓	↓	↓	↓	↓	↓	↓	↓	
↓	237	Le Mans	3516	↓	↓	↓	52.6	↓	↓	↓	↓	↓	↓	↓	↓	↓	↓	
↓	239	Tempest Safari	3837	↓	211	76.3	54.3	↓	↓	↓	↓	↓	↓	↓	↓	↓	↓	121
↓	242	GTO	3672	112	201.2	75.8	52.3	↓	↓	↓	↓	↓	4M, THM	↓	↓	3.55	123	111, 124, 134
↓	252	Catalina	4144	122	217.5	79.8	54.8	64	64	↓	↓	↓	THM	↓	↓	3.23	112	111, 117, 127, 129
↓	256	Executive	4244	125	223.5	↓	55	↓	↓	↓	↓	↓	↓	↓	↓	↓	↓	

Year	Series	Model	Dimensions					Track		Suspension		Transmission		Brakes		Axle Ratio	Engines	
			Curb Wt.	Wheel Base	Length	Width	Height	Front	Rear	Front	Rear	Std.	Opt.	Front	Rear		Std.	Opt.
1969	262	Bonneville	4379	125	224	79.8	55	64	64	SLA, C	RA, C	3M	THM	drum	drum	3.23	117	111, 129
↓	276	Grand Prix	3885	118 ↓	210.2 ↓	75.7 ↓	52.1 ↓	62 ↓	60	↓	↓	↓	4M, THM	↓	↓	↓	115 ↓	111, 129, 135
1970	223	Firebird	3241	108	191.6	73.4	50.4	61.3	↓	↓	RA, SE	↓	2A, THM	↓	↓	3.08	136	137
↓	224	Esprit	3534	↓	↓	↓	↓	61.6	60.3	↓	↓	↓	4M,2A THM	↓	↓	3.36	137	138
↓	226	Formula 400	3571	↓	↓	↓	↓	↓	↓	↓	↓	↓	4M, THM	↓	↓	3.55	141	142
↓	228	Trans Am	3651	↓	↓	↓	↓	61.7	60.4	↓	↓	4M	THM	disc	↓	↓	142	—
↓	233	Tempest	3396	116	206.5	76.7	52.6	61	60	↓	RA, C	3M	4M,2A, THM	drum	↓	3.23	136	137, 138, 140
↓	235	Le Mans	3451	↓	↓	↓	↓	↓	↓	↓	↓	↓	↓	↓	↓	↓	↓	↓
↓	237	Le Mans Sport	3551	↓	↓	↓	↓	↓	↓	↓	↓	↓	↓	↓	↓	↓	↓	↓
↓	242	GTO	3781	112	202.9	↓	52	↓	↓	↓	↓	↓	4M, THM	↓	↓	3.55	143	144-146
↓	252	Catalina	4167	122 ↓	217.9 ↓	79.8	54.8 ↓	64	64	↓	↓	↓	THM	↓	↓	3.23	137 ↓	138-140, 146, 147
↓	256	Executive	4266	125	223.9 ↓	↓	55	↓	↓	↓	↓	↓	↓	↓	↓	↓	139 ↓	138, 140, 146, 147
↓	262	Bonneville	4358	↓	224.6	↓	↓	↓	↓	↓	↓	↓	↓	↓	↓	↓	146	138, 147
↓	276	Grand Prix	3936	118	210.2	75.7	52	62	60	↓	↓	↓	4M, THM	disc	↓	↓	143	↓
1971	223	Firebird	3240	108	191.6	73.4	50.4	61.3	↓	↓	RA, SE	↓	4M,2A, 3A	↓	↓	3.08	148	149
↓	224	Esprit	3495	↓	↓	↓	↓	↓	↓	↓	↓	↓	↓	↓	↓	3.42	149	150
↓	226	Formula 350	3550	↓	↓	↓	↓	61.6	60.3	↓	↓	↓	↓	↓	↓	↓	↓	—
↓		Formula 400	3595	↓	↓	↓	↓	↓	↓	↓	↓	↓	4M,3A	↓	↓	↓	151	—
↓		Formula 455	3680	↓	↓	↓	↓	↓	↓	↓	↓	3A	3M,4M	↓	↓	↓	152	153
↓	228	Trans Am	3695	↓	↓	↓	↓	61.7	60.4	↓	↓	3M	4M,3A	↓	↓	↓	153	—
↓	233	T-37	3402	116	206.8	76.7	52.6	61	60	↓	RA, C	↓	4M,2A, 3A	drum	↓	3.23	148	149, 150, 151, 152, 153
↓	235	Le Mans	3458	↓	↓	↓	↓	↓	↓	↓	↓	↓	↓	↓	↓	↓	↓	
↓	237	Le Mans Sport	3562	↓	↓	↓	↓	↓	↓	↓	↓	↓	↓	↓	↓	↓	↓	
↓	242	GTO	3788	112	203.3	↓	52	↓	↓	↓	↓	↓	4M,3A	↓	↓	3.55	151	152, 153

Appendix I. (continued)

Year	Series	Model	Dimensions					Track		Suspension		Transmission		Brakes		Axle Ratio	Engines	
			Curb Wt.	Wheel Base	Length	Width	Height	Front	Rear	Front	Rear	Std.	Opt.	Front	Rear		Std.	Opt.
1971	252	Catalina	4173	123.5	220.2	79.5	54.3	64	64	SLA, C	RA, C	3M	2A,3A	drum	drum	3.42	149	150, 151, 152, 155
↓	258	Catalina Brougham	4237	↓	↓	↓	↓	↓	↓	↓	↓	3A	3M	↓	↓	2.73	150 ↓	151, 152, 155
↓	262	Bonneville	4427	126	224.2	↓	54.4	↓	↓	↓	↓	↓	↓	↓	↓	↓	155	152
↓	268	Grand Ville	4455	↓	↓	↓	↓	↓	↓	↓	↓	↓	↓	↓	↓	3.08	152	—
↓	252	Safari	4856	127	230.2	↓	54.2	↓	↓	↓	RA, SE	3M	3A	↓	↓	3.23	149	150, 151, 152, 155
↓	262	Grand Safari	4977	↓	↓	↓	↓	↓	↓	↓	↓	3A	3M	↓	↓	3.08	155	152
↓	276	Grand Prix	3950	118	212	76.1	52	62	60	↓	RA, C	3M	4M,3A	disc	↓	3.23	151	↓
↓	2Y	Ventura II	3032	111	194.5	72.4	53.9	59	58.9	↓	RA, SE	↓	2A,3A	drum	↓	3.08	148	154
1972	2S	Firebird	3240	108	191.6	73.4	50.4	61.3	60	↓	↓	↓	2A, THM	disc	↓	↓	↓	157
↓	2T	Esprit	3490	↓	↓	↓	↓	↓	↓	↓	↓	↓	4M,2A, THM	↓	↓	3.42	157	158a
↓	2U	Formula 350	3563	↓	↓	↓	↓	61.6	60.3	↓	↓	↓	4M, THM	↓	↓	↓	↓	—
↓		Formula 400	3600	↓	↓	↓	↓	↓	↓	↓	↓	↓	↓	↓	↓	↓	159b	—
↓		Formula 455	3680	↓	↓	↓	↓	↓	↓	↓	↓	4M	THM	↓	↓	↓	162	—
↓	2V	Trans Am	3695	↓	↓	↓	↓	61.7	60.4	↓	↓	↓	↓	↓	↓	↓	↓	—
↓	2Y	Ventura II	3032	111	194.5	72.4	53.9	59	58.9	↓	↓	3M	2A, THM	drum	↓	3.08	148	156, 157a
↓	2D	Le Mans	3363	116	207.2	76.7	52.6	61	60	↓	RA, C	↓	4M,2A, THM	↓	↓	3.23	↓	157, 158, 159, 161, 162
↓	2G	Luxury Le Mans	3707	↓	↓	↓	↓	↓	↓	↓	↓	↓	↓	↓	↓	↓	157 ↓	158, 159, 161
↓	2L	Catalina	4309	123.5	221.3	79.3	54.2	64	64	↓	↓	THM	—	disc	↓	2.73	158	159, 160, 161
↓	2M	Catalina Brougham	4322	↓	↓	↓	54.3	↓	↓	↓	↓	↓	↓	↓	↓	↓	↓	
↓	2N	Bonneville	4388	126	225.3	↓	54.4	↓	↓	↓	↓	↓	↓	↓	↓	↓	160	161
↓	2P	Grand Ville	4438	↓	↓	↓	54.2	↓	↓	↓	↓	↓	↓	↓	↓	3.08	161	—
↓	2K	Grand Prix	3962	118	213.6	76.4	52	62	60	↓	↓	↓	↓	↓	↓	↓	159b	161b

Appendix I. (continued)

Year	Series	Model	Dimensions					Track		Suspension		Transmission		Brakes		Axle Ratio	Engines	
			Curb Wt.	Wheel Base	Length	Width	Height	Front	Rear	Front	Rear	Std.	Opt.	Front	Rear		Std.	Opt.
1973	2FS	Firebird	3248	108	192.1	73.4	50.4	61.3	60	SLA, C	RA, SE	3M	4M, THM	disc	drum	3.08	163	164
↓	2FT	Esprit	3511	↓	↓	↓	↓	↓	↓	↓	↓	↓	↓	↓	↓	↓	164	165a
↓	2FU	Formula 350	3528	↓	↓	↓	↓	61.6	60.3	↓	↓	↓	↓	↓	↓	↓	↓	—
↓		Formula 400	3580	↓	↓	↓	↓	↓	↓	↓	↓	4M	THM	↓	↓	3.42	166b	—
↓		Formula 455	3655	↓	↓	↓	↓	↓	↓	↓	↓	↓	↓	↓	↓	↓	167b	168
↓	2FV	Trans Am	3711	↓	↓	↓	↓	↓	↓	↓	↓	↓	↓	↓	↓	↓	↓	↓
↓	2XY	Ventura	3234	111	197.5	72.4	53.9	59.9	59.6	↓	↓	3M	4M,2A, THM	drum	↓	3.08	163	164
↓	2XZ	Ventura Custom	3267	↓	↓	↓	↓	↓	↓	↓	↓	↓	↓	↓	↓	↓	↓	↓
↓	2AD	Le Mans	3715	116	211.4	77.7	54.3	61.5	60.7	↓	RA, C	↓	4M, THM	disc	↓	3.23	↓	164-168
↓	2AF	Le Mans Sport Coupe	3633	112	207.4	↓	52.9	↓	↓	↓	↓	↓	↓	↓	↓	↓	↓	↓
↓	2AG	Luxury Le Mans	3977	116	211.4	↓	54.3	↓	↓	↓	↓	↓	↓	↓	↓	↓	164	165-167
↓	2AH	Grand Am	4150	↓	212.6	↓	↓	61.9	61.1	↓	↓	↓	↓	↓	↓	↓	165	166-168
↓	2BL	Catalina	4370	124	224.8	79.6	54.2	64.1	64	↓	↓	THM	—	↓	↓	3.08	164	165-167
↓	2BN	Bonneville	4469	↓	↓	↓	54.4	↓	↓	↓	↓	↓	↓	↓	↓	2.73	165	166, 167
↓	2BP	Grand Ville	4512	↓	↓	↓	53.8	↓	↓	↓	↓	↓	↓	↓	↓	2.93	167	—
↓	2GK	Grand Prix	4145	116	216.6	78.7	52.9	61.9	61.1	↓	↓	↓	↓	↓	↓	↓	166b	167b, 168
1974	2FS	Firebird	3390	108	196	73	49.2	61.3	60	↓	RA, SE	3M	4M, THM	↓	↓	3.08	163	169
↓	2FT	Esprit	3647	↓	↓	73.4	49.4	↓	↓	↓	↓	↓	↓	↓	↓	↓	169a	169b, 171
↓	2FU	Formula	3655	↓	↓	73	↓	61.6	60.3	↓	↓	↓	↓	↓	↓	↓	169b	167b, 171b, 172b, 173
↓	2FV	Trans Am	3762	↓	↓	73.2	49.6	61.7	60.4	↓	↓	4M	THM	↓	↓	3.42	172b	167b, 173
↓	2XY	Ventura	3276	111	199.4	72.5	53.1	59.9	59.6	↓	↓	3M	4M, THM	drum	↓	3.08	163	169, 170
↓	2XZ	Ventura Custom	3313	↓	↓	↓	↓	↓	↓	↓	↓	↓	↓	↓	↓	↓	↓	
↓	2AD	Le Mans	3628	116	212	77.9	52.9	61.5	60.7	↓	RA, C	↓	↓	disc	↓	3.23	↓	167b, 169, 170, 171, 172b
↓	2AF	Le Mans Sport Coupe	3580	112	208	↓	52.3	↓	↓	↓	↓	↓	↓	↓	↓	↓	↓	

Appendix I. (continued)

Year	Series	Model	Dimensions: Curb Wt.	Dimensions: Wheel Base	Dimensions: Length	Dimensions: Width	Dimensions: Height	Track: Front	Track: Rear	Suspension: Front	Suspension: Rear	Transmission: Std.	Transmission: Opt.	Brakes: Front	Brakes: Rear	Axle Ratio	Engines: Std.	Engines: Opt.
1974	2AG	Luxury Le Mans	3904	116	212	77.9	52.9	61.5	60.7	SLA, C	RA, C	3M	4M, THM	disc	drum	3.23	169b	167b, 169a, 170, 171, 172b
↓	2AD	Le Mans Safari	4333	↓	215.7	78	53.7	↓	↓	↓	↓	↓	↓	↓	↓	↓	169a	167b, 171, 172b
↓	2AH	Grand Am	4073	↓	214.9	77.3	52.9	61.9	61.1	↓	↓	THM	4M	↓	↓	2.93	171a	167b, 171b, 172b
↓	2BL	Catalina	4434	124	225.2	79.6	54	64.1	64	↓	↓	↓	—	↓	↓	↓	↓	167, 172a
↓	2BN	Bonneville	4524	↓	↓	↓	↓	↓	↓	↓	↓	↓	↓	↓	↓	↓	↓	↓
↓	2BP	Grand Ville	4655	↓	226	↓	↓	↓	↓	↓	↓	↓	↓	↓	↓	↓	167a	167b
↓	2BL	Catalina Safari	5089	127	230.6	↓	58.1	↓	↓	↓	RA, SE	↓	↓	↓	↓	3.08	171a	—
↓	2BP	Grand Safari	5127	↓	↓	↓	↓	↓	↓	↓	↓	↓	↓	↓	↓	↓	167a	↓
↓	2GK	Grand Prix	4096	116	217.5	77.9	52.6	61.9	61.1	↓	RA, C	↓	↓	↓	↓	2.93	172b	167b
1975	2FS	Firebird	3386	108	196	73	49.1	60.9	60	↓	RA, SE	3M	4M, THM	↓	↓	3.08	177	181, 182
↓	2FT	Esprit	3431	↓	↓	↓	49.4	↓	↓	↓	↓	↓	↓	↓	↓	↓	↓	↓
↓	2FU	Formula	3631	↓	↓	↓	↓	61.3	60.4	↓	↓	4M	THM	↓	↓	↓	182	184
↓	2FW	Trans Am	3716	↓	↓	↓	49.6	61.2	60.3	↓	↓	↓	↓	↓	↓	↓	184	—
↓	2HV	Astre	2492	97	175.4	65.4	50	54.7	53.6	↓	RA, C	3M	4M, THM	↓	↓	↓	174	175
↓	2HX	Astre SJ	2584	↓	176.4	↓	↓	↓	↓	↓	↓	4M	THM	↓	↓	↓	175	—
↓	2X	Ventura	3335	111	199.6	72.4	53.2	61.2	59	↓	RA, SE	3M	↓	↓	↓	↓	177	178, 179, 180
↓	2AD	Le Mans	3729	116	212	77.4	52.9	61.2	60.7	↓	RA, C	↓	↓	↓	↓	↓	↓	181, 182, 184
↓	2AF	Le Mans Sport Coupe	3688	112	208	↓	52.3	↓	↓	↓	↓	↓	↓	↓	↓	↓	↓	↓
↓	2AG	Grand Le Mans	3786	116	212	↓	52.9	↓	↓	↓	↓	↓	↓	↓	↓	↓	↓	↓
↓	2AD	Le Mans Safari	4401	↓	215.4	↓	53.7	61.6	61.1	↓	↓	THM	—	↓	↓	2.56	183	184
↓	2AH	Grand Am	4055	↓	215	77	↓	61.1	↓	↓	↓	↓	↓	↓	↓	↓	↓	184, 185
↓	2BL	Catalina	4347	123.4	226	79.6	54.2	63.8	64	↓	↓	↓	↓	↓	↓	↓	↓	↓
↓	2BP	Bonneville	4503	↓	↓	↓	↓	↓	↓	↓	↓	↓	↓	↓	↓	↓	↓	↓
↓	2BR	Grand Ville Brougham	4558	↓	↓	↓	↓	↓	↓	↓	↓	↓	↓	↓	↓	2.73	184	183, 185

Appendix I. (continued)

Year	Series	Model	Dimensions					Track		Suspension		Transmission		Brakes		Axle Ratio	Engines	
			Curb Wt.	Wheel Base	Length	Width	Height	Front	Rear	Front	Rear	Std.	Opt.	Front	Rear		Std.	Opt.
1975	2BL	Catalina Safari	4933	127	231.3	79.6	57.8	63.8	64	SLA, C	RA, SE	THM	—	disc	drum	2.73	184	185
↓	2BP	Grand Safari	5035	↓	↓	↓	↓	↓	↓	↓	↓	↓	↓	↓	↓	↓	↓	↓
↓	2GK	Grand Prix	4032	116	217.5	77.8	52.6	61.6	61.1	↓	RA, C	↓	↓	↓	↓	2.56	↓	↓
1976	2FS	Firebird	3493	108	196.8	73	49.1	60.9	60	↓	RA, SE	3M	4M, THM	↓	↓	2.73	191	184, 195, 196
↓	2FT	Esprit	3541	↓	↓	↓	49.4	↓	↓	↓	↓	↓		↓	↓	↓	↓	
↓	2FU	Formula	3735	↓	↓	↓	↓	61.3	60.4	↓	↓	THM	4M	↓	↓	2.41	195	184, 196
↓	2FW	Trans Am	3750	↓	↓	↓	49.6	61.2	60.3	↓	↓	4M	THM	↓	↓	3.08	184	185
↓	2HC	Astre	2519	97	177.6	65.4	51.8	55.2	54.1	↓	RA, C	3M	4M,5M, THM	↓	↓	2.92	186	187
↓	2HV	Astre Custom	2596	↓	↓	↓	↓	↓	↓	↓	↓	↓	↓	↓	↓	↓	↓	↓
↓	2HM	Sunbird	2733	↓	177.8	↓	49.8	↓	↓	↓	↓	↓	↓	↓	↓	↓	↓	188, 190
↓	2XY	Ventura	3381	111.1	199.6	72.4	53.2	61.8	59.6	↓	RA, SE	↓	5M, THM	↓	↓	2.73	191	192, 193, 194
↓	2XZ	Ventura SJ	3436	↓	↓	↓	↓	61.2	59	↓	↓	↓		↓	↓	↓	↓	
↓	2AD	Le Mans	3876	116	212	77.4	53.5	61.6	61.1	↓	RA, C	↓	THM	↓	↓	↓	↓	183, 184, 185, 192, 195, 196
↓	2AF	Le Mans Sport Coupe	3784	112	208	↓	52.7	↓	↓	↓	↓	↓	5M, THM	↓	↓	↓	↓	
↓	2AG	Grand Le Mans	3976	116	212	↓	53.5	↓	↓	↓	↓	THM	—	↓	↓	↓	↓	
↓	2AD	Le Mans Safari	4452	↓	215.4	↓	56.3	↓	↓	↓	↓	↓	↓	↓	↓	2.41	183	184, 185
↓	2BL	Catalina	4416	123.4	226	79.6	54.2	63.9	64	↓	↓	↓	↓	↓	↓	↓	↓	↓
↓	2BP	Bonneville	4600	↓	↓	↓	↓	↓	↓	↓	↓	↓	↓	↓	↓	↓	↓	↓
↓	2BR	Bonneville Brougham	4654	↓	↓	↓	↓	↓	↓	↓	↓	↓	↓	↓	↓	2.56	184	185
↓	2BL	Catalina Safari	5060	127	231.3	79.4	57.8	↓	↓	↓	RA, SE	↓	↓	↓	↓	↓	185	—
↓	2BP	Grand Safari	5151	↓	↓	↓	↓	↓	↓	↓	↓	↓	↓	↓	↓	↓	↓	↓
↓	2GJ	Grand Prix	4183	116	212.7	77.8	52.6	61.6	61.1	↓	RA, C	↓	↓	↓	↓	2.41	195	183, 184, 185
↓	2GK	Grand Prix SJ	4187	↓	↓	↓	↓	↓	↓	↓	↓	↓	↓	↓	↓	↓	184	183, 185
1977	2FS	Firebird	3374	108	196.8	73	49.1	60.9	60	↓	RA, SE	3M	4M, THM	↓	↓	3.08	199	200, 202, 203
↓	2FT	Esprit	3422	↓	↓	↓	49.4	↓	↓	↓	↓	↓		↓	↓	↓	↓	
↓	2FU	Firebird Formula	3521	↓	↓	↓	↓	61.3	60.4	↓	↓	4M	THM	↓	↓	3.23	200	202, 203,

Appendix I. (continued)

Year	Series	Model	Dimensions: Curb Wt.	Dimensions: Wheel Base	Dimensions: Length	Dimensions: Width	Dimensions: Height	Track: Front	Track: Rear	Suspension: Front	Suspension: Rear	Transmission: Std.	Transmission: Opt.	Brakes: Front	Brakes: Rear	Axle Ratio	Engines: Std.	Engines: Opt.
1977	2FU	Firebird Formula	3521	108	196.8	73	49.4 ↓	61.3 ↓	60.4 ↓	SLA, C	RA, SE	4M ↓	THM ↓	disc	drum	3.23 ↓	200 ↓	205, 206, 207
↓	2FW	Trans Am	3636	↓	↓	↓	49.6	61.2	60.3	↓	↓	THM	4M	↓	↓	2.41	205	206, 207
↓	2HC	Astre	2560	97	177.6	65.4	51.8	55.2	54.1	↓	RA, C	4M	5M, THM	↓	↓	2.92	197	198
↓	2HM	Sunbird	2742	↓	177.8	↓	49.8	↓	↓	↓	↓	↓	↓	↓	↓	2.73	198	197, 199
↓	2XY	Ventura	3277	111.1	199.3	72.4	53.2	61.8 ↓	59.6 ↓	↓	RA, SE	3M	4M, 5M, THM ↓	↓	↓	3.08	199	198, 200, 201, 203, 204
↓	2XZ	Ventura SJ	3346	↓	↓	↓	↓	61.2	59	↓	↓	↓	4M, THM ↓	↓	↓	↓	↓	200, 201, 203, 204
↓	2XY	Phoenix	3355	↓	203.4 ↓	↓	↓	↓	↓	↓	↓	↓	THM	↓	↓	↓	↓	198, 201, 203, 204
↓	2AD	Le Mans	3754	116	212	77.4	53.5	61.6	61.1	↓	RA, C	↓	↓	↓	↓	↓	↓	200, 202, 203, 205, 207
↓	2AF	Le Mans Sport Coupe	3674	112	208	↓	52.7	↓	↓	↓	↓	↓	↓	↓	↓	↓	↓	
↓	2AG	Grand Le Mans	3856	116	↓	↓	↓	↓	↓	↓	↓	↓	↓	↓	↓	↓	↓	
↓	2AD	Le Mans Safari	4251	↓	215.4 ↓	↓	55.3 ↓	↓	↓	↓	↓	THM	—	↓	↓	2.56 ↓	200 ↓	203, 205, 207
↓	2BL	Catalina	3611	115.9	214.3	75.7	53.2	61.7	60.7	↓	↓	↓	↓	↓	↓	2.73 ↓	199 ↓	200, 202, 203, 205, 207
↓	2BN	Bonneville	3726	↓	↓	↓	↓	↓	↓	↓	↓	↓	↓	↓	↓	2.41	200	202, 203, 205, 207
↓	2BQ	Bonneville Brougham	3790	↓	↓	↓	↓	↓	↓	↓	↓	↓	↓	↓	↓	↓	↓	
↓	2BL	Catalina Safari	4143	↓	214.7	↓	57.3	62.1	64.1	↓	↓	↓	↓	↓	↓	2.56	↓	205, 207
↓	2BN	Grand Safari	4182	↓	↓	↓	↓	↓	↓	↓	↓	↓	↓	↓	↓	↓	↓	
↓	2GJ	Grand Prix	3939	116	218.1	77.8	52.6	61.6	61.1	↓	↓	↓	↓	↓	↓	↓	↓	202, 203, 205, 207
↓	2GK	Grand Prix LJ	3950	↓	↓	↓	↓	↓	↓	↓	↓	↓	↓	↓	↓	↓	↓	
↓	2GH	Grand Prix SJ	4111	↓	↓	↓	↓	↓	↓	↓	↓	↓	↓	↓	↓	2.41	205	207
1978	2FS	Firebird	3364	108.2	196.8	73.4	49.3	61.3	60	↓	RA, SE	3M	4M, THM	↓	↓	3.08	210	213, 215
↓	2FT	Esprit	3395	↓	↓	↓	↓	↓	↓	↓	↓	↓		↓	↓	↓	↓	

Year	Series	Model	Dimensions					Track		Suspension		Transmission		Brakes		Axle Ratio	Engines	
			Curb Wt.	Wheel Base	Length	Width	Height	Front	Rear	Front	Rear	Std.	Opt.	Front	Rear		Std.	Opt.
1978	2FU	Firebird Formula	3652	108.2	196.8	73.4	49.5	61.6	60.3	SLA, C,	RA, SE	4M	THM	disc	drum	3.08	213	215, 219, 220, 221
↓	2FW	Trans Am	3621	↓	↓	↓	↓	↓	↓	↓	↓	THM	4M	↓	↓	2.56	219	220, 221
↓	2HE	Sunbird	2742	97	117.8	65.4	49.6	55.3	54.1	↓	RA, C	4M	5M, THM	↓	↓	2.73	208	210, 213
↓	2HM	Sunbird Sport		↓	↓	↓	↓	↓	↓	↓	↓	↓		↓	↓	↓	↓	
↓	2XY	Phoenix	3279	111.1	203.4	73.2	53.2	61.8	59.6	↓	RA, SE	3M	4M, 5M, THM	↓	↓	3.08	210	208, 213, 216
↓	2XZ	Phoenix LJ	3387	↓	↓	↓	↓	↓	↓	↓	↓	↓		↓	↓	↓	↓	
↓	2AD	Le Mans	3137	108.1	198.5	72.4	54.4	58.5	57.8	↓	RA, C	↓	4M, THM	↓	↓	2.93	↓	213
↓	2AF	Grand Le Mans	3188	↓	↓	↓	↓	↓	↓	↓	↓	↓		↓	↓	↓	↓	↓
↓	2AG	Grand Am	3328	↓	↓	↓	↓	↓	58	↓	↓	THM	—	↓	↓	2.29	211	212, 213
↓	2AD	Le Mans Safari	3314	↓	197.8	72.6	54.8	↓	↓	↓	↓	↓	↓	↓	↓	2.73	210	213, 215
↓	2BL	Catalina	3580	115.9	214.3	78	54.5	61.7	60.7	↓	↓	↓	↓	↓	↓	↓	211, 217, 218, 219, 221	
↓	2BN	Bonneville	3748	↓	↓	↓	↓	↓	↓	↓	↓	↓	↓	↓	↓	2.41	211	217, 218, 219, 221
↓	2BQ	Bonneville Brougham	3778	↓	↓	↓	↓	↓	↓	↓	↓	↓	↓	↓	↓	↓	↓	↓
↓	2BL	Catalina Safari	4097	↓	215.1	80	57.3	62.1	64.1	↓	↓	↓	↓	↓	↓	2.56	↓	↓
↓	2BN	Grand Safari	4122	↓	↓	↓	↓	↓	↓	↓	↓	↓	↓	↓	↓	↓	↓	↓
↓	2GJ	Grand Prix	3190	108.1	201.2	72.8	53.3	58.5	57.8	↓	↓	3M	THM	↓	↓	2.93	210	211, 213
↓	2GK	Grand Prix LJ	3306	↓	↓	↓	↓	↓	↓	↓	↓	THM	—	↓	↓	2.29	211	212, 213
↓	2GH	Grand Prix SJ	3319	↓	↓	↓	↓	↓	↓	↓	↓	↓	↓	↓	↓	2.41	212	213
1979	2FS	Firebird	3368	108.2	198.1	73	49.3	61.3	60	↓	RA, SE	3M	4M, THM	↓	↓	3.08	223	224, 225, 226, 229
↓	2FT	Esprit	3377	↓	↓	↓	↓	↓	↓	↓	↓	↓	↓	↓	↓	↓	↓	
↓	2FU	Firebird Formula	3466	↓	↓	↓	↓	↓	↓	↓	↓	THM	4M	↓	↓	2.41	224	220, 221, 225, 226, 229
↓	2FW	Trans Am	3601	↓	↓	↓	↓	↓	↓	↓	↓	↓	↓	↓	↓	↓	221	220, 225
↓	2HE	Sunbird	2694	97	179.2	65.4	49.6	55.3	54.1	↓	RA, C	4M	5M	↓	↓	2.73	222	209

Appendix I. (continued)

Year	Series	Model	Dimensions: Curb Wt.	Dimensions: Wheel Base	Dimensions: Length	Dimensions: Width	Dimensions: Height	Track: Front	Track: Rear	Suspension: Front	Suspension: Rear	Transmission: Std.	Transmission: Opt.	Brakes: Front	Brakes: Rear	Axle Ratio	Engines: Std.	Engines: Opt.
1979	2HM	Sunbird Sport	2700	97	179.2	65.4	49.6	55.3	54.1	SLA, C	RA, C	4M	THM	disc	drum	2.73	222	223, 226
↓		Sunbird Sport Safari	2736	↓	178	↓	51.8	↓	↓	↓	↓	↓	↓	↓	↓	↓	↓	209, 223
↓	2XY	Phoenix	3288	111.1	203.4	72.4	53.2	61.9	59.6	↓	RA, SE	3M	4M, THM	↓	↓	3.08	223	226, 229
↓	2XZ	Phoenix LJ	3396	↓	↓	↓	↓	↓	↓	↓	↓	↓		↓	↓	↓	↓	
↓	2AD	Le Mans	3135	108.1	198.6	↓	54.4	58.5	57.8	↓	RA, C	↓	↓	↓	↓	2.93	↓	224, 225, 228
↓	2AF	Grand Le Mans	3180	↓	↓	↓	↓	↓	↓	↓	↓	↓	↓	↓	↓	↓	↓	
↓	2AG	Grand Am	3178	↓	↓	↓	↓	↓	↓	↓	↓	↓	↓	↓	↓	↓	↓	224, 225
↓	2AD	Le Mans Safari	3300	↓	197.8	72.4	54.8	↓	58	↓	↓	THM	—	↓	↓	2.73	↓	224, 225, 228, 229
↓	2BL	Catalina	3617	116	214.3	76.4	54.9	61.7	60.7	↓	↓	↓	↓	↓	↓	↓	↓	217, 218, 221, 224, 225
↓	2BN	Bonneville	3782	↓	↓	↓	↓	↓	↓	↓	↓	↓	↓	↓	↓	2.29	224	217, 218, 221, 225
↓	2BQ	Bonneville Brougham	3850	↓	↓	↓	↓	↓	↓	↓	↓	↓	↓	↓	↓	↓	↓	
↓	2BL	Catalina Safari	4134	↓	215.1	79.9	57.3	62	64.1	↓	↓	↓	↓	↓	↓	2.56	↓	↓
↓	2BN	Bonneville Safari	4140	↓	↓	↓	↓	↓	↓	↓	↓	↓	↓	↓	↓	↓	↓	↓
↓	2GJ	Grand Prix	3168	108.1	201.4	72.7	53.3	58.5	57.8	↓	↓	3M	4M, THM	↓	↓	2.93	223	224, 225, 228
↓	2GK	Grand Prix LJ	3246	↓	↓	↓	↓	↓	↓	↓	↓	THM	3M,4M	↓	↓	2.14	224	223, 225, 228
↓	2GH	Grand Prix SJ	3307	↓	↓	↓	↓	↓	↓	↓	↓	↓	4M	↓	↓	2.29	225	228
1980	2FS	Firebird	3379	108.2	198.1	73	50.3	61.3	60	↓	RA, SE	3M	THM	↓	↓	3.08	223	225, 234, 237
↓	2FT	Esprit	3414	↓	↓	↓	↓	↓	↓	↓	↓	↓	↓	↓	↓	↓	↓	
↓	2FV	Firebird Formula	3521	↓	↓	↓	↓	↓	↓	↓	↓	THM	4M	↓	↓	2.41	225	235, 236, 237
↓	2FW	Trans Am	3540	↓	↓	↓	↓	↓	↓	↓	↓	↓	↓	↓	↓	↓	↓	
↓	2HE	Sunbird	2698	97	179.2	65.4	50.5	55.3	55.1	↓	RA, C	4M	THM	↓	↓	2.73	230	223
↓	2HM	Sunbird Sport	2704	↓	↓	↓	↓	↓	↓	↓	↓	↓	↓	↓	↓	↓	↓	↓
↓	2XY	Phoenix	2527	104.9	182.1	69.1	53.5	58.7	57	MS, C	TA, C	↓	↓	↓	↓	3.34	231	232

Appendix I. (continued)

Year	Series	Model	Dimensions					Track		Suspension		Transmission		Brakes		Axle Ratio	Engines	
			Curb Wt.	Wheel Base	Length	Width	Height	Front	Rear	Front	Rear	Std.	Opt.	Front	Rear		Std.	Opt.
1980	2XZ	Phoenix LJ	2559	104.9	182.1	69.1	53.5	58.7	57	MS, C	TA, C	4M	THM	disc	drum	3.34	231	232
	2AD	Le Mans	3131	108.1	198.6	72.4	55.6	58.5	57.8	SLA, C	RA, C	3M				2.93	233	225, 234
	2AF	Grand Le Mans	3182															
	2AG	Grand Am	3424									THM	—				235	—
	2AD	Le Mans Safari	3325		197.8	72.6	55.9		58							2.73	233	225, 234
	2AF	Grand Le Mans Safari	3358															
	2BL	Catalina	3528	116	214.3	76.4	56.7	61.7	60.7								223	
	2BN	Bonneville	3586															
	2BR	Bonneville Brougham	3748													2.56	234	225, 239
	2BL	Catalina Safari	4038		216	79.9	57.1	62	64.1								225	218, 239
	2BN	Bonneville Safari	4058															
	2GJ	Grand Prix	3232	108.1	201.4	72.7	54.5	58.5	57.8							2.41	223	225, 234
	2GK	Grand Prix LJ	3372															
	2GH	Grand Prix SJ	3384													2.93	235	—
1981	2FS	Firebird	3385	108.2	198.1	73	50.3	61.3	60		RA, SE	3M	3A			3.08	242	225, 234
	2FT	Esprit	3423															
	2FV	Firebird Formula	3507									3A	4M			2.41	234	225, 244, 245
	2FW	Trans Am	3529													3.08	225	244, 245
	2XY	Phoenix	2518	104.9	182.1	69.1	53.5	58.7	57	MS, C	TA, C	4M	3A			3.32	240	241
	2XZ	Phoenix LJ	2559															
	2AD	Le Mans	3093	108.1	198.5	71.9	55.8	58.5	57.8	SLA, C	RA, C	3M				3.08	242	234
	2AF	Grand Le Mans	3147															
	2AD	Le Mans Safari	3308		197.8		56.1					3A	—			3.23		234, 243
	2AF	Grand Le Mans Safari	3342															
	2BL	Catalina	2977	116	214	76.4	56.7	61.7	60.7				4A					234, 246, 247
	2BN	Bonneville	3022															
	2BR	Bonneville Brougham	3053															

Appendix I. (continued)

Year	Series	Model	Dimensions					Track		Suspension		Transmission		Brakes		Axle Ratio	Engines	
			Curb Wt.	Wheel Base	Length	Width	Height	Front	Rear	Front	Rear	Std.	Opt.	Front	Rear		Std.	Opt.
1981	2BL	Catalina Safari	3388	116	216.7	79.9	57.1	62.1	64.1	SLA, C	RA, C	4A	3A	disc	drum	3.23	246	247
↓	2BN	Bonneville Safari	3413	↓	↓	↓	↓	↓	↓	↓	↓	↓	↓	↓	↓	↓	↓	↓
↓	2AJ	Grand Prix	3259	108.1	201.8	72.1	54.7	58.5	57.8	↓	↓	3A	—	↓	↓	3.08	242	234, 247
↓	2AK	Grand Prix LJ	3288	↓	↓	↓	↓	↓	↓	↓	↓	↓	↓	↓	↓	↓	↓	↓
↓	2AH	Grand Prix Brougham	3317	↓	↓	↓	↓	↓	↓	↓	↓	↓	↓	↓	↓	↓	↓	↓
1982	2TM	T1000	2133	97.1	164.7	61.8	52.9	51.2	51.2	↓	↓	4M	5M, 3A	↓	↓	3.36	248	—
↓	2JB	J2000	2432	101.2	175.7	66.2	53.6	55.4	55.2	MS, C	TA, C	↓	↓	↓	↓	3.32	250	249
↓	2JC	J2000 LE	2441	↓	↓	↓	↓	↓	↓	↓	↓	↓	↓	↓	↓	↓	↓	↓
↓	2JD	J2000 SE	2447	↓	↓	↓	↓	↓	↓	↓	↓	↓	↓	↓	↓	3.65	↓	↓
↓	2AF	6000	2731	104.9	188.8	72	53.7	58.7	57	↓	↓	3A	—	↓	↓	2.39	251	241, 256
↓	2AG	6000 LE	2738	↓	↓	↓	↓	↓	↓	↓	↓	↓	↓	↓	↓	↓	↓	↓
↓	2XY	Phoenix	2550	↓	179.3	69.1	53.4	↓	↓	↓	↓	4M	3A	↓	↓	3.32	↓	241
↓	2XZ	Phoenix LJ	2593	↓	↓	↓	↓	↓	↓	↓	↓	↓	↓	↓	↓	↓	↓	↓
↓	2XT	Phoenix SJ	2683	↓	↓	↓	↓	↓	↓	↓	↓	↓	↓	↓	↓	3.65	253	—
↓	2GN	Bonneville Model G	3296	108.1	198.5	71.6	55.8	58.5	57.8	SLA,C	RA, C	3A	—	↓	↓	2.41	242	247, 255
↓	2GR	Bonneville Model G Brougham	3321	↓	↓	↓	↓	↓	↓	↓	↓	↓	↓	↓	↓	↓	↓	↓
↓	2GN	Bonneville Model G Wagon	3468	↓	197.8	71.2	56.1	↓	58	↓	↓	↓	↓	↓	↓	↓	↓	247
↓	2GJ	Grand Prix	3320	↓	201.9	72.3	54.7	↓	57.8	↓	↓	↓	↓	↓	↓	↓	↓	247, 255
↓	2GK	Grand Prix LJ	3331	↓	↓	↓	↓	↓	↓	↓	↓	↓	↓	↓	↓	↓	↓	↓
↓	2GP	Grand Prix Brougham	3372	↓	↓	↓	↓	↓	↓	↓	↓	↓	↓	↓	↓	↓	↓	↓
↓	2FS	Firebird	2864	101	190.3	72.4	49.8	60.7	61.6	MS, C	↓	4M	3A	↓	↓	3.42	252	254
↓	2FX	Firebird S/E	2946	↓	↓	↓	↓	↓	↓	↓	↓	↓	↓	↓	↓	3.23	254	245, 252
↓	2FW	Trans Am	3171	↓	↓	↓	↓	↓	↓	↓	↓	↓	↓	↓	↓	↓	245	257
1983	2TL	1000	2137	97.1	164.7	61.8	52.8	51.2	51.2	SLA, C	↓	↓	5M,3A	↓	↓	3.36	258	—
↓	2JB	2000	2413	101.2	175.7	66.2	53.6	55.4	55.2	MS, C	TA, C	5M	3A,4M	↓	↓	3.83	249	259
↓	2JC	2000 LE	2437	↓	↓	↓	↓	↓	↓	↓	↓	↓	↓	↓	↓	↓	↓	↓
↓	2JD	2000 SE	2471	↓	173.7	66.6	51.7	↓	↓	↓	↓	↓	↓	↓	↓	3.19	↓	↓
↓	2AF	6000	2735	104.9	188.8	72	53.7	58.7	57	↓	↓	3A	—	↓	↓	2.39	260	241, 256

Appendix I. (continued)

Year	Series	Model	Dimensions					Track		Suspension		Transmission		Brakes		Axle Ratio	Engines	
			Curb Wt.	Wheel Base	Length	Width	Height	Front	Rear	Front	Rear	Std.	Opt.	Front	Rear		Std.	Opt.
1983	2AG	6000 LE	2749	104.9	188.8	72	53.7	58.7	57	MS, C	TA, C	3A	—	disc	drum	2.39	260	256
↓	2AH	6000 STE	2965	↓	↓	↓	↓	↓	↓	↓	↓	↓	↓	↓	↓	3.33	253	—
↓	2XY	Phoenix	2531	↓	183.1	69.1	53.3	↓	↓	↓	↓	4M	3A	↓	↓	3.32	260	241
↓	2XZ	Phoenix LJ	2580	↓	↓	↓	↓	↓	↓	↓	↓	↓	↓	↓	↓	↓	↓	↓
↓	2XT	Phoenix SJ	2670	↓	↓	↓	↓	↓	↓	↓	↓	↓	↓	↓	↓	3.65	253	—
↓	2N	Bonneville	3297	108.1	198.5	71.6	55.8	58.5	57.8	SLA, C	RA, C	3A	—	↓	↓	2.41	242	245, 247
↓	2R	Bonneville Brougham	3321	↓	↓	↓	↓	↓	↓	↓	↓	↓	↓	↓	↓	↓	↓	↓
↓	2N	Bonneville Wagon	3468	↓	197.8	71.2	56.1	↓	58	↓	↓	↓	↓	↓	↓	2.73	↓	↓
↓	2J	Grand Prix	3321	↓	201.9	72.3	54.7	↓	57.8	↓	↓	↓	↓	↓	↓	2.41	↓	↓
↓	2K	Grand Prix LJ	3331	↓	↓	↓	↓	↓	↓	↓	↓	↓	↓	↓	↓	↓	↓	↓
↓	2P	Grand Prix Brougham	3372	↓	↓	↓	↓	↓	↓	↓	↓	↓	↓	↓	↓	↓	↓	↓
↓	2FS	Firebird	2867	101	189.9	72.4	49.7	60.7	61.6	MS, C	↓	4M	5M,3A, 4A	↓	↓	3.42	252	245, 254
↓	2FX	Firebird S/E	2966	↓	↓	↓	↓	↓	↓	↓	↓	5M	3A,4A	↓	↓	3.73	261	245, 252
↓	2FW	Trans Am	3108	↓	↓	↓	↓	↓	↓	↓	↓	↓	4A	↓	↓	↓	245	257, 262
↓	2BL	Parisienne	3482	116	212	75.3	56.4	61.7	60.7	SLA, C	↓	3A	↓	↓	↓	2.73	233	245, 247
↓	2BT	Parisienne Brougham	3530	↓	↓	↓	↓	↓	↓	↓	↓	↓	↓	↓	↓	↓	↓	↓
↓		Parisienne Brougham Wagon	4128	↓	215	79.3	58.1	62.2	64.1	↓	↓	4A	3A	↓	↓	↓	245	247
1984	2TL	1000	2138	97.3	164.8	61.8	52.8	51.2	51.2	↓	↓	4M	5M,3A	↓	↓	3.36	258	—
↓	2JB	2000 Sunbird	2406	101.2	175.4	66.2	53.8	55.4	55.2	MS, C	TA, C	5M	4M,3A	↓	↓	3.45	249	259, 263
↓	2JC	2000 Sunbird LE	2436	↓	↓	↓	↓	↓	↓	↓	↓	↓	↓	↓	↓	↓	↓	↓
↓	2JD	2000 Sunbird S/E	2528	↓	↓	↓	↓	↓	↓	↓	↓	4M	3A	↓	↓	3.65	263	—
↓	2AF	6000	2748	104.9	188.8	72	53.7	58.7	57	↓	↓	3A	—	↓	↓	2.39	264	241, 256
↓	2AG	6000 LE	2772	↓	↓	↓	↓	↓	↓	↓	↓	↓	↓	↓	↓	2.84	↓	
↓	2AH	6000 STE	2990	↓	↓	↓	↓	↓	↓	↓	↓	↓	↓	↓	disc	3.33	253	—
↓	2XY	Phoenix	2554	↓	183.1	69.1	53.1	↓	↓	↓	↓	4M	3A	↓	drum	3.32	264	241, 253
↓	2XZ	Phoenix LE	2573	↓	↓	↓	↓	↓	↓	↓	↓	↓	↓	↓	↓	↓	↓	
↓	2XT	Phoenix SE	2681	↓	182.1	↓	53.3	↓	↓	↓	↓	↓	↓	↓	↓	3.65	253	—

Appendix I. (continued)

Year	Series	Model	Dimensions					Track		Suspension		Transmission		Brakes		Axle Ratio	Engines	
			Curb Wt.	Wheel Base	Length	Width	Height	Front	Rear	Front	Rear	Std.	Opt.	Front	Rear		Std.	Opt.
1984	2GN	Bonneville	3155	108.1	200.2	71.6	55.8	58.5	57.8	SLA, C	RA, C	3A	4A	disc	drum	2.41	242	247, 267
↓	2GS	Bonneville LE	3164	↓	↓	↓	↓	↓	↓	↓	↓	↓	↓	↓	↓	↓	↓	↓
↓	2GR	Bonneville Brougham	3176	↓	↓	↓	↓	↓	↓	↓	↓	↓	↓	↓	↓	↓	↓	↓
↓	2GJ	Grand Prix	3207	↓	201.9	72.3	54.7	↓	↓	↓	↓	↓	↓	↓	↓	↓	↓	↓
↓	2GK	Grand Prix LE	3227	↓	↓	↓	↓	↓	↓	↓	↓	↓	↓	↓	↓	↓	↓	↓
↓	2GP	Grand Prix Brougham	3265	↓	↓	↓	↓	↓	↓	↓	↓	↓	↓	↓	↓	↓	↓	↓
↓	2FS	Firebird	2859	101	189.9	72.4	49.7	60.7	61.6	MS, C	↓	4M	5M,4A	↓	↓	3.42	265	254, 267
↓	2FX	Firebird S/E	2915	↓	↓	↓	↓	↓	↓	↓	↓	5M	4A	↓	↓	3.23	266	265, 267
↓	2FW	Trans Am	3191	↓	↓	↓	↓	↓	↓	↓	↓	↓	↓	↓	↓	3.73	267	262
↓	2BL	Parisienne	3484	116	212.2	75.3	56.4	61.8	60.8	SLA, C	↓	3A	↓	↓	↓	2.73	242	247, 267
↓	2BT	Parisienne Brougham	3531	↓	↓	↓	↓	↓	↓	↓	↓	↓	↓	↓	↓	↓	↓	↓
↓	2BL	Parisienne Wagon	4080	↓	215.1	79.3	58.1	62.2	64.1	↓	↓	4A	—	↓	↓	↓	267	247
↓	2PM	Fiero	2459	93.4	160.7	68.9	46.9	57.8	58.7	↓	MS, C	4M	3A	↓	disc	4.10	264	—
↓	2PF	Fiero SE	2461	↓	↓	↓	↓	↓	↓	↓	↓	↓	↓	↓	↓	↓	↓	↓
1985	2TL	1000	2142	97.3	164.8	61.8	52.8	51.2	51.2	↓	RA, C	↓	5M,3A	↓	drum	3.36	258	↓
↓	2JB	Sunbird	2371	101.2	175.7	66.2	53.8	55.5	55.1	MS, C	↓	5M	3A	↓	↓	3.45	249	263
↓	2JC	Sunbird LE	2435	↓	↓	↓	↓	↓	↓	↓	↓	↓	↓	↓	↓	↓	↓	↓
↓	2JD	Sunbird S/E	2478	↓	↓	↓	↓	↓	↓	↓	↓	4M	↓	↓	↓	4.10	263	—
↓	2AF	6000	2776	104.9	188.8	72	53.7	58.7	57	↓	↓	3A	—	↓	↓	2.39	264	256, 269, 270
↓	2AG	6000 LE	2799	↓	↓	↓	↓	↓	↓	↓	↓	↓	↓	↓	↓	2.84	↓	
↓	2AH	6000 STE	3065	↓	↓	↓	↓	↓	↓	↓	↓	↓	↓	↓	disc	3.18	270	—
↓	2GN	Bonneville	3217	108.1	200.2	71.6	55.8	58.5	57.8	SLA, C	↓	↓	4A	↓	drum	2.41	242	275
↓	2GS	Bonneville LE	3231	↓	↓	↓	↓	↓	↓	↓	↓	↓	↓	↓	↓	↓	↓	↓
↓	2GR	Bonneville Brougham	3259	↓	↓	↓	↓	↓	↓	↓	↓	↓	↓	↓	↓	↓	↓	↓
↓	2PE	Fiero Coupe	2505	93.4	160.7	69	46.9	57.8	58.7	↓	MS, C	5M	3A	↓	disc	3.35	264	272
↓	2PM	Fiero Sport Coupe		↓	↓	↓	↓	↓	↓	↓	↓	↓	↓	↓	↓	↓	↓	↓
↓	2PF	Fiero SE		↓	↓	↓	↓	↓	↓	↓	↓	↓	↓	↓	↓	3.18	↓	↓
↓	2PG	Fiero GT	2572	↓	165.8	↓	↓	58.4	59.3	↓	↓	4M	↓	↓	↓	3.65	272	—

Appendix I. (continued)

Year	Series	Model	Dimensions					Track		Suspension		Transmission		Brakes		Axle Ratio	Engines	
			Curb Wt.	Wheel Base	Length	Width	Height	Front	Rear	Front	Rear	Std.	Opt.	Front	Rear		Std.	Opt.
1985	2FS	Firebird	2868	101	190.5	72.4	49.7	60.7	61.6	MS, C	RA, C	5M	4A	disc	drum	3.73	265	271, 275
↓	2FX	Firebird SE	2991	↓	↓	↓	↓	↓	↓	↓	↓	↓	↓	↓	↓	3.42	271	275
↓	2FW	Trans Am	3212	↓	191.8	↓	↓	↓	↓	↓	↓	↓	↓	↓	↓	3.27	275	262, 277
↓	2NE	Grand Am	2488	103.4	177.5	66.9	52.5	55.6	55.1	↓	↓	↓	3A	↓	↓	3.35	268	273
↓	2NV	Grand Am LE	2516	↓	↓	67.5	↓	↓	↓	↓	↓	↓	↓	↓	↓	2.84	↓	↓
↓	2GJ	Grand Prix	3231	108.1	201.9	72.3	54.7	58.5	57.8	SLA, C	↓	3A	—	↓	↓	2.41	242	275
↓	2GK	Grand Prix LE	3252	↓	↓	↓	↓	↓	↓	↓	↓	↓	↓	↓	↓	↓	↓	↓
↓	2GP	Grand Prix Brougham	3270	↓	↓	↓	↓	↓	↓	↓	↓	↓	↓	↓	↓	↓	↓	↓
↓	2BL	Parisienne	3485	116	212.3	75.3	56.6	61.8	60.8	↓	↓	↓	4A	↓	↓	2.56	274	247, 276
↓	2BT	Parisienne Brougham	3513	↓	↓	↓	↓	↓	↓	↓	↓	↓	↓	↓	↓	↓	↓	↓
1986	2TL	1000	2174	97.3	164.9	61.8	52.8	51.2	51.2	↓	↓	4M	5M,3A	↓	↓	3.36	258	—
↓	2JB	Sunbird	2404	101.2	175.7	66.3	53.8	55.6	55.2	MS, C	↓	5M	4M,3A	↓	↓	3.45	249	263
↓	2JD	Sunbird SE	2353	↓	↓	↓	↓	↓	↓	↓	↓	↓	↓	↓	↓	↓	↓	↓
↓	2JU	Sunbird GT	2466	↓	↓	↓	↓	↓	↓	↓	↓	4M	3A	↓	↓	3.65	263	—
↓	2AF	6000	2786	104.9	188.9	72	53.7	58.7	57.0	↓	↓	↓	3A,4A	↓	↓	↓	264	269, 270
↓	2AG	6000 LE	2804	↓	↓	↓	↓	↓	↓	↓	↓	↓	↓	↓	↓	↓	↓	
↓	2AH	6000 STE	3095	↓	↓	↓	↓	↓	↓	↓	↓	3A	4A	↓	disc	3.18	270	—
↓	2GN	Bonneville	3226	108.1	200.2	71.6	55.8	58.5	57.8	SLA, C	↓	↓	↓	↓	drum	2.41	242	275
↓	2GS	Bonneville LE	3235	↓	↓	↓	↓	↓	↓	↓	↓	↓	↓	↓	↓	↓	↓	↓
↓	2GR	Bonneville Brougham	3255	↓	↓	↓	↓	↓	↓	↓	↓	↓	↓	↓	↓	↓	↓	↓
↓	2PE	Fiero Coupe	2493	93.4	160.7	69.0	46.9	58.3	59.3	↓	MS, C	5M	—	↓	disc	3.35	264	—
↓	2PM	Fiero Sport Coupe		↓	↓	↓	↓	57.8	58.7	↓	↓	↓	3A	↓	↓	↓	↓	↓
↓	2PF	Fiero SE	2499	↓	↓	↓	↓	↓	↓	↓	↓	↓	4M,3A	↓	↓	↓	↓	272
↓	2PG	Fiero GT	2652	↓	165.1	↓	↓	58.3	59.3	↓	↓	4M	3A	↓	↓	3.65	272	—
↓	2FS	Firebird	2886	101	190.5	72.4	49.7	60.7	61.6	MS, C	RA, C	5M	4A	↓	drum	3.73	265	271, 275
↓	2FX	Firebird SE	3022	↓	↓	↓	↓	↓	↓	↓	↓	↓	↓	↓	↓	3.42	271	275
↓	2FW	Trans Am	3239	↓	191.8	↓	↓	↓	↓	↓	↓	↓	↓	↓	↓	3.27	275	262, 277
↓	2NE	Grand Am	2565	103.4	177.5	67.5	52.5	55.6	55.1	↓	TA, C	↓	3A	↓	↓	3.35	268	273
↓	2NV	Grand Am LE	2590	↓	↓	↓	↓	↓	↓	↓	↓	↓	↓	↓	↓	↓	↓	↓

Notes:
1. 1000 Coupe wheelbase is 94.3 in.
2. Rear disc brakes optional on Firebird.

Appendix I. (continued)

Year	Series	Model	Dimensions: Curb Wt.	Wheel Base	Length	Width	Height	Track: Front	Rear	Suspension: Front	Rear	Transmission: Std.	Opt.	Brakes: Front	Rear	Axle Ratio	Engines: Std.	Opt.
1986	2NW	Grand Am SE	2752	103.4	177.5	67.5	52.5	55.6	55.1	MS, C	TA, C	5M	3A	disc	drum	3.35	2.68	273
↓	2GJ	Grand Prix	3244	108.1	201.8	72.3	54.7	58.5	57.8	SLA, C	RA, C	3A	4A	↓	↓	2.41	242	275
↓	2GK	Grand Prix LE	3261	↓	↓	↓	↓	↓	↓	↓	↓	↓	↓	↓	↓	↓	↓	↓
↓	2GP	Grand Prix Brougham	3284	↓	↓	↓	↓	↓	↓	↓	↓	↓	↓	↓	↓	↓	↓	↓
↓	2BL	Parisienne	3563	116	212.3	75.4	56.7	61.7	60.7	↓	↓	↓	↓	↓	↓	2.56	278	276
↓	2BT	Parisienne Brougham	3591	↓	↓	↓	↓	↓	↓	↓	↓	↓	↓	↓	↓	↓	↓	↓
1987	2TL	1000	2143	97.3	164.9	61.8	52.8	51.2	51.2	↓	↓	4M	5M,3A	↓	↓	3.36	258	—
↓	2JB	Sunbird	2370	101.2	175.7	66.3	53.8	55.6	55.2	MS, C	↓	5M	3A	↓	↓	3.45	279	—
↓	2JD	Sunbird SE	2356	↓	↓	↓	↓	↓	↓	↓	↓	↓	↓	↓	↓	↓	↓	280
↓	2JU	Sunbird GT	2519	↓	↓	↓	↓	↓	↓	↓	↓	↓	↓	↓	↓	3.61	280	—
↓	2AF	6000	2760	104.9	188.9	72	53.7	58.7	57	↓	↓	3A	4A	↓	↓	2.84	264	270
↓	2AG	6000 LE	2762	↓	↓	↓	↓	↓	↓	↓	↓	↓	↓	↓	↓	↓	↓	↓
↓	2AH	6000 STE	3036	↓	↓	↓	↓	↓	↓	↓	↓	5M	3A,4A	↓	disc	3.61	270	—
↓	2HX	Bonneville	3289	110.8	198.7	72.4	55.5	60.3	59.8	↓	MS, C	4A	—	↓	drum	2.73	281	—
↓	2HZ	Bonneville LE	3312	↓	↓	↓	↓	↓	↓	↓	↓	↓	↓	↓	↓	↓	↓	↓
↓	2CHZ	Bonneville SE	3325	↓	↓	↓	↓	↓	↓	↓	↓	↓	↓	↓	↓	↓	↓	↓
↓	2PE	Fiero Coupe	2567	93.4	163.1	69	46.9	58.3	59.3	SLA, C	↓	5M	3A	↓	disc	3.35	264	—
↓	2PM	Fiero Sport Coupe	2570	↓	↓	↓	↓	57.8	58.7	↓	↓	↓	↓	↓	↓	↓	↓	↓
↓	2PF	Fiero SE	2581	↓	↓	↓	↓	↓	↓	↓	↓	↓	↓	↓	↓	3.61	↓	272
↓	2PG	Fiero GT	2723	↓	164.8	↓	↓	58.3	59.3	↓	↓	↓	↓	↓	↓	↓	272	—
↓	2FP	Firebird	3111	101	190.5	72.4	49.7	60.7	61.6	MS, C	RA, C	↓	4A	↓	drum	3.42	271	276, 277
↓	2FW	Firebird Formula	3383	↓	↓	↓	↓	↓	↓	↓	↓	↓	↓	↓	↓	3.23	276	277, 282
↓	2FW	Trans Am	3312	↓	191.8	↓	↓	↓	↓	↓	↓	↓	↓	↓	↓	↓	↓	↓
↓	2NE	Grand Am	2566	103.4	177.5	67.5	52.5	55.6	55.1	↓	TA, C	↓	3A	↓	↓	3.35	268	273
↓	2NV	Grand Am LE		↓	↓	↓	↓	↓	↓	↓	↓	↓	↓	↓	↓	↓	↓	↓
↓	2NW	Grand Am SE		↓	↓	↓	↓	↓	↓	↓	↓	↓	↓	↓	↓	↓	273	280
↓	2GJ	Grand Prix	3245	108.1	201.8	72.3	54.7	58.5	57.8	SLA, C	RA, C	3A	4A	↓	↓	2.41	242	275, 278
↓	2GK	Grand Prix LE	3263	↓	↓	↓	↓	↓	↓	↓	↓	↓	↓	↓	↓	↓	↓	275
↓	2GP	Grand Prix Brougham	3278	↓	↓	↓	↓	↓	↓	↓	↓	↓	↓	↓	↓	↓	↓	↓
↓	2BL	Safari	4191	116	215.1	79.3	57.4	62	64.1	↓	↓	4A	—	↓	↓	2.73	246	—

Notes:
1. 1000 Coupe wheelbase is 94.3 in.
2. Rear disc brakes optional on Firebird.

Appendix II. **ENGINE SPECIFICATIONS**

Notes

1. All power ratings 1946–70 are SAE gross ratings.
2. All power ratings 1972–88 are SAE net ratings.
3. Both gross and net ratings are shown for the 1971 model year—net ratings in parentheses.
4. For model years 1972–74, suffix "a" on the engine number indicates single exhaust; suffix "b" indicates dual exhaust. The type of exhaust system made no difference in the SAE gross power ratings used prior to 1972; from 1975 the use of catalytic converters mandated the equivalent of a single exhaust system.
5. A "c" suffix in parentheses behind the power rating indicates an engine designed specifically for California emissions standards.
6. GM engine codes are included for all years subsequent to 1976.

Explanation of terms

Engine number: locates this engine in Appendix I table.
Displacement: engine total swept volume in cubic inches.
Bore x stroke: in inches.
Carburetion: the number of carburetors per engine, followed by the number of throats per carburetor.
Power rating: maximum power of the engine at the peaking speed in rpm. See notes 1–5 above.

List of abbreviations

OHV: overhead valves
OHC: overhead camshaft
L6, L8: inline engine of six or eight cylinders
FI: fuel injection
turbo: turbocharged

Year Introduced	Engine Number	Type	Displacement	Bore × stroke	Compression Ratio	Carburetion	Power Rating
1946	1	L 6	239.2	3.56 × 4.00	6.5	1 × 1	90 @ 3200
	2	L 8	248.9	3.25 × 3.75	↓	1 × 2	103 @ 3500
	3	L 6	239.2	3.56 × 4.00	7.5	1 × 1	93 @ 3400
↓	4	L 8	248.9	3.25 × 3.75	↓	1 × 2	106 @ 3800
1948	5	L 6	239.2	3.56 × 4.00	6.5	1 × 1	90 @ 3400
↓	6	L 8	248.9	3.25 × 3.75		1 × 2	104 @ 3800
1950	7	L 8	268.2	3.38 × 3.75	↓		108 @ 3600
↓	8	L 8	↓	↓	7.5	↓	113 @ 3600
1951	9	L 6	239.2	3.56 × 4.00	6.5	1 × 1	96 @ 3400
	10	↓	↓	↓	7.5	↓	98 @ 3400
	11	L 8	268.4	3.38 × 3.75	6.5	1 × 2	116 @ 3600
↓	12	L 8	↓	↓	7.5	↓	120 @ 3600
1952	13	L 6	239.2	3.56 × 4.00	6.8	1 × 1	100 @ 3400
	14	↓	↓	↓	7.7	↓	102 @ 3400
	15	L 8	268.4	3.38 × 3.75	6.8	1 × 2	118 @ 3600
↓	16	↓	↓	↓	7.7		122 @ 3600
1953	17	L 6	239.2	3.56 × 4.00	7.0		115 @ 3800
↓	18	↓	↓	↓	7.7		118 @ 3800
1954	19	L 8	268.4	3.38 × 3.75	6.8		122 @ 3800
↓	20	↓	↓	↓	7.7	↓	127 @ 3800

Year Introduced	Engine Number	Type	Displacement	Bore × stroke	Compression Ratio	Carburetion	Power Rating
1955	21	OHV V-8	287.2	3.75 × 3.25	7.4	1 × 2	173 @ 4400
	22				8.0	↓	180 @ 4600
↓	23		↓	↓	↓	1 × 4	200 @ 4600
1956	24		316.6	3.94 × 3.25	7.9	1 × 2	N.S.
	25				8.9	↓	205 @ 4600
	26				↓	1 × 4	227 @ 4800
↓	27		↓	↓	10	2 × 4	285 @ 5100
1957	28		347	3.94 × 3.56	8.5	1 × 2	227 @ 4600
	29				↓	1 × 4	244 @ 4800
	30				10	1 × 2	252 @ 4600
	31					1 × 4	270 @ 4800
	32					3 × 2	290 @ 5000
	33				↓	↓	317 @ 5200
↓	34		↓	↓	10.25	FI	N.S.
1958	35		370	4.06 × 3.56	8.6	1 × 2	240 @ 4500
	36				↓	1 × 4	255 @ 4500
	37				10	1 × 2	270 @ 4600
	38				↓	1 × 4	285 @ 4600
	39				10.5	3 × 2	300 @ 4600
↓	40	↓	↓	↓	↓	FI	310 @ 4800

Appendix II. (continued)

Year Introduced	Engine Number	Type	Displacement	Bore × stroke	Compression Ratio	Carburetion	Power Rating
1958	41	OHV V-8	370	4.06 × 3.56	10.5	1 × 4	315 @ 5000
	42	↓	↓	↓	↓	3 × 2	330 @ 5200
1959	43		389	4.06 × 3.75	8.6	1 × 2	245 @ 4200
↓	44		↓	↓	↓	1 × 4	260 @ 4200
	45				10	1 × 2	280 @ 4400
	46				↓	1 × 4	300 @ 4600
	47				10.5	3 × 2	315 @ 4600
	48				↓	1 × 4	330 @ 4800
	49					3 × 2	345 @ 4800
1960	50				8.6	1 × 2	215 @ 3600
↓	51				↓	↓	230 @ 3600
	52					1 × 4	235 @ 3600
	53					↓	281 @ 4400
	54				10.25	1 × 2	283 @ 4400
	55				↓	1 × 4	303 @ 4600
	56				10.75	3 × 2	318 @ 4600
	57				↓	1 × 4	333 @ 4800
	58					3 × 2	348 @ 4800
1961	59				8.6	1 × 2	230 @ 4000
↓	60				10.25	↓	267 @ 4200
	61				↓	1 × 4	287 @ 4400
	62	OHV 4	194.5		8.6	1 × 1	110 @ 3800
	63	↓	↓		10.25	↓	120 @ 3800
	64				8.6		130 @ 4400
	65				10.25		140 @ 4400
	66				↓	1 × 4	155 @ 4800
	67	OHV V-8	215	3.50 × 2.80	8.8	1 × 2	155 @ 4600
1962	68	OHV 4	194.5	4.06 × 3.75	8.6	1 × 1	115 @ 4000
↓	69		↓	↓	10.25	1 × 4	166 @ 4800
	70	OHV V-8	215	3.50 × 2.80	↓	↓	185 @ 4800
	71	↓	↓	↓	11.0		190 @ 4800
1963	72		326	3.72 × 3.75	10.25	1 × 2	260 @ 4800
↓	73		↓	↓	↓	1 × 4	280 @ 4800

Year Introduced	Engine Number	Type	Displacement	Bore × stroke	Compression Ratio	Carburetion	Power Rating
1963	74	OHV V-8	389	4.06 × 3.75	10.25	3 × 2	313 @ 4600
↓	75		421	4.09 × 4.00	↓	1 × 4	320 @ 4400
	76	↓	↓	↓	10.75	↓	353 @ 5000
	77				↓	3 × 2	370 @ 5200
1964	78	OHV 6	215	3.75 × 3.25	8.6	1 × 1	140 @ 4200
↓	79	OHV V-8	326	3.72 × 3.75	↓	1 × 2	250 @ 4600
	80	↓	↓	↓	10.5	1 × 4	280 @ 4800
	81		389	4.06 × 3.75	10.75	↓	325 @ 4800
	82		↓	↓	↓	3 × 2	348 @ 4900
	83				8.6	1 × 2	235 @ 4000
	84				10.5	↓	267 @ 4200
	85				↓		283 @ 4400
	86					1 × 4	303 @ 4600
	87					↓	306 @ 4800
	88				10.75	3 × 2	330 @ 4600
	89		421	4.09 × 4.00	10.5	1 × 4	320 @ 4400
	90		↓	↓	10.75	3 × 2	350 @ 4600
1965	91		326	3.72 × 3.75	9.2	1 × 2	250 @ 4600
↓	92		↓	↓	10.5	1 × 4	285 @ 5000
	93		389	4.06 × 3.75	10.75	↓	335 @ 5000
	94		↓	↓	↓	3 × 2	360 @ 5200
	95				8.6	1 × 2	256 @ 4600
	96				10.5	↓	290 @ 4600
	97				↓	1 × 4	325 @ 4800
	98					↓	333 @ 5000
	99				10.75	3 × 2	338 @ 4800
	100		421	4.09 × 4.00	10.5	1 × 4	338 @ 4600
	101		↓	↓	10.75	3 × 2	356 @ 4800
	102				↓	↓	376 @ 5000
1966	103	OHC 6	230	3.88 × 3.25	9	1 × 1	165 @ 4700
↓	104	↓	↓	↓	10.5	1 × 4	207 @ 5200
1967	105				↓	↓	215 @ 5200

Appendix II. (continued)

Year Intro-duced	Engine Number	Type	Dis-place-ment	Bore × stroke	Com-pression Ratio	Carbu-retion	Power Rating
1967	106	OHV V-8	400	4.12 × 3.75	10.75	1 × 4	325 @ 4800
↓	107	↓	↓	↓	8.6	1 × 2	255 @ 4400
↓	108	↓	↓	↓	10.75	1 × 4	335 @ 5000
↓	109	↓	↓	↓	↓	↓	360 @ 5100
↓	110	↓	↓	↓	↓	↓	360 @ 5400
↓	111	↓	↓	↓	8.6	1 × 2	265 @ 4600
↓	112	↓	↓	↓	10.5	↓	290 @ 4600
↓	113	↓	↓	↓	↓	1 × 4	325 @ 4800
↓	114	↓	↓	↓	↓	↓	333 @ 5000
↓	115	↓	↓	↓	↓	↓	350 @ 5000
↓	116	↓	↓	↓	↓	↓	350 @ 4800
↓	117	↓	428	4.12 × 4.00	↓	↓	360 @ 4600
↓	118	↓	↓	↓	10.75	↓	376 @ 5100
1968	119	OHC 6	250	3.88 × 3.53	9	1 × 1	175 @ 4800
↓	120		↓	↓	10.5	1 × 4	215 @ 5200
↓	121	OHV V-8	350	3.88 × 3.75	9.2	1 × 2	265 @ 4600
↓	122	↓	↓	↓	10.5	1 × 4	320 @ 5100
↓	123	↓	400	4.12 × 3.75	10.75	↓	350 @ 5000
↓	124	↓	↓	↓	↓	↓	366 @ 5400
↓	125	↓	↓	↓	↓	↓	330 @ 4800
↓	126	↓	↓	↓	↓	↓	335 @ 5300
↓	127	↓	↓	↓	10.5	↓	340 @ 4800
↓	128	↓	428	4.12 × 4.00	↓	↓	375 @ 4800
↓	129	↓	↓	↓	10.75	↓	390 @ 5200
1969	130	OHC 6	250	3.88 × 3.53	10.5	↓	230 @ 5400
↓	131	OHV V-8	350	3.88 × 3.75	↓	↓	325 @ 5100
↓	132	↓	↓	↓	↓	↓	330 @ 5100
↓	133	↓	400	4.12 × 3.75	10.75	↓	345 @ 5400
↓	134	↓	↓	↓	↓	↓	370 @ 5500
↓	135	↓	428	4.12 × 4.00	10.5	↓	370 @ 4800
1970	136	OHV 6	250	3.88 × 3.53	8.5	1 × 1	155 @ 4200
↓	137	OHV V-8	350	3.88 × 3.75	8.8	1 × 2	255 @ 4600
1970	138	OHV V-8	400	4.12 × 3.75	8.8	1 × 2	265 @ 4600
↓	139	↓	↓	↓	10	↓	290 @ 4600
↓	140	↓	↓	↓	↓	1 × 4	330 @ 4800
↓	141	↓	↓	↓	10.25	↓	330 @ 4800
↓	142	↓	↓	↓	10.5	↓	345 @ 5000
↓	143	↓	↓	↓	10.25	↓	350 @ 5000
↓	144	↓	↓	↓	10.5	↓	366 @ 5100
↓	145	↓	↓	↓	↓	↓	370 @ 5500
↓	146	↓	455	4.15 × 4.21	10	↓	360 @ 4300
↓	147	↓	↓	↓	10.25	↓	370 @ 4600
1971	148	OHV 6	250	3.88 × 3.53	8.5	1 × 1	145 @ 4200 (110 @ 3800)
↓	149	OHV V-8	350	3.88 × 3.75	8	1 × 2	250 @ 4400 (165 @ 4200) (180 @ 4400)
↓	150	↓	400	4.12 × 3.75	8.2	↓	265 @ 4400 (180 @ 3800)
↓	151	↓	↓	↓	↓	1 × 4	300 @ 4800 (250 @ 4400)
↓	152	↓	455	4.15 × 4.21	↓	↓	325 @ 4400 (255 @ 4000)
↓	153	↓	↓	↓	8.4	↓	335 @ 4800 (305 @ 4400)
1972	154	↓	307	3.88 × 3.25	8.5	1 × 2	200 @ 4600 (140 @ 4400)
↓	155	↓	455	4.15 × 4.21	8.2	↓	280 @ 4400
↓	156	↓	307	3.88 × 3.25	8.5	↓	130 @ 4400
↓	157a	↓	350	3.88 × 3.75	8	↓	160 @ 4400
↓	157b	↓	↓	↓	↓	↓	175 @ 4400
↓	158a	↓	400	4.12 × 3.75	8.2	↓	175 @ 4000
↓	158b	↓	↓	↓	↓	↓	200 @ 4000
↓	159a	↓	↓	↓	↓	1 × 4	200 @ 4000
↓	159b	↓	↓	↓	↓	↓	250 @ 4400
↓	160a	↓	455	4.15 × 4.21	↓	1 × 2	185 @ 4000
↓	160b	↓	↓	↓	↓	↓	200 @ 4000
↓	161a	↓	↓	↓	↓	1 × 4	220 @ 3600
↓	161b	↓	↓	↓	↓	↓	250 @ 3600

Appendix II. (continued)

Year Introduced	Engine Number	Type	Displacement	Bore × stroke	Compression Ratio	Carburetion	Power Rating
1972	162	OHV V-8	455	4.15 × 4.21	8.4	1 × 4	300 @ 4000
1973	163	OHV 6	250	3.88 × 3.53	8.2	1 × 1	100 @ 3600
↓	164a	OHV V-8	350	3.88 × 3.75	7.6	1 × 2	150 @ 4000
↓	164b	↓	↓	↓	↓	↓	175 @ 4400
↓	165a	↓	400	4.12 × 3.75	8	↓	170 @ 3600
↓	165b	↓	↓	↓	↓	↓	185 @ 4000
↓	166a	↓	↓	↓	↓	1 × 4	200 @ 4000
↓	166b	↓	↓	↓	↓	↓	230 @ 4400
↓	167a	↓	455	4.15 × 4.21	↓	↓	215 @ 3600
↓	167b	↓	↓	↓	↓	↓	250 @ 4000
↓	168	↓	↓	↓	8.4	↓	310 @ 4000
1974	169a	↓	350	3.88 × 3.75	7.6	1 × 2	155 @ 3600
↓	169b	↓	↓	↓	↓	↓	170 @ 4000
↓	170a	↓	↓	↓	↓	1 × 4	
↓	170b	↓	↓	↓	↓	↓	200 @ 4400
↓	171a	↓	400	4.12 × 3.75	8	1 × 2	175 @ 3600
↓	171b	↓	↓	↓	↓	↓	190 @ 4000
↓	172a	↓	↓	↓	↓	1 × 4	200 @ 4000
↓	172b	↓	↓	↓	↓	↓	225 @ 4000
↓	173	↓	455	4.15 × 4.21	8.4	↓	290 @ 4000
1975	174	OHC 4	140	3.50 × 3.63	8	1 × 1	78 @ 4200
↓	175	↓	↓	↓	↓	1 × 2	87 @ 4400
↓	176	↓	↓	↓	↓	↓	80 @ 4400 (C)
↓	177	OHV 6	250	3.88 × 3.53	8.25	1 × 1	105 @ 3800
↓	178	OHV V-8	260	3.50 × 3.39	8	1 × 2	110 @ 3400
↓	179	↓	350	3.80 × 3.85	↓	↓	145 @ 3200
↓	180	↓	↓	↓	↓	1 × 4	165 @ 3800
↓	181	↓	↓	3.88 × 3.75	7.6	1 × 2	155 @ 4000
↓	182	↓	↓	↓	↓	1 × 4	175 @ 4000
↓	183	↓	400	4.12 × 3.75	↓	1 × 2	170 @ 4000
↓	184	↓	↓	↓	↓	1 × 4	185 @ 3600

Year Introduced	Engine Number	Type	Displacement	Bore × stroke	Compression Ratio	Carburetion	Power Rating	GM Engine Code
1975	185	OHV V-8	455	4.15 × 4.21	7.6	1 × 4	200 @ 3500	
1976	186	OHC 4	140	3.50 × 3.63	7.9	1 × 1	70 @ 4400	
↓	187	↓	↓	↓	↓	1 × 2	84 @ 4400	
↓	188	↓	↓	↓	↓	↓	87 @ 4400	
↓	189	↓	↓	↓	↓	↓	79 @ 4400 (C)	
↓	190	OHV V-6	231	3.80 × 3.40	8	↓	105 @ 3400	
↓	191	OHV 6	250	3.88 × 3.53	8.3	1 × 1	110 @ 3600	
↓	192	OHV V-8	260	3.50 × 3.39	7.5	1 × 2	110 @ 3400	
↓	193	↓	350	3.80 × 3.85	8	↓	140 @ 3200	
↓	194	↓	↓	↓	↓	1 × 4	155 @ 3400	
↓	195	↓	↓	3.88 × 3.75	7.6	1 × 2	160 @ 4000	
↓	196	↓	↓	↓	↓	1 × 4	165 @ 4000	
1977	197	OHC 4	140	3.50 × 3.63	8	1 × 2	84 @ 4400	L11
↓	198	OHV 4	151	4.00 × 3.00	8.3	↓	88 @ 4400	LX6
↓	199	OHV V-6	231	3.80 × 3.40	8	↓	105 @ 3200	LD7
↓	200	OHV V-8	301	4.00 × 3.00	8.2	↓	135 @ 4000	L27
↓	201	↓	305	3.74 × 3.48	8.5	↓	145 @ 3800	LG3
↓	202	↓	350	3.88 × 3.75	7.6	1 × 4	170 @ 4000	L76
↓	203	↓	↓	4.06 × 3.39	8	↓	170 @ 3800	L34
↓	204	↓	↓	4.00 × 3.48	8.5	↓	170 @ 3800	LM1
↓	205	↓	400	4.12 × 3.75	7.6	↓	180 @ 3600	L78
↓	206	↓	↓	↓	8.0	↓	200 @ 3600	L78 T/A
↓	207	↓	403	4.35 × 3.39	↓	↓	185 @ 3600	L80
1978	208	OHV 4	151	4.00 × 3.00	8.3	1 × 2	85 @ 4400	LX6
↓	209	↓	↓	↓	↓	↓	85 @ 4400 (C)	LS6
↓	210	OHV V-6	231	3.80 × 3.40	8	↓	105 @ 3400	LD5
↓	211	OHV V-8	301	4.00 × 3.00	8.2	↓	140 @ 3600	L27

Appendix II. (continued)

Year Intro-duced	Engine Number	Type	Dis-place-ment	Bore × stroke	Com-pression Ratio	Carbu-retion	Power Rating	GM Engine Code
1978	212	OHV V-8	301	4.00 × 3.00	8.2	1 × 4	150 @ 4000	L37
↓	213	↓	305	3.74 × 3.48	8.4	1 × 2	145 @ 3800	LG3
↓	214	↓	↓	↓	↓	↓	135 @ 3800 (C)	LG3
↓	215	↓	350	4.00 × 3.48	8.2	1 × 4	170 @ 3800	LM1
↓	216	↓	↓	↓	↓	↓	160 @ 3800 (C)	LM1
↓	217	↓	↓	4.06 × 3.39	7.9	↓	170 @ 3800	L34
↓	218	↓	↓	3.80 × 3.85	8	↓	155 @ 3400	L77
↓	219	↓	400	4.12 × 3.75	7.7	↓	180 @ 3600	L78
↓	220	↓	↓	↓	8.1	↓	220 @ 4000	L78 W72
↓	221	↓	403	4.35 × 3.39	7.9	↓	185 @ 3600	L80
1979	222	OHV 4	151	4.00 × 3.00	8.2	1 × 2	90 @ 4400	LX8
↓	223	OHV V-6	231	3.80 × 3.40	8	↓	115 @ 3800	LD5
↓	224	OHV V-8	301	4.00 × 3.00	8.1	↓	135 @ 3800	L27
↓	225	↓	↓	↓	↓	1 × 4	150 @ 4000	L37
↓	226	↓	305	3.74 × 3.48	8.4	1 × 2	130 @ 3200	LG3
↓	227	↓	↓	↓	↓	↓	125 @ 3200 (C)	LG3
↓	228	↓	↓	↓	↓	1 × 4	155 @ 4000	LG4
↓	229	↓	350	4.00 × 3.48	8.2	↓	165 @ 3800	LM1
1980	230	OHV 4	151	4.00 × 3.00	↓	1 × 2	90 @ 4000	LX8
↓	231		↓	↓	↓	↓		LW9
↓	232	OHV V-6	173	3.50 × 2.99	8.5	↓	115 @ 4800	LE2
↓	233		229	3.74 × 3.48	8.6	↓	110 @ 4200	LC3
↓	234	OHV V-8	265	3.75 × 3.00	8.3	↓	120 @ 3600	LS5
↓	235	↓	301	4.00 × 3.00	8.1	1 × 4	170 @ 4400	L37 W72
↓	236	↓	↓	↓	7.6	1 × 4/ turbo	210 @ 4000	LU8
↓	237	↓	305	3.74 × 3.48	8.4	1 × 4	150 @ 3800	LG4
↓	238	↓	350	4.06 × 3.39	8	↓	160 @ 3600	L34
↓	239	↓	↓	↓	22.5	FI	125 @ 3600	LF9

Year Intro-duced	Engine Number	Type	Dis-place-ment	Bore × stroke	Com-pression Ratio	Carbu-retion	Power Rating	GM Engine Code
1981	240	OHV 4	151	4.00 × 3.00	8.2	1 × 2	84 @ 4000	LW9
↓	241	OHV V-6	173	3.50 × 2.99	8.5	↓	110 @ 4800	LE2
↓	242		231	3.80 × 3.40	8	↓	110 @ 3800	LD5
↓	243	OHV V-8	301	4.00 × 3.00	8.1	1 × 4	135 @ 3600	L37
↓	244	↓	↓	↓	7.5	1 × 4/ turbo	200 @ 4000	LU8
↓	245	↓	305	3.74 × 3.48	8.6	1 × 4	145 @ 3800	LG4
↓	246	↓	307	3.80 × 3.385	8	↓	↓	LV2
↓	247	↓	350	4.06 × 3.39	22.5	FI	105 @ 3200	LF9
1982	248	OHC 4	98	3.23 × 2.98	9.2	1 × 2	62 @ 5200	L17
↓	249		110	3.34 × 3.12	9.0	FI	84 @ 5200	LH8
↓	250	OHV 4	112	3.50 × 2.91	↓	1 × 2	88 @ 5100	L46
↓	251		151	4.00 × 3.00	8.2	FI	90 @ 4000	LR8
↓	252	↓	↓	↓	↓	↓	↓	LQ9
↓	253	OHV V-6	173	3.50 × 2.99	8.9	1 × 2	135 @ 5400	LH7
↓	254	↓	↓	↓	8.5	↓	105 @ 4800	LC1
↓	255	↓	252	3.97 × 3.40	8	↓	125 @ 4000	LC4
↓	256	↓	263	4.06 × 3.39	22.7	FI	85 @ 3600	LT7
↓	257	OHV V-8	305	3.74 × 3.48	9.5	↓	165 @ 4200	LU5
1983	258	OHC 4	98	3.23 × 2.98	9	1 × 2	65 @ 5200	L17
↓	259	OHV 4	121	3.50 × 3.15	9.3	FI	88 @ 4800	LQ5
↓	260		151	4.00 × 3.00	8.2		94 @ 4000	LR8
↓	261	OHV V-6	173	3.50 × 2.99	8.9	1 × 2	135 @ 5400	LL1
↓	262	OHV V-8	305	3.74 × 3.48	9.5	1 × 4	190 @ 4800	L69
1984	263	OHC 4	110	3.34 × 3.12	8	MPFI/ turbo	150 @ 5600	LA5
↓	264	OHV 4	151	4.00 × 3.00	9	EFI	92 @ 4400	LR8
↓	265		↓	↓	↓		↓	LQ9
↓	266	OHV V-6	173	3.50 × 2.99	8.9	1 × 2	125 @ 5400	LL1
↓	267	OHV V-8	305	3.74 × 3.48	8.6	1 × 4	150 @ 4000	LG4

Appendix II. (continued)

Year Intro-duced	Engine Number	Type	Dis-place-ment	Bore × stroke	Com-pression Ratio	Carbu-retion	Power Rating	GM Engine Code
1985	268	OHV 4	151	4.00 × 3.00	9	EFI	92 @ 4400	L68
↓	269	OHV V-6	173	3.50 × 2.99	8.5	1 × 2	112 @ 4800	LE2
	270	↓	↓	↓	↓	MPFI	125 @ 4800	LB6
	271				8.9	↓	135 @ 5100	LB8
	272				8.4		140 @ 5200	L44
	273		181	3.80 × 2.66	9		125 @ 4900	LN7
	274		262	4.00 × 3.48	9.3	TBI	140 @ 4000	LB4
	275	OHV V-8	305	3.74 × 3.48	9.5	1 × 4	155 @ 4200	LG4
	276	↓	↓	↓	↓	↓	165 @ 4200	LG4
	277					EFI	205 @ 4400	LB9

Year Intro-duced	Engine Number	Type	Dis-place-ment	Bore × stroke	Com-pression Ratio	Carbu-retion	Power Rating	GM Engine Code
1986	278	OHV V-6	262	4.00 × 3.48	9.3	TBI	130 @ 3600	LB4
1987	279	OHC 4	122	3.39 × 3.39	8.8	↓	96 @ 4800	LT2
↓	280	↓	↓	↓	8	MPFI/ turbo	165 @ 5600	LT3
	281	OHV V-6	231	3.80 × 3.40	8.5	EFI	150 @ 4400	LG3
	282	OHV V-8	350	3.74 × 3.48	9.3	↓	210 @ 4400	B2L

Appendix III. **PRODUCTION FIGURES**

Notes

1. The "chassis" figures for model years 1959–75 are for full-size models only.
2. The front-wheel-drive Phoenix was a designated 1980 model introduced in April 1979. Its production through August 31, 1979, is included in the 1979 model year.
3. The 1980-model Sunbird remained in production until December 1980. Its production from Sept. 1, 1979 to August 31, 1980 is included in the 1980 model year; production from Sept. 1, 1980 until termination is included in the 1981 model year.
4. The J2000 was a designated 1982 model introduced in May 1981. Its production from its introduction until Aug. 31, 1981, is included in the 1981 model year.

	1946	1947	1948
Torpedo 6	26,636	67,125	39,262
Torpedo 8	18,273	34,815	35,300
Streamliner 6	43,430	42,336	37,742
Streamliner 8	49,301	86,324	123,115
Total	137,640	230,600	235,419

	1949	1950	1951
Chieftain 6, Streamliner 6	69,654	115,542	53,748
Chieftain 8, Streamliner 8	235,165	330,887	316,411
Total	304,819	446,429	370,159

	1952	1953	1954
Chieftain 6	19,809	38,914	22,670
Chieftain 8	251,564	379,705	149,986
Star Chief	–	–	115,088
Total	271,373	418,619	287,744

	1955	1956
Chieftain 860	138,520	184,232
Chieftain 870	212,184	93,872
Star Chief	64,562	31,856
Star Chief Custom	138,542	95,469
Total	553,808	405,429

	1957
Bonneville	630
Chieftain	162,575
Star Chief	16,563
Star Chief Custom	89,205
Super Chief	64,500
Total	333,473

	1958
Bonneville	12,240
Chieftain	128,819
Star Chief	48,795
Super Chief	27,128
Total	216,982

	1959
Bonneville	82,564
Catalina	231,561
Star Chief	68,815
Chassis	380
Total	383,320

Appendix III. (continued)

1960	
Bonneville	85,277
Catalina	210,934
Star Chief	43,691
Ventura	56,277
Chassis	537
Total	396,716

1961	
Bonneville	69,323
Catalina	113,354
Star Chief	29,581
Tempest	100,783
Ventura	27,209
Chassis	385
Total	340,635

1962	
Bonneville	101,753
Catalina	204,654
Grand Prix	30,195
Star Chief	41,642
Tempest	143,193
Chassis	496
Total	521,933

1963	
Bonneville	109,539
Catalina	234,549
Grand Prix	72,959
Le Mans	61,658
Star Chief	40,757
Tempest	69,832
Chassis	777
Total	590,071

1964	
Bonneville	120,259
Catalina	257,768
Grand Prix	63,810
GTO	32,450
Le Mans	80,186
Star Chief	37,653
Tempest	48,026
Tempest Custom	74,464
Chassis	645
Total	715,261

1965	
Bonneville	134,020
Catalina	271,058
Grand Prix	57,881
GTO	75,352
Le Mans	107,553
Star Chief	31,315
Tempest	39,525
Tempest Custom	84,653
Chassis	643
Total	802,000

1966	
Bonneville	135,401
Catalina	254,310
Grand Prix	36,757
GTO	96,946
Le Mans	121,740
Star Chief Executive	45,212
Tempest	43,753
Tempest Custom	96,659
Chassis	553
Total	831,331

1967	
Bonneville	102,996
Catalina	240,750
Executive	46,987
Firebird	82,560
Grand Prix	42,981
GTO	81,722
Le Mans	104,902
Tempest	39,120
Tempest Custom	75,325
Chassis	483
Total	817,826

1968	
Bonneville	104,436
Catalina	276,182
Executive	44,635
Firebird	107,112
Grand Prix	31,711
GTO	87,684
Le Mans	140,711
Tempest	31,581
Tempest Custom	86,430
Chassis	495
Total	910,977

Appendix III. (continued)

1969	
Bonneville	96,315
Catalina	246,596
Executive	39,061
Firebird	87,708
Grand Prix	112,486
GTO	72,287
Le Mans	104,116
Tempest	26,922
Tempest Custom	84,590
Chassis	447
Total	870,528

1970	
Bonneville	82,031
Catalina	223,380
Executive	32,426
Firebird	48,739
Grand Prix	65,750
GTO	40,149
Le Mans	84,252
Le Mans Sport	72,179
Tempest	42,047
Chassis	350
Total	691,303

1971	
Bonneville	41,269
Catalina	149,596
Catalina Brougham	23,893
Firebird	53,124
Grand Prix	58,325
Grand Ville	46,330
GTO	10,532
Le Mans	69,179
Le Mans Sport	40,941
T-37	44,986
Ventura II	48,484
Chassis	194
Total	586,853

1972	
Bonneville	50,293
Catalina	200,948
Catalina Brougham	27,314
Firebird	29,951
Grand Prix	91,961
Grand Ville	63,411
GTO	5,807
Le Mans	117,930
Luxury Le Mans	46,256
Ventura II	72,787
Chassis	320
Total	706,978

1973	
Bonneville	46,898
Catalina	237,065
Firebird	46,313
Grand Am	43,136
Grand Prix	153,899
Grand Ville	90,172
Le Mans	111,357
Le Mans Sport	50,999
Luxury Le Mans	43,293
Ventura	96,500
Chassis	240
Total	919,872

1974	
Bonneville	20,560
Catalina	110,599
Firebird	73,729
Grand Am	17,083
Grand Prix	99,817
Grand Ville	44,494
Le Mans	62,074
Le Mans Sport	37,955
Luxury Le Mans	32,525
Ventura	81,799
Chassis	113
Total	580,748

Appendix III. (continued)

1975	
Astre	64,601
Bonneville	27,815
Catalina	70,998
Firebird	84,063
Grand Am	10,679
Grand Le Mans	27,110
Grand Prix	86,582
Grand Ville Brougham	27,682
Le Mans	42,082
Le Mans Sport	23,817
Ventura	66,554
Chassis	60
Total	532,043

1976	
Astre	50,384
Bonneville	33,769
Bonneville Brougham	30,702
Catalina	72,745
Firebird	110,775
Grand Le Mans	23,168
Grand Prix	228,091
Le Mans	57,479
Le Mans Sport	15,582
Sunbird	52,031
Ventura	74,116
Total	748,842

1977	
Astre	32,788
Bonneville	69,818
Bonneville Brougham	63,366
Catalina	74,736
Firebird	155,736
Grand Le Mans	18,558
Grand Prix	288,430
Le Mans	49,179
Le Mans Sport	12,277
Sunbird	55,398
Ventura	90,764
Total	911,050

1978	
Bonneville	85,004
Bonneville Brougham	54,140
Catalina	61,750
Firebird	187,285
Grand Am	10,608
Grand Le Mans	50,810
Grand Prix	228,444
Le Mans	59,023
Phoenix	76,527
Sunbird	86,789
Total	900,380

1979	
Bonneville	122,958
Bonneville Brougham	56,458
Catalina	46,884
Firebird	211,454
Grand Am	5,886
Grand Le Mans	62,380
Grand Prix	210,050
Le Mans	68,672
Phoenix ('79)	24,900
Phoenix ('80)	52,744
Sunbird	97,770
Total	960,156

1980	
Bonneville	48,192
Bonneville Brougham	33,623
Catalina	16,658
Firebird	107,340
Grand Am	1,647
Grand Le Mans	39,870
Grand Prix	114,714
Le Mans	42,507
Phoenix	125,547
Sunbird	143,070
Total	673,168

Appendix III. (continued)

1981	
T1000	70,194
J2000	48,306
Bonneville	53,851
Bonneville Brougham	37,712
Catalina	10,442
Firebird	70,899
Grand Le Mans	43,743
Grand Prix	147,711
Le Mans	38,122
Phoenix	127,869
Sunbird	44,909
Total	693,758

1982	
T1000	44,469
J2000	70,553
6000	57,534
Bonneville G	80,513
Firebird	116,362
Grand Prix	80,367
Phoenix	49,167
Total	498,965

1983	
1000	25,977
2000	78,329
6000	68,464
Bonneville	83,889
Firebird	74,884
Grand Prix	85,798
Parisienne	17,445
Phoenix	27,493
Total	462,279

1984	
1000	36,746
2000 Sunbird	169,290
6000	122,192
Bonneville	73,389
Fiero	136,840
Firebird	128,304
Grand Prix	77,444
Parisienne	60,524
Phoenix	22,847
Total	827,576

1985	
1000	16,863
2000 Sunbird	111,899
6000	156,322
Bonneville	53,394
Fiero	76,371
Firebird	95,880
Grand Am	82,542
Grand Prix	59,783
Parisienne	82,107
Total	735,161

1986	
1000	20,066
6000	196,209
Bonneville	41,636
Fiero	71,283
Firebird	96,208
Grand Am	190,994
Grand Prix	40,842
Parisienne	72,909
Sunbird	109,807
Total	839,954